& PROCESSIONALS
RECESSIONALS

100 PIECES FOR ORGAN

Kevin Mayhew

We hope you enjoy the music in *Processionals and Recessionals*.
Further copies are available from your local
music shop or Christian bookshop.

In case of difficulty, please contact the publisher direct by writing to:

The Sales Department
KEVIN MAYHEW LTD
Buxhall
Stowmarket
Suffolk IP14 3BW

Phone 01449 737978
Fax 01449 737834
E-mail info@kevinmayhewltd.com

Please ask for our complete catalogue of outstanding Church Music.

Front Cover: *Flight Into Egypt* (tapestry).
Courtesy of SuperStock, London.
Reproduced by kind permission.

Cover designed by Jaquetta Sergeant

First published in Great Britain in 1995 by Kevin Mayhew Ltd

ISBN 0 86209 595 6
Catalogue No: 1400033

Music Editor: Joanne Clarke
Music setting by Kate Emerson, Louise Hill and Kevin Whomes

Printed and bound in Great Britain

Contents

FESTIVE SCHERZO

Malcolm Archer

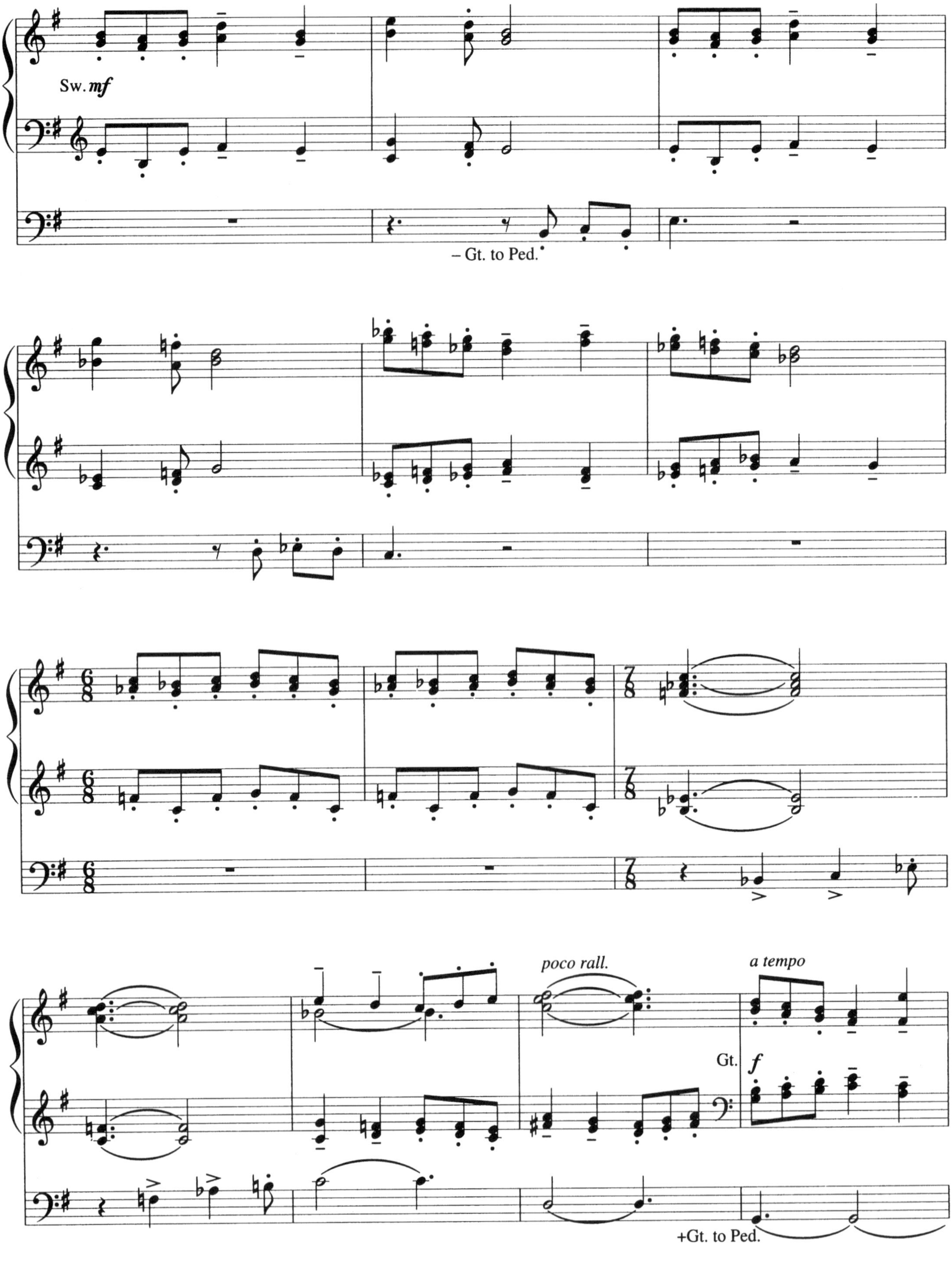
Sw. mf
– Gt. to Ped.
poco rall.
a tempo
Gt. f
+Gt. to Ped.

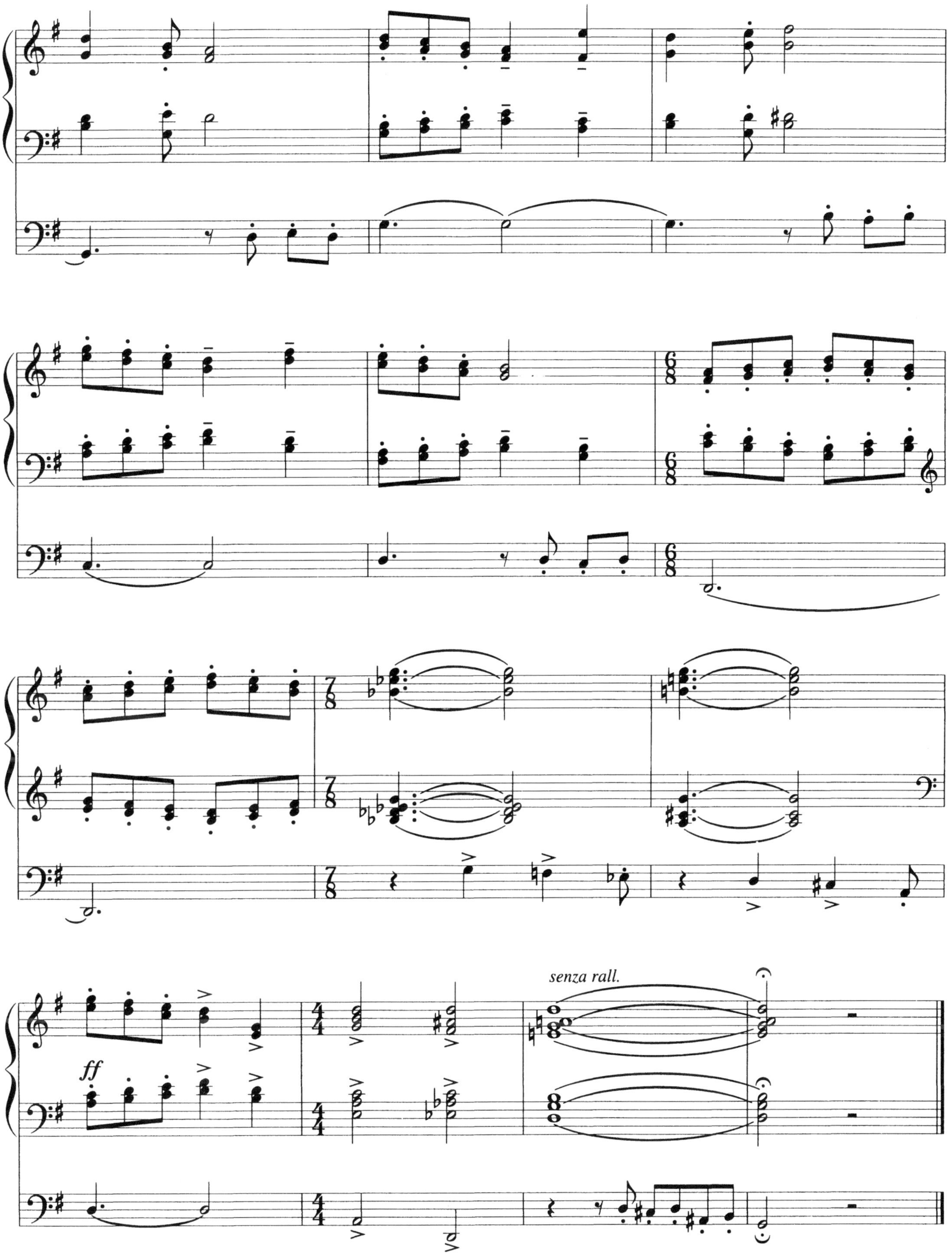
ff
senza rall.

for Julia and Paul
AVANT-PROPOS
Richard Lloyd

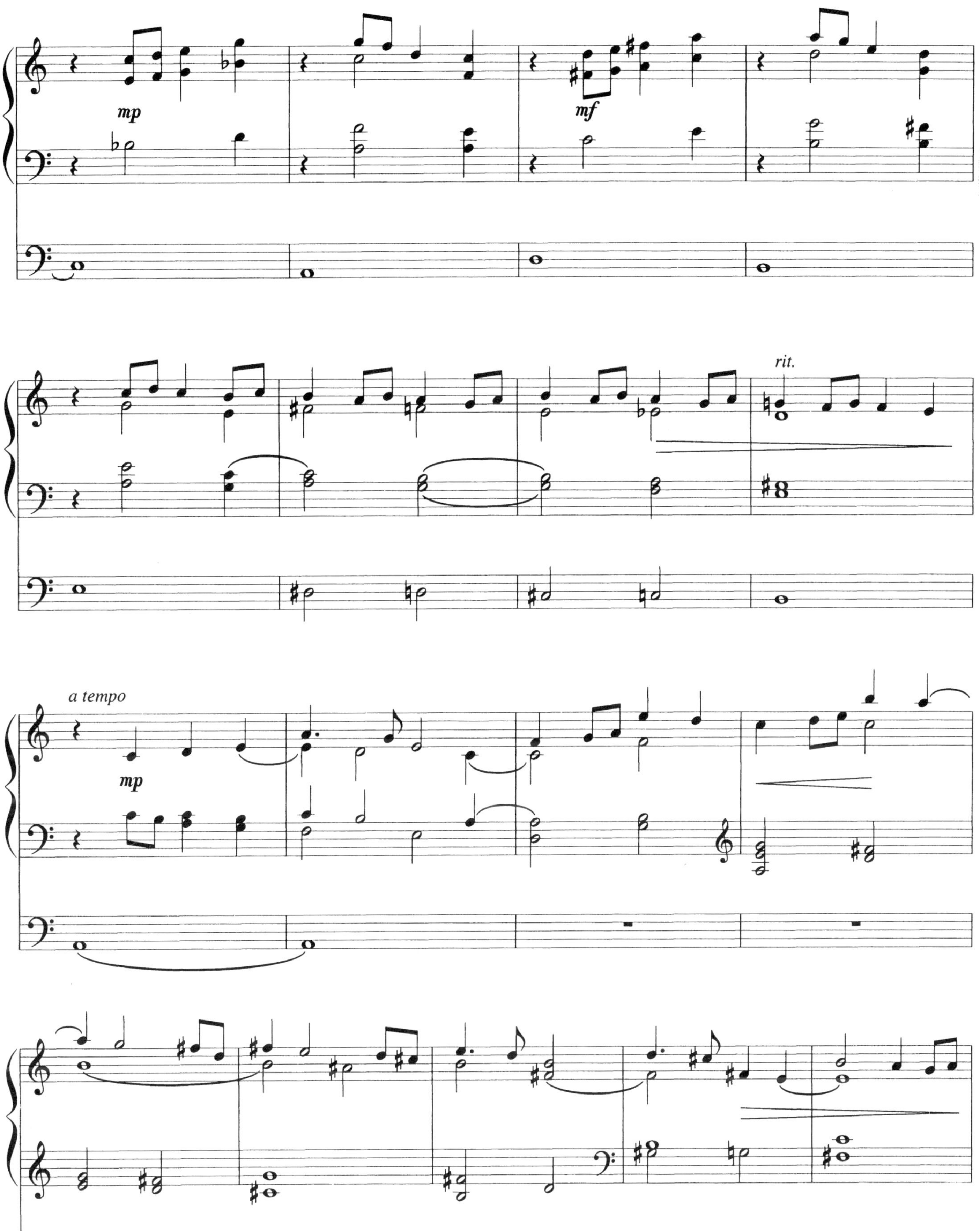
mp
mf
rit.
a tempo
mp

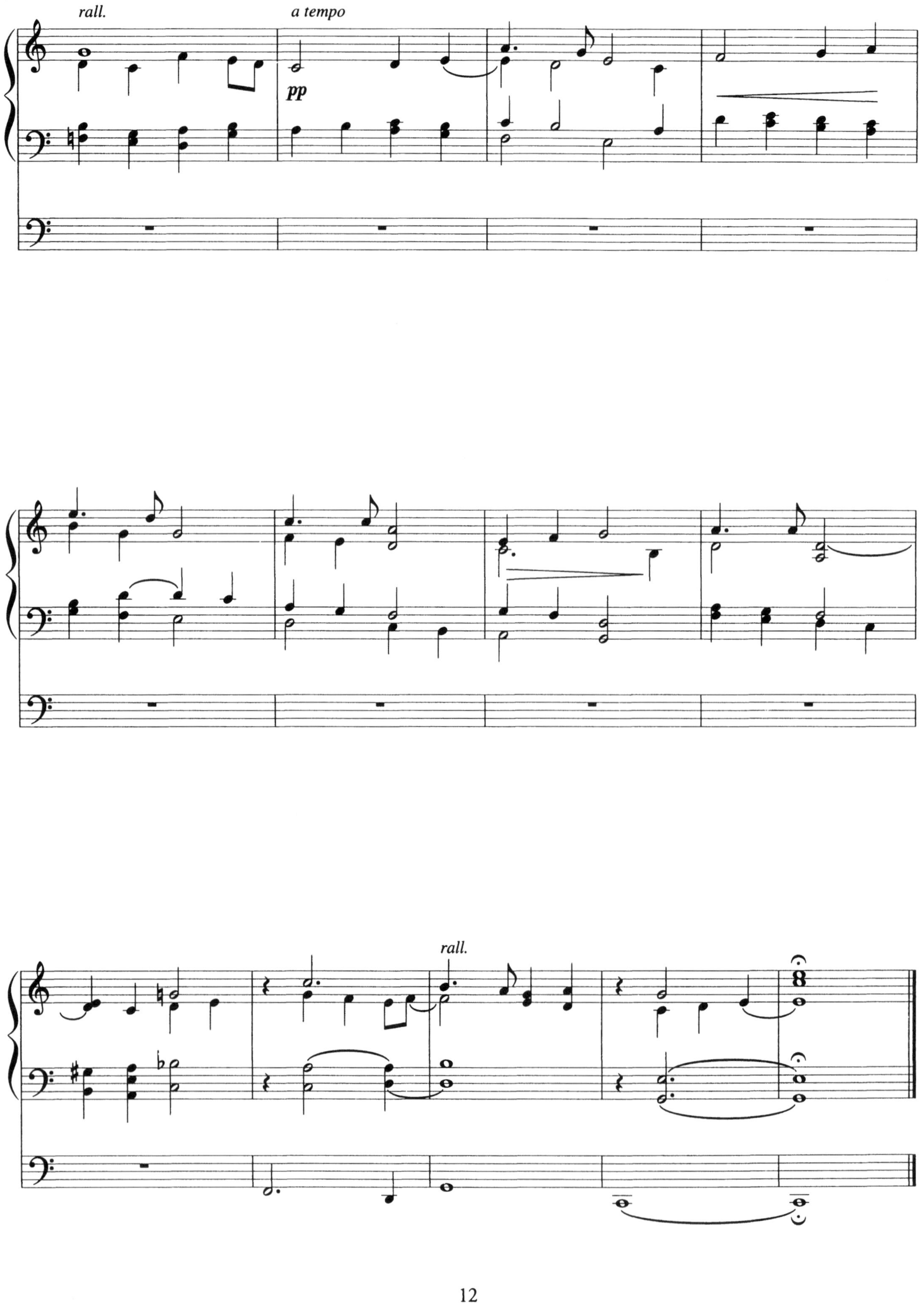
rall.
a tempo
pp
rall.

SORTIE

Andrew Moore

Gt.
last time to Coda
Sw. mf
Gt. mf
Sw.
Gt.
Sw.
(2nd time rit. e dim.)
mf
1.
Gt.
2.
poco meno mosso
Gt.
Sw.

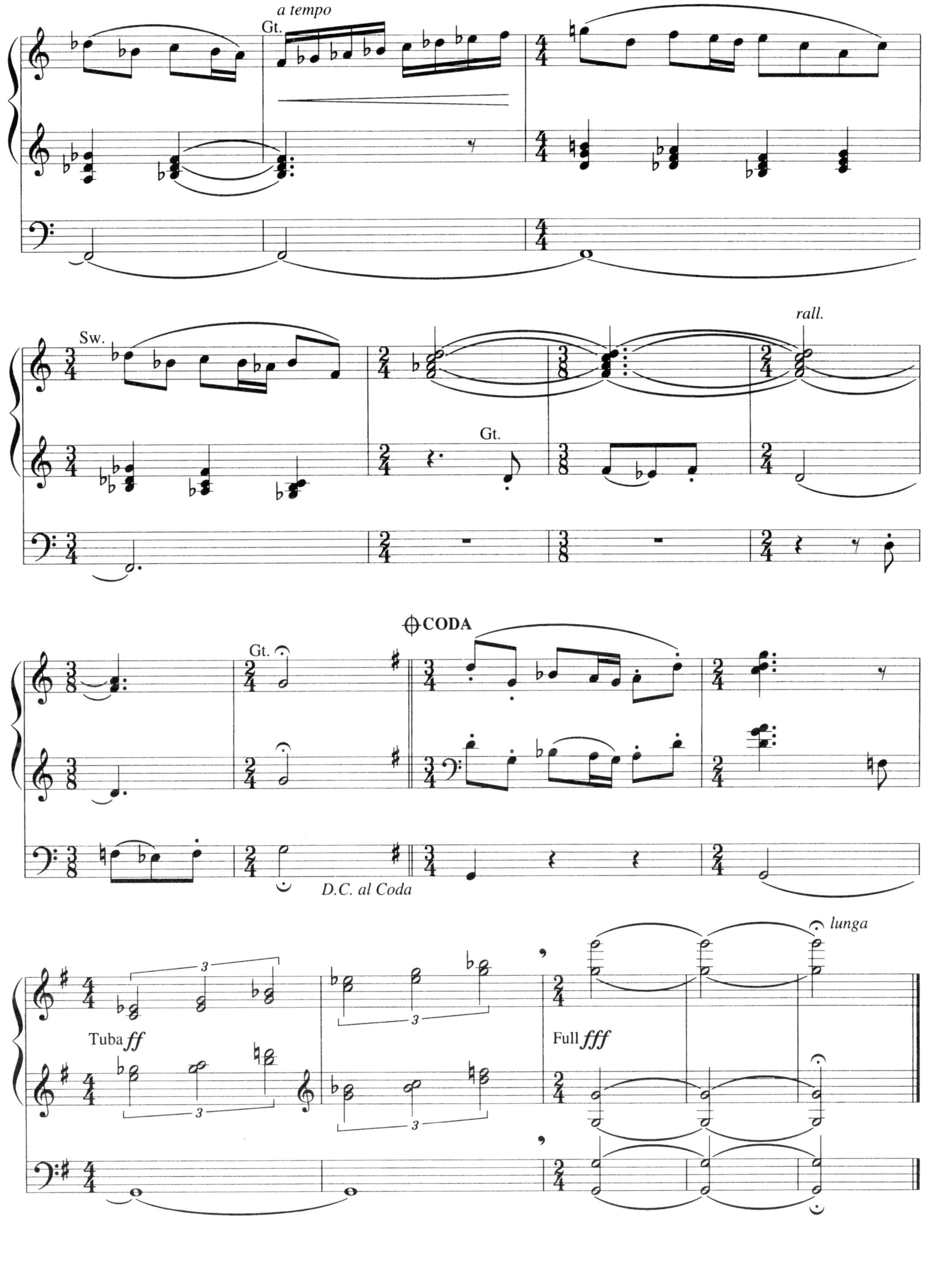
a tempo
Gt.
Sw.
Gt.
rall.
CODA
Gt.
D.C. al Coda
lunga
Tuba ff
Full fff

POSTLUDE

Andrew Fletcher

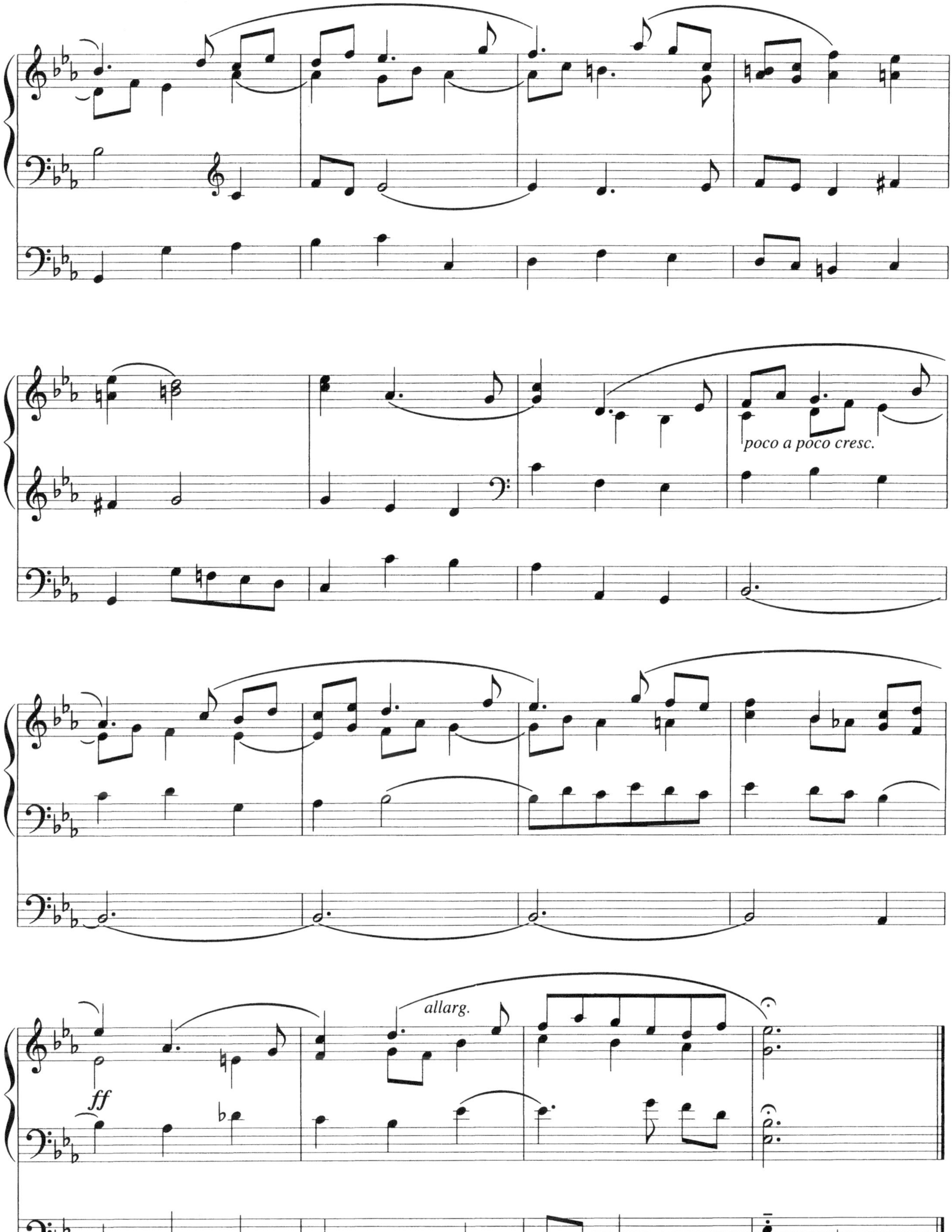
poco a poco cresc.
allarg.
ff

PILGRIMAGE

Colin Hand

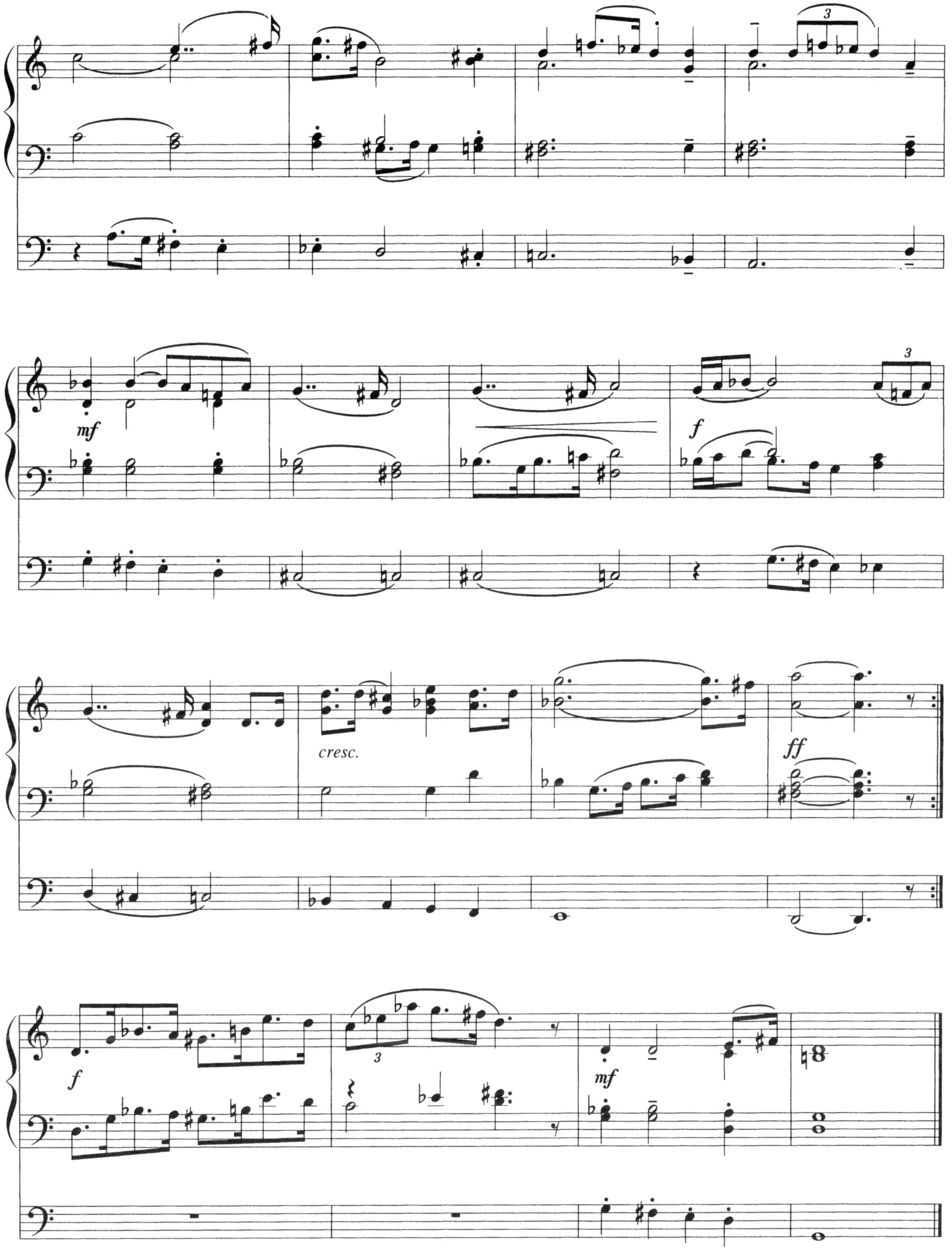
mf
f
cresc.
ff
f
mf

JOYFUL RECESSIONAL

Rosalie Bonighton

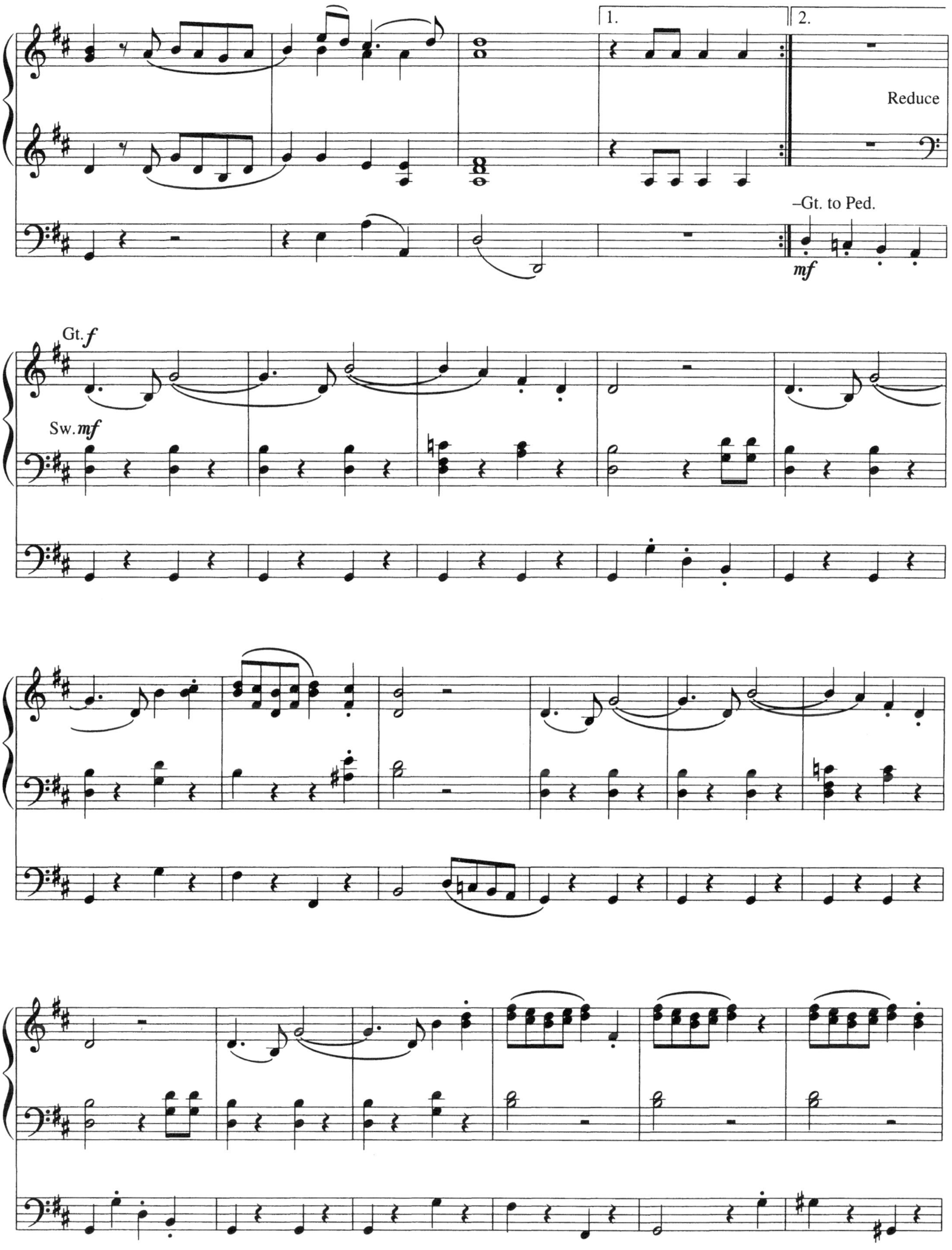
1.
2.
Reduce
–Gt. to Ped.
mf
Gt. f
Sw. mf

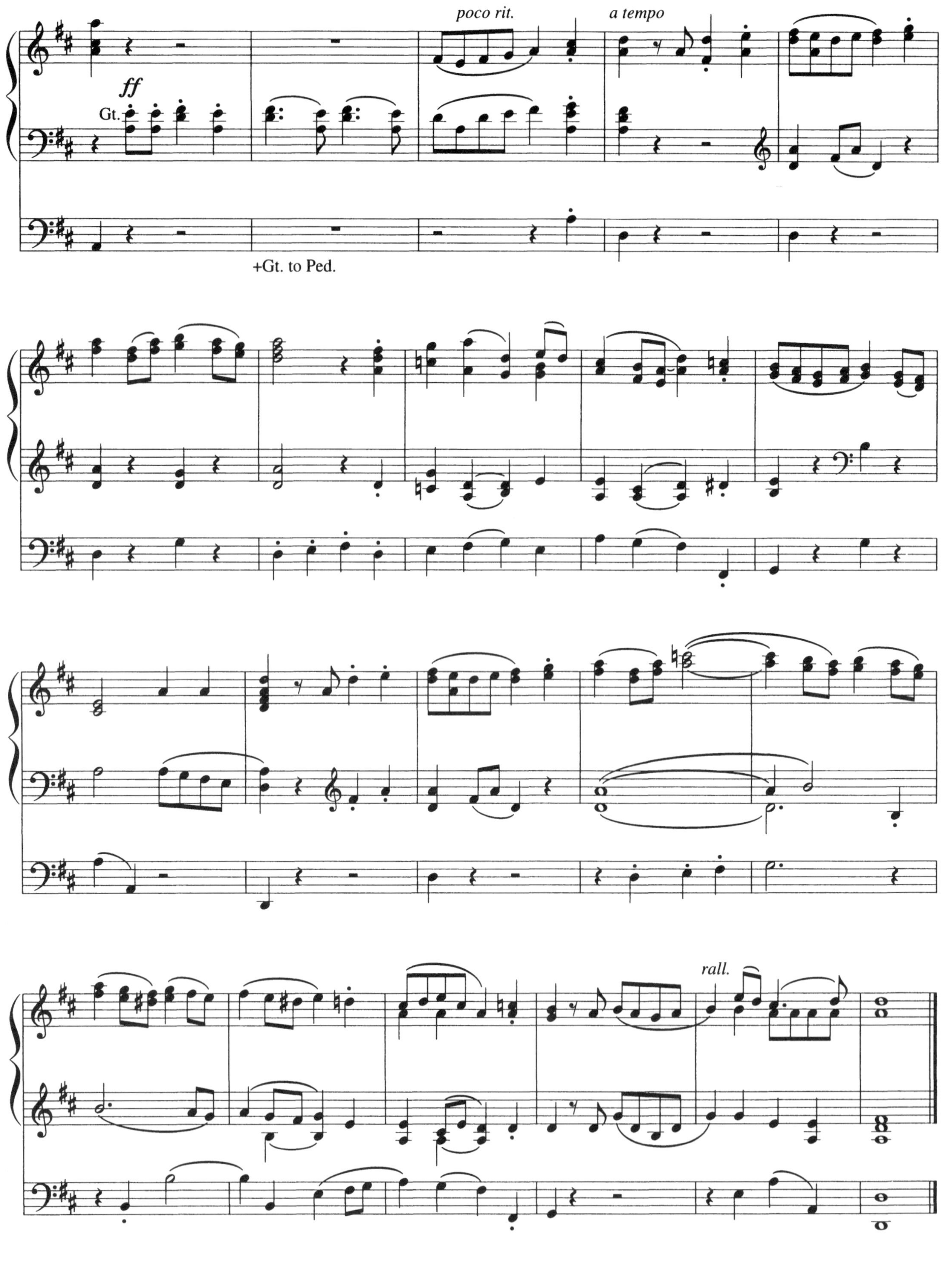
poco rit.
a tempo
ff
Gt.
+Gt. to Ped.
rall.

PAGEANT

Philip Moore

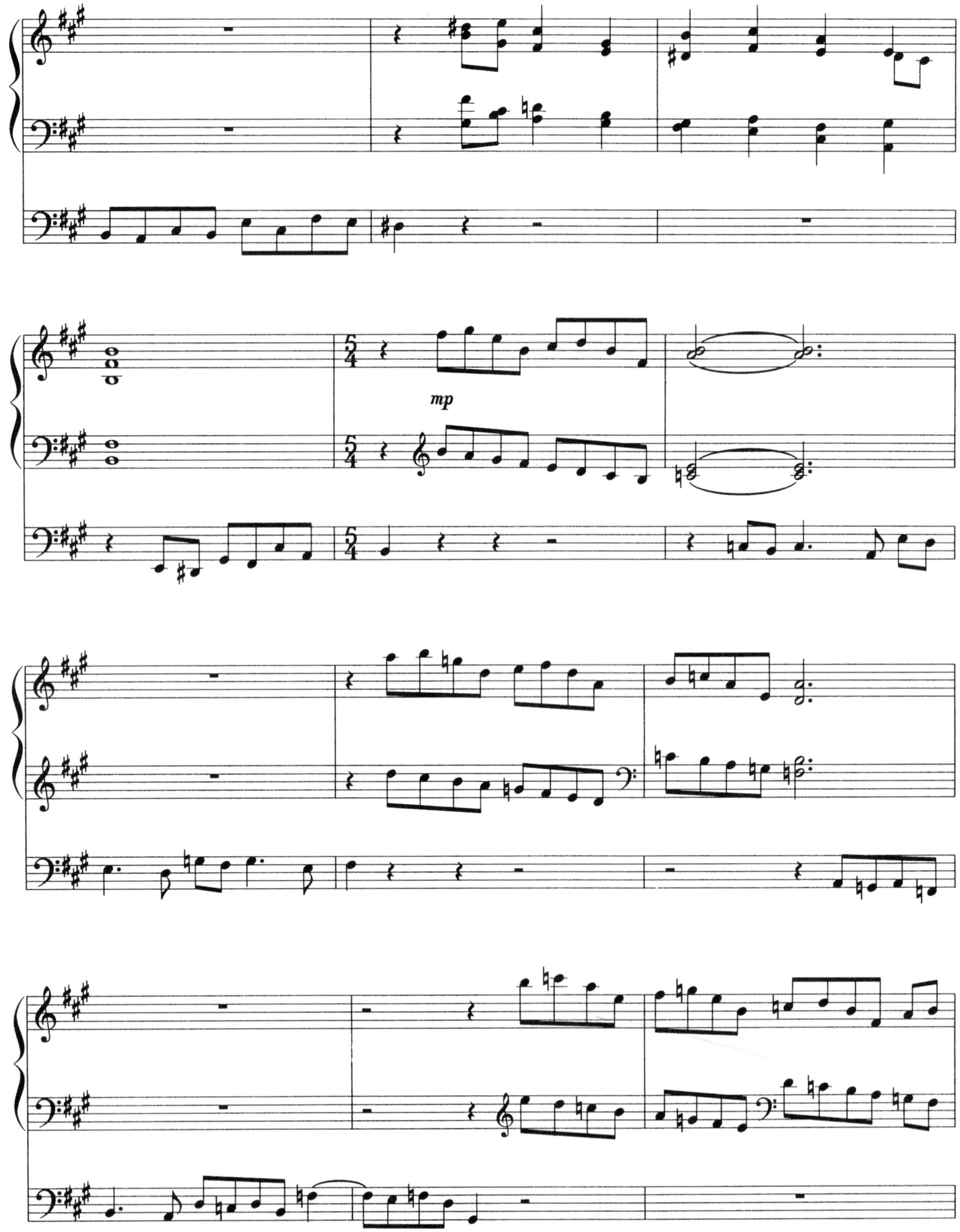
mp

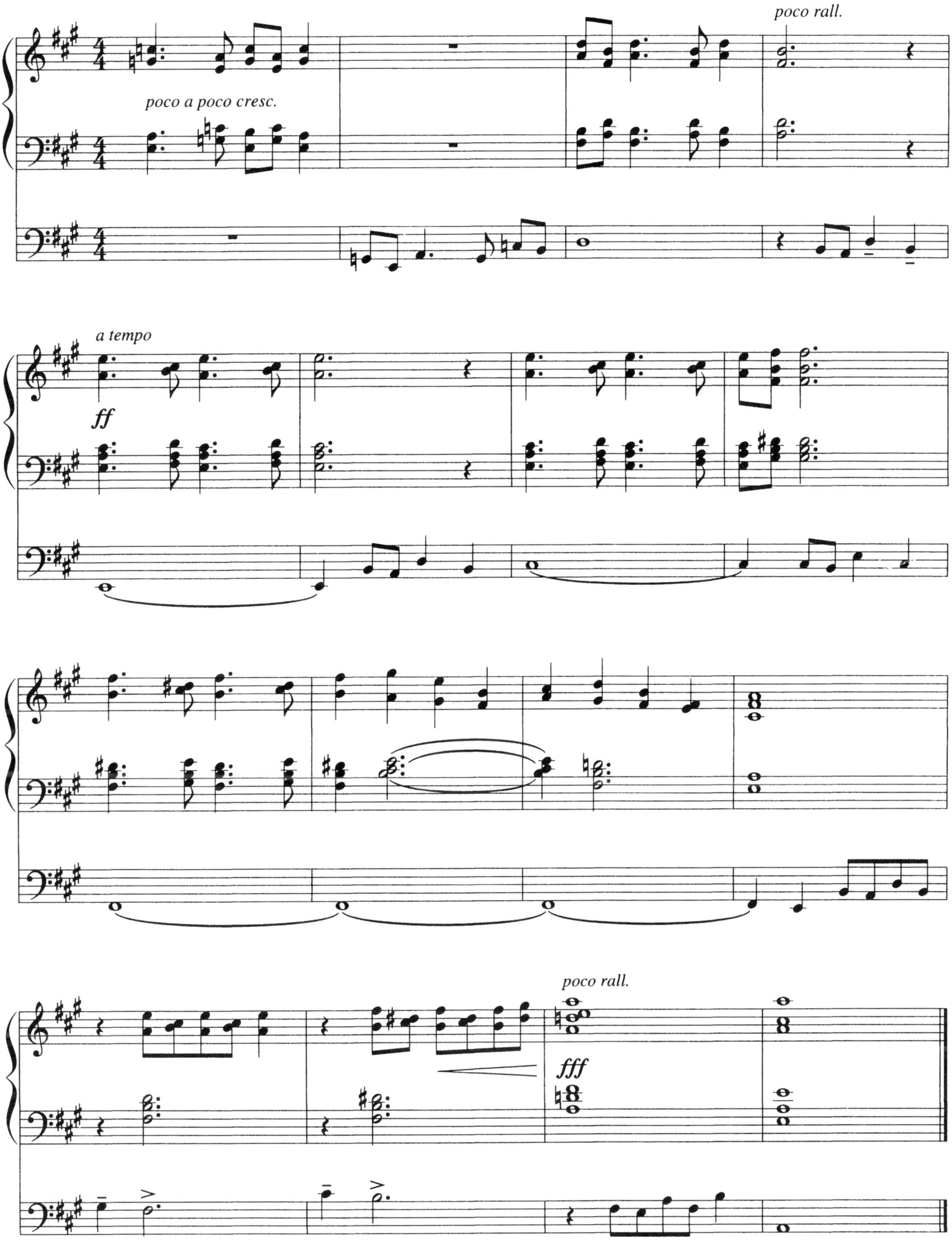
poco rall.
poco a poco cresc.
a tempo
ff
poco rall.
fff

for John W Gearhart III

BRANLE

Stephen Kemp

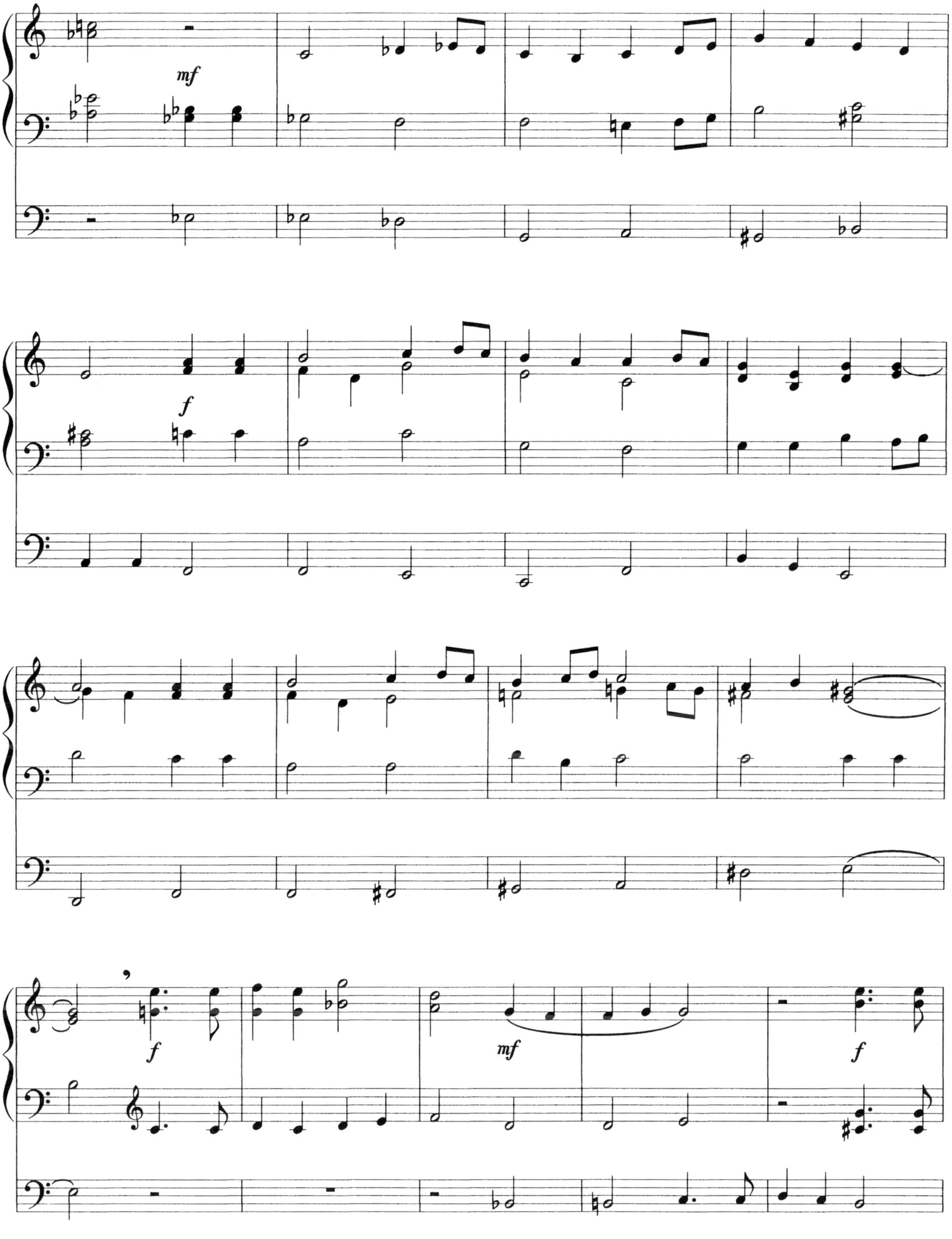
mf
f
f
mf
f

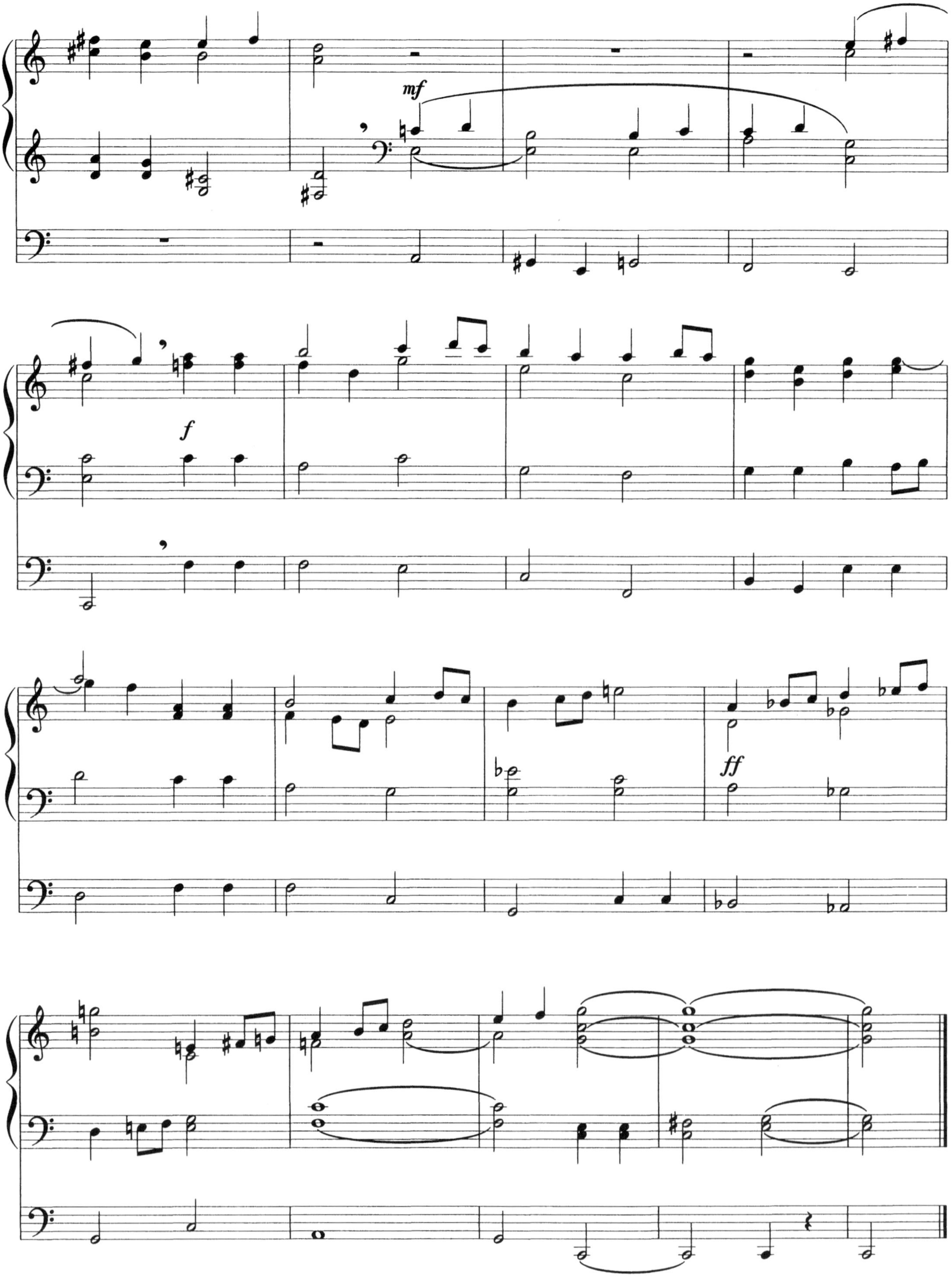
mf
f
ff

FANFARES

Richard Pantcheff

rit.
Slightly slower
mp
mp
poco a poco cresc.
accel.
ff cresc. marcato

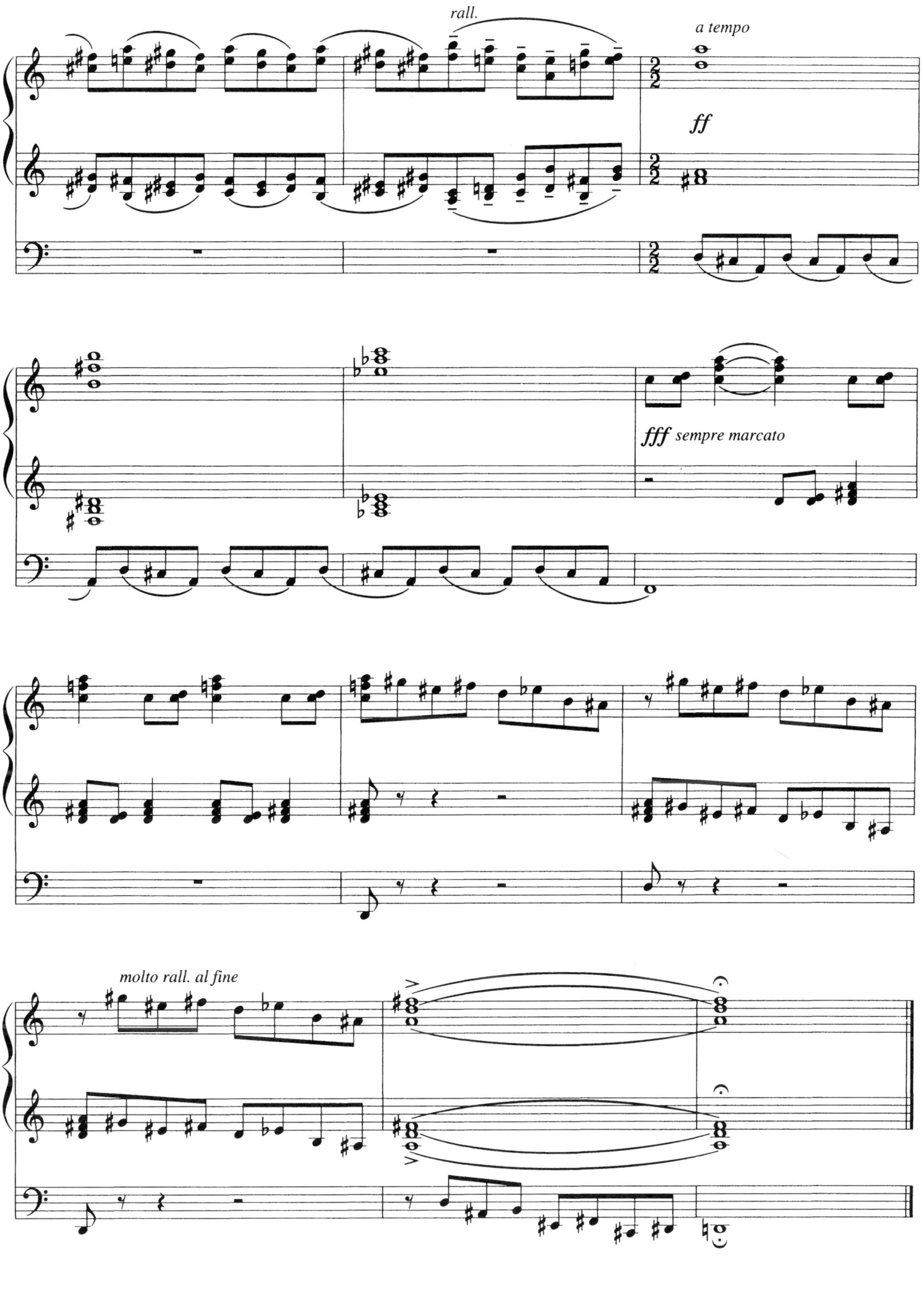
rall.
a tempo
ff
fff sempre marcato
molto rall. al fine

PASSACAGLIA
Paul Bryan

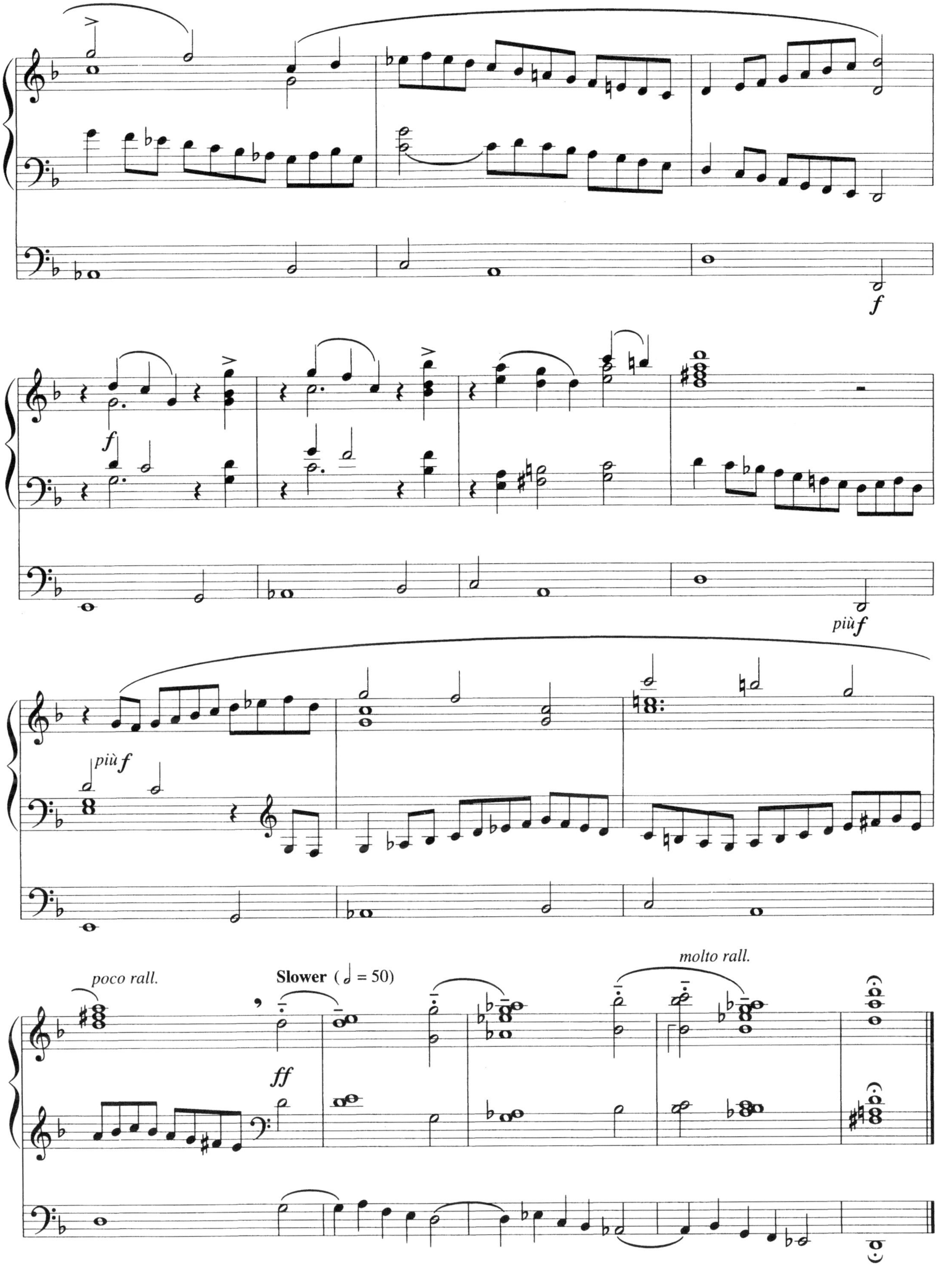
f
f
più f
più f
poco rall.
Slower (𝅗𝅥 = 50)
ff
molto rall.

for Noël
FROM THE SOUTH SEA ISLANDS
Alan Ridout

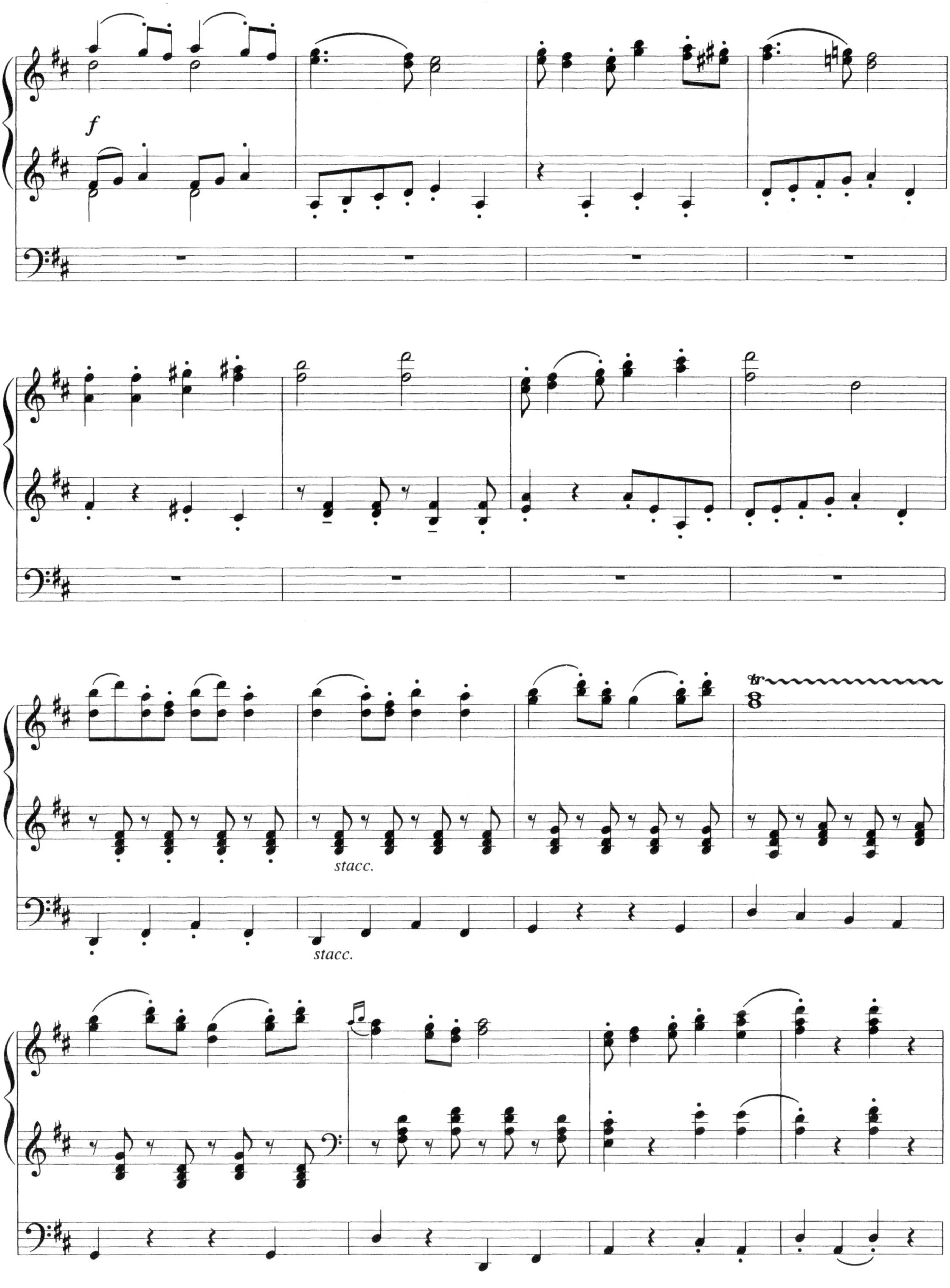
f
stacc.
stacc.

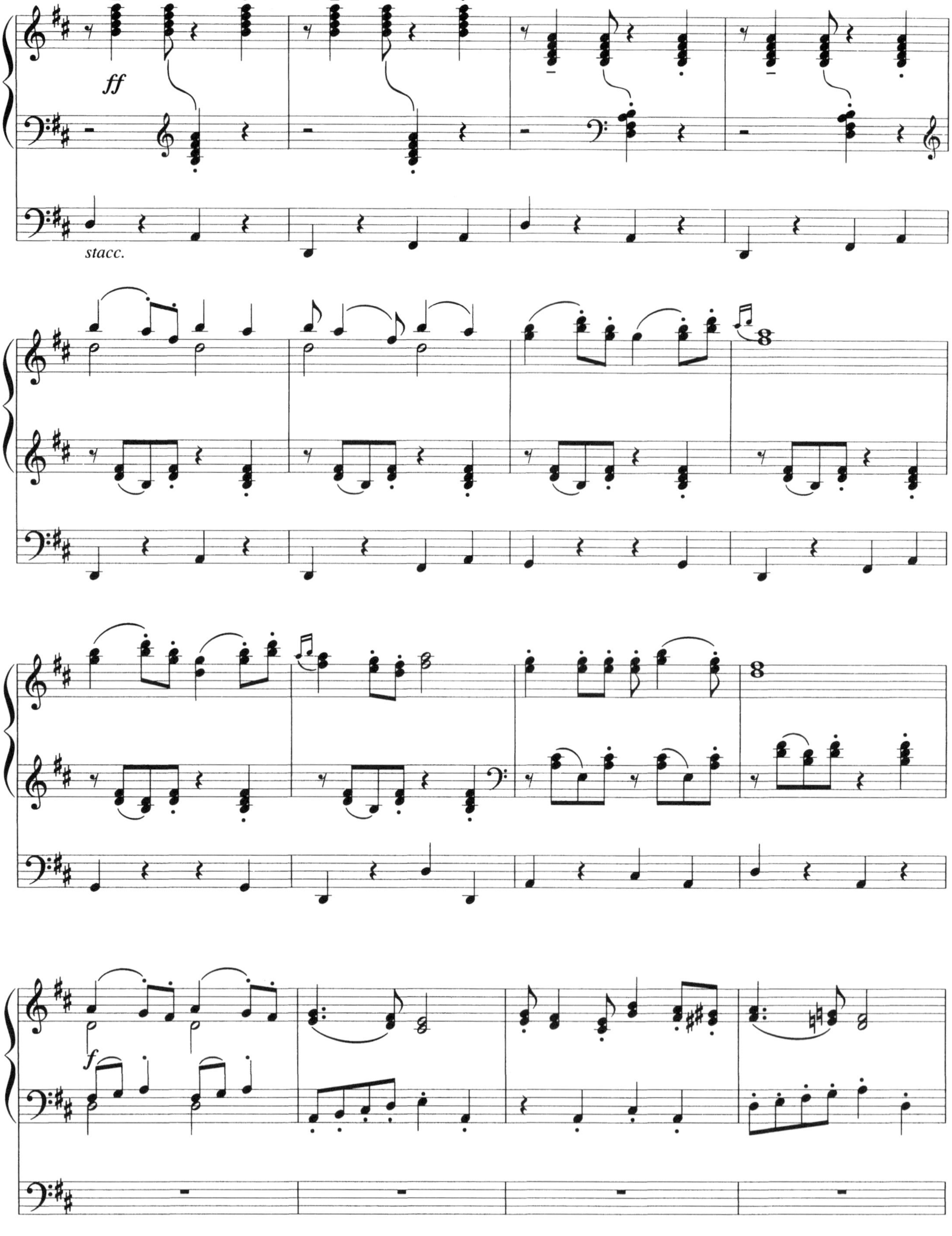
ff
stacc.
f

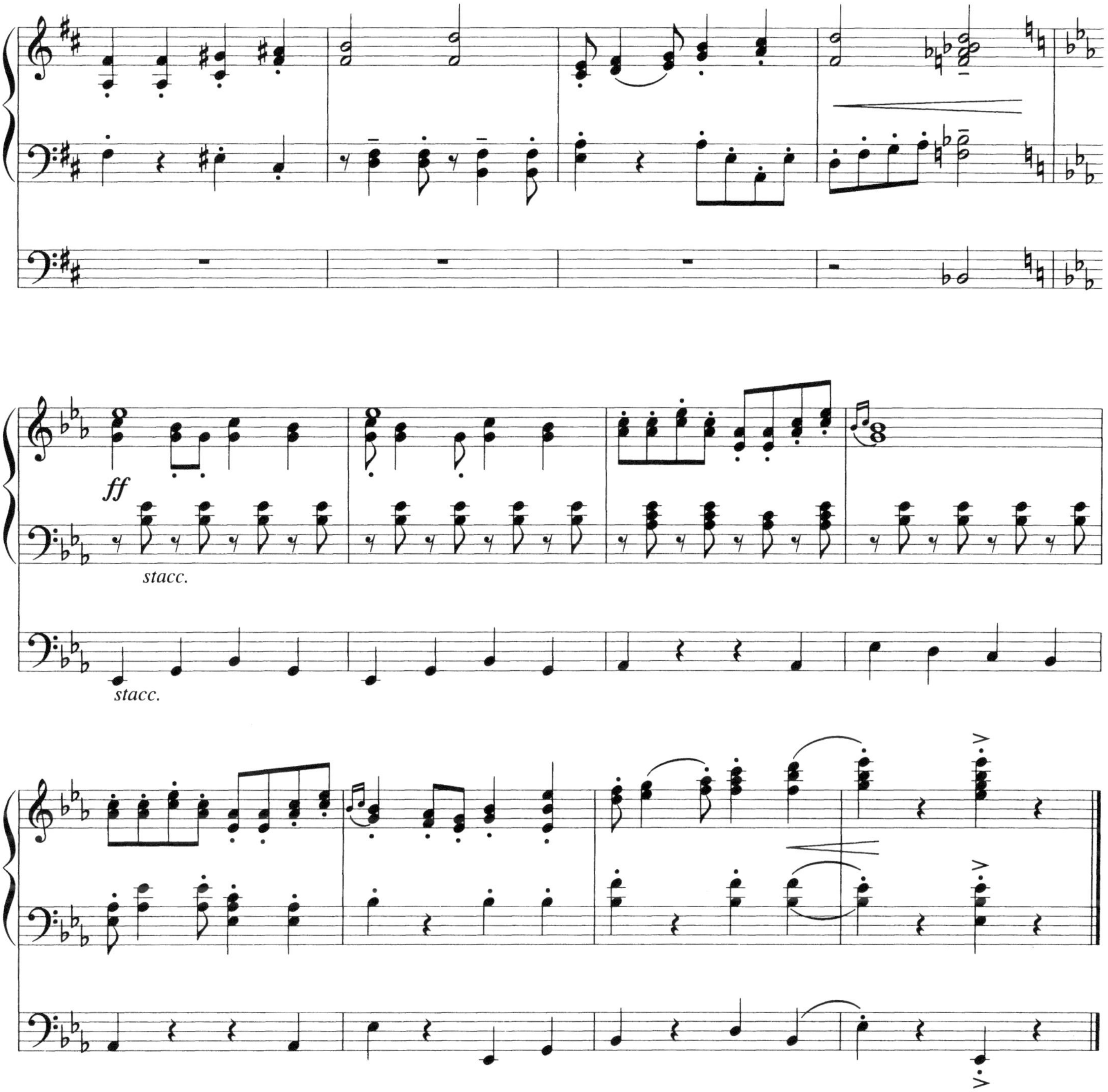
ff
stacc.
stacc.

REFLECTIVE PROCESSIONAL

Owain Edwards

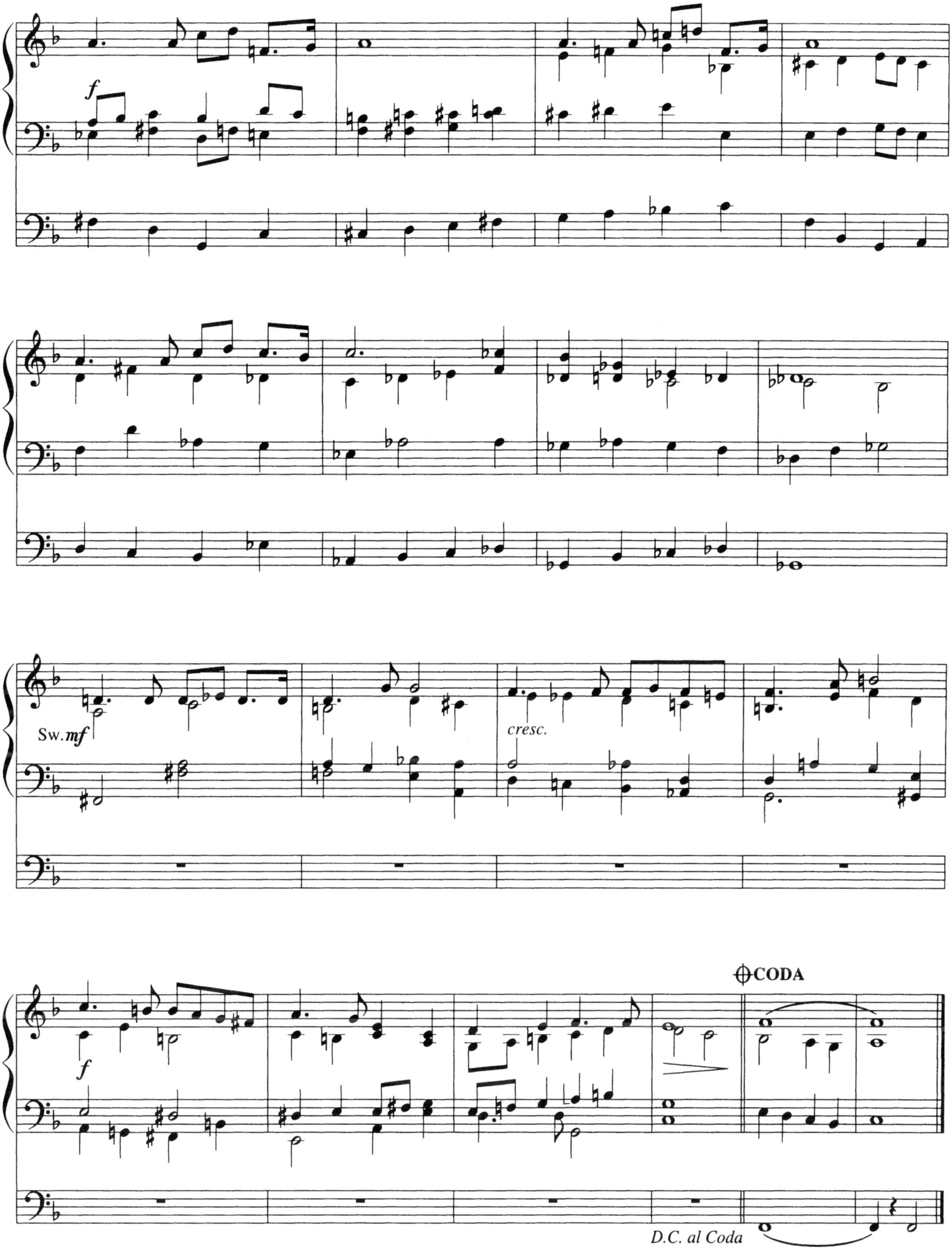
f
Sw. mf
cresc.
f
CODA
D.C. al Coda

PETIT CHORALE

Robert Fielding

41

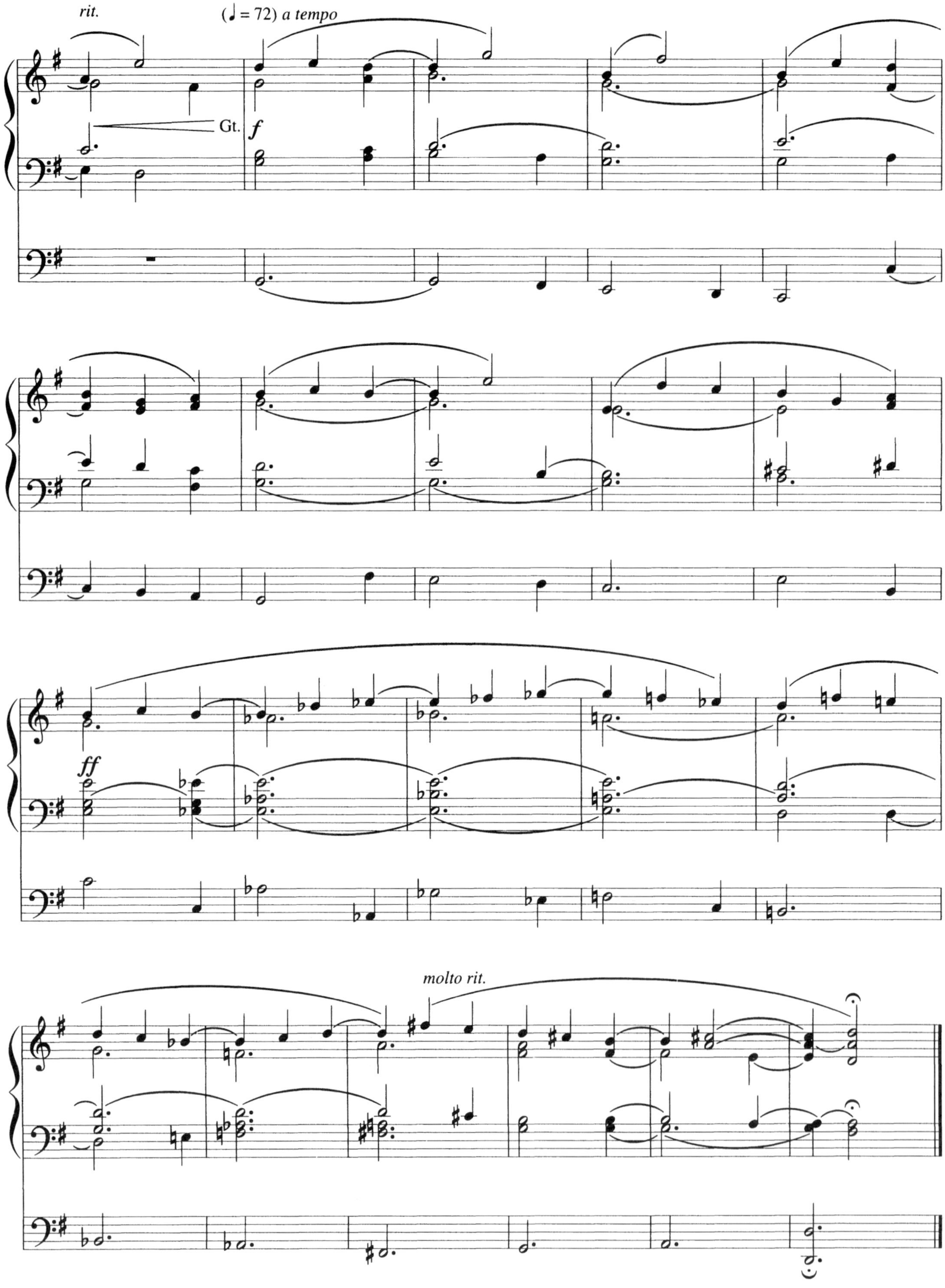
rit.
(♩ = 72) a tempo
Gt.
f
ff
molto rit.

PAEAN

Richard Knight

Allegro con bravura

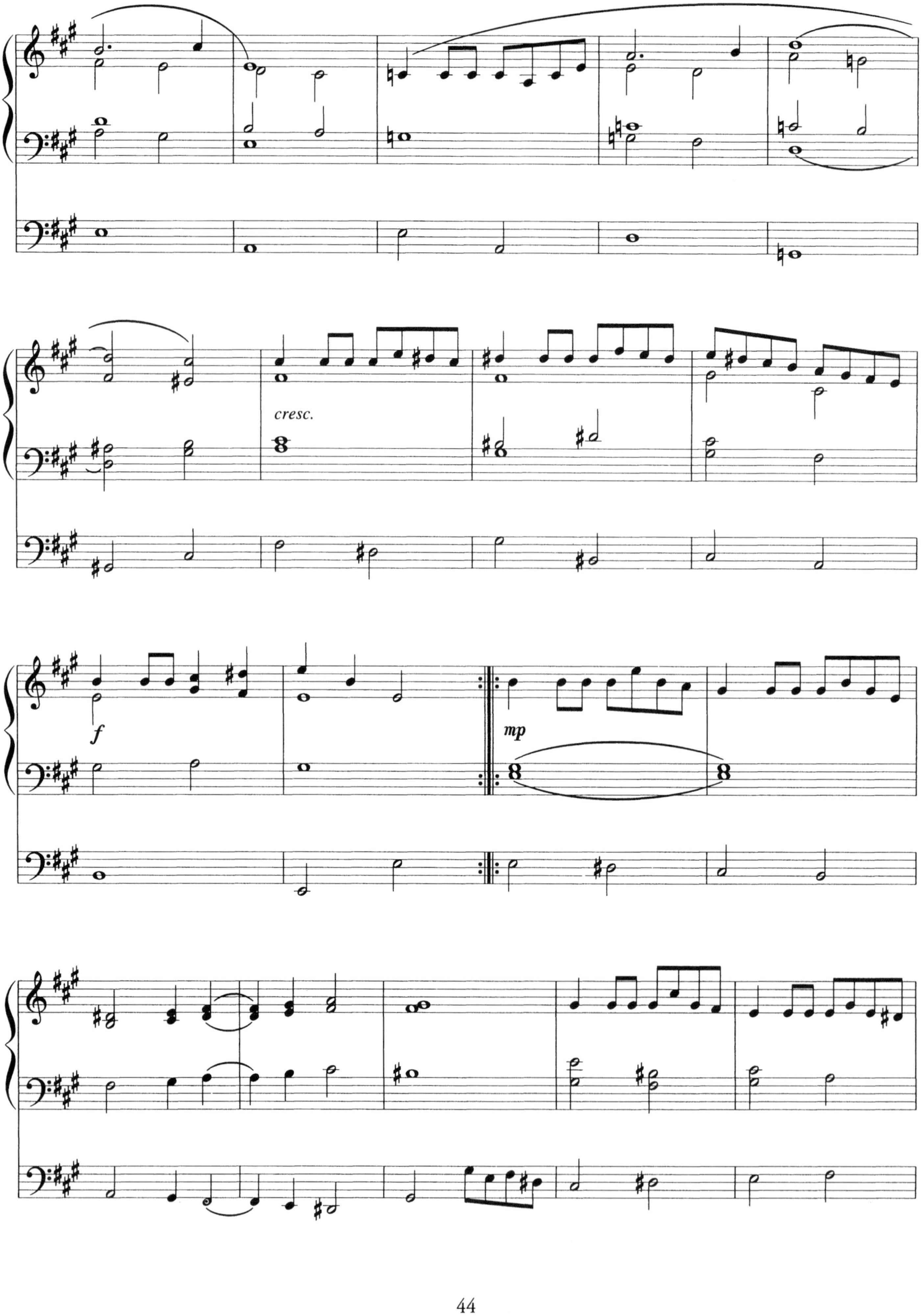
cresc.
f
mp

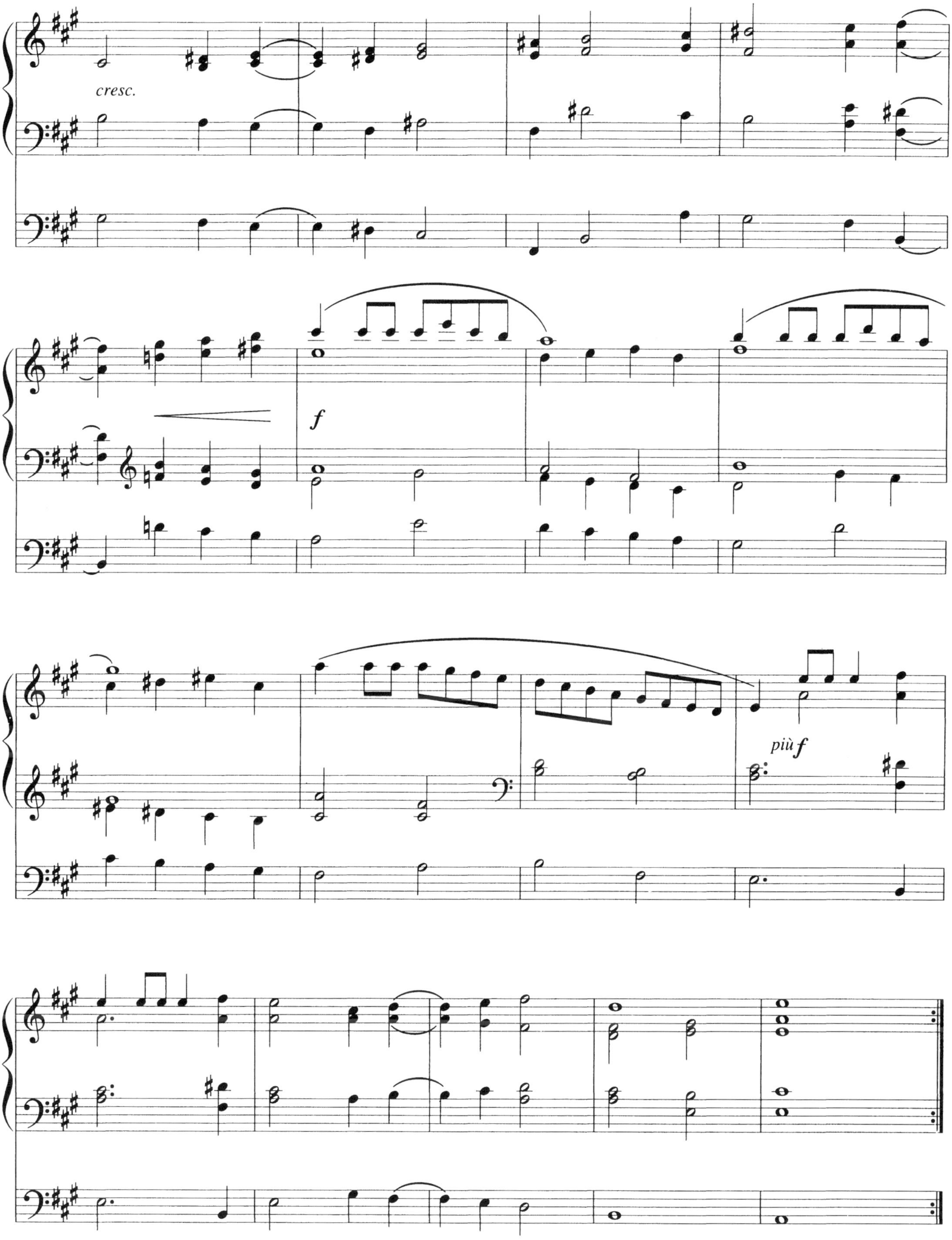
cresc.
f
più f

DIGNITATE

Andrew Moore

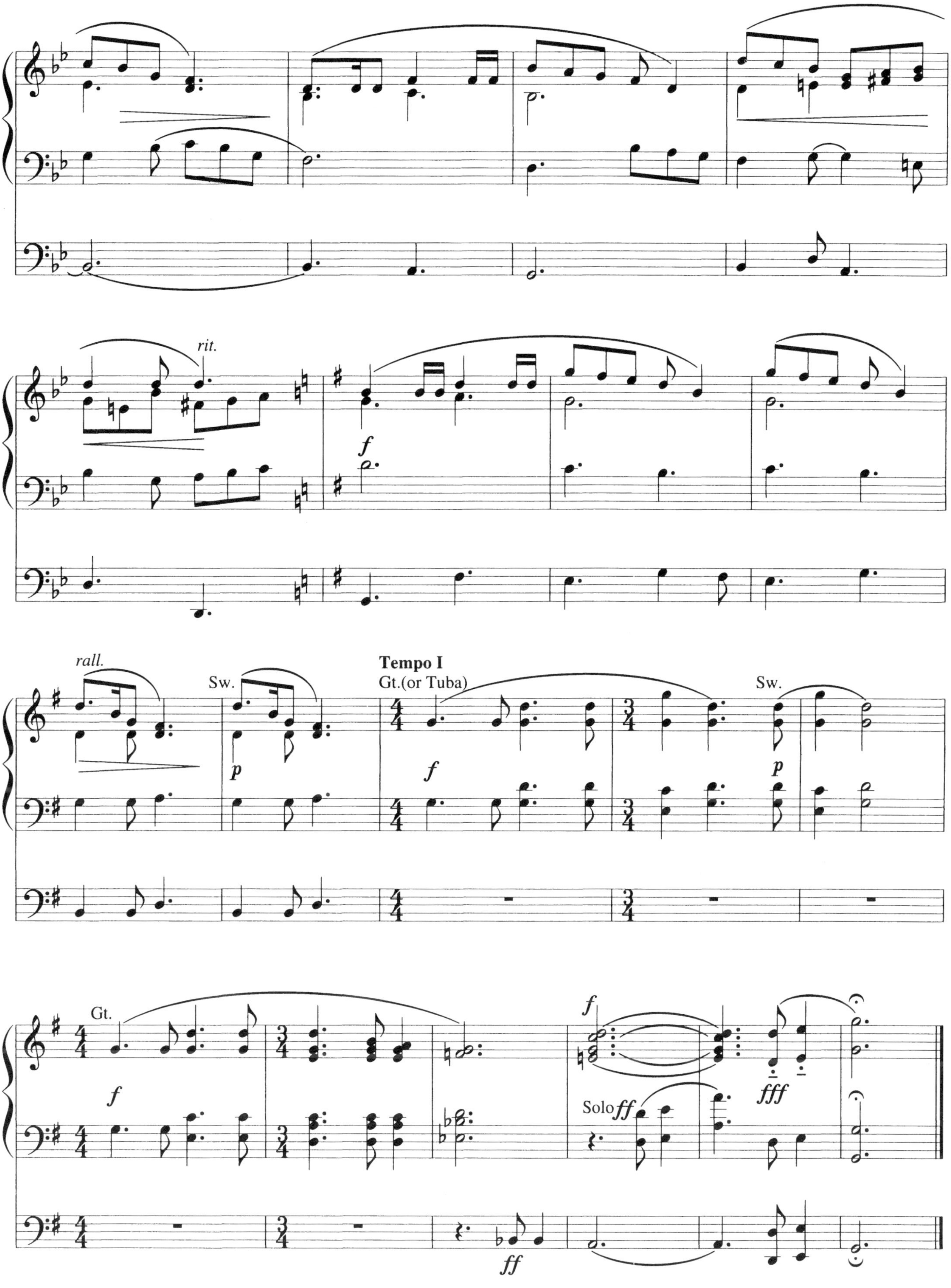
rit.
f
rall.
Sw.
p
Tempo I
Gt.(or Tuba)
f
Sw.
p
Gt.
f
f
Solo ff
fff
ff

for Frances and Winston

GRAZIOSO

Betty Roe

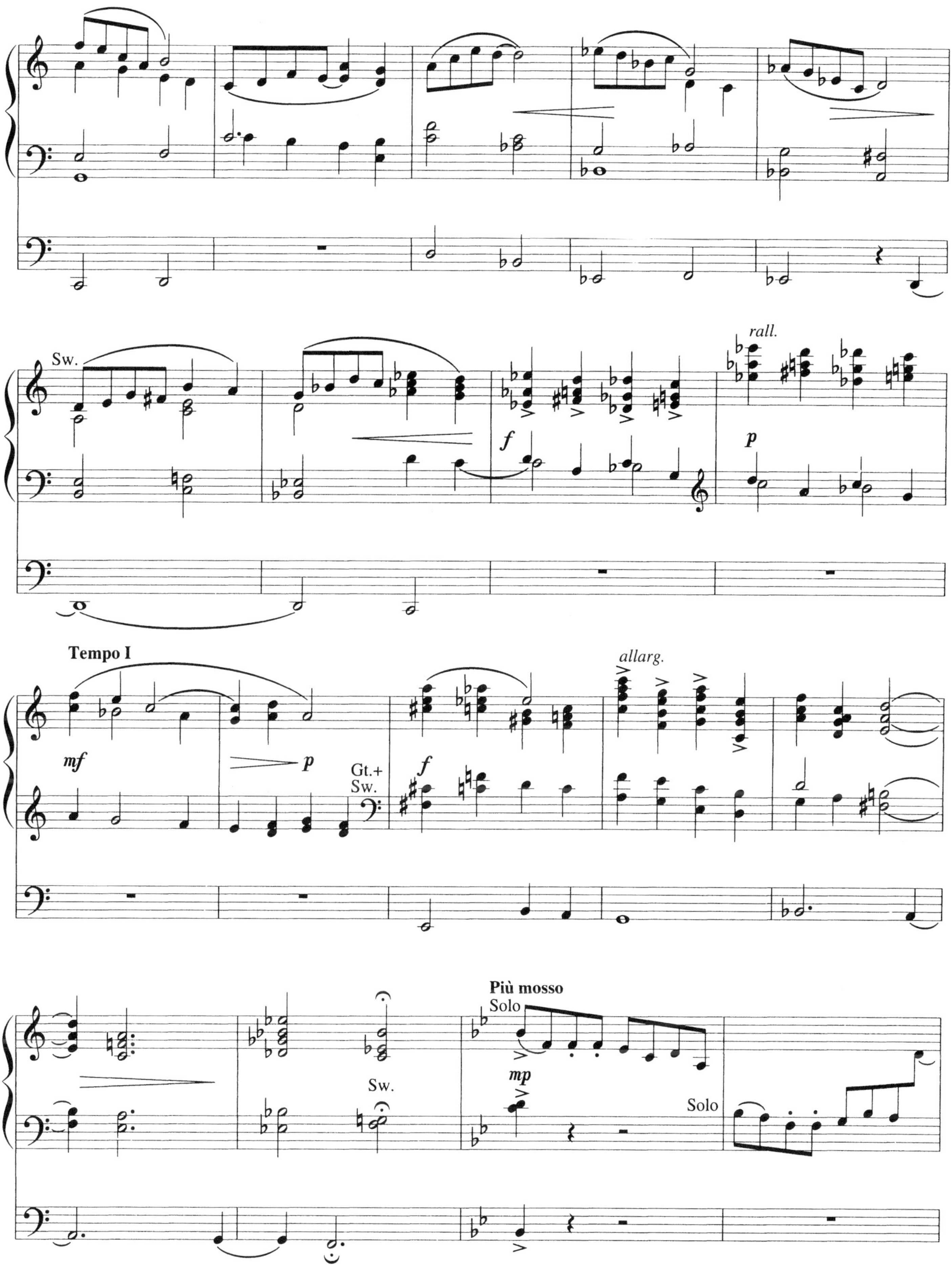
Sw.
rall.
f
p
Tempo I
mf
p
Gt.+
Sw.
f
allarg.
Più mosso
Solo
mp
Sw.
Solo

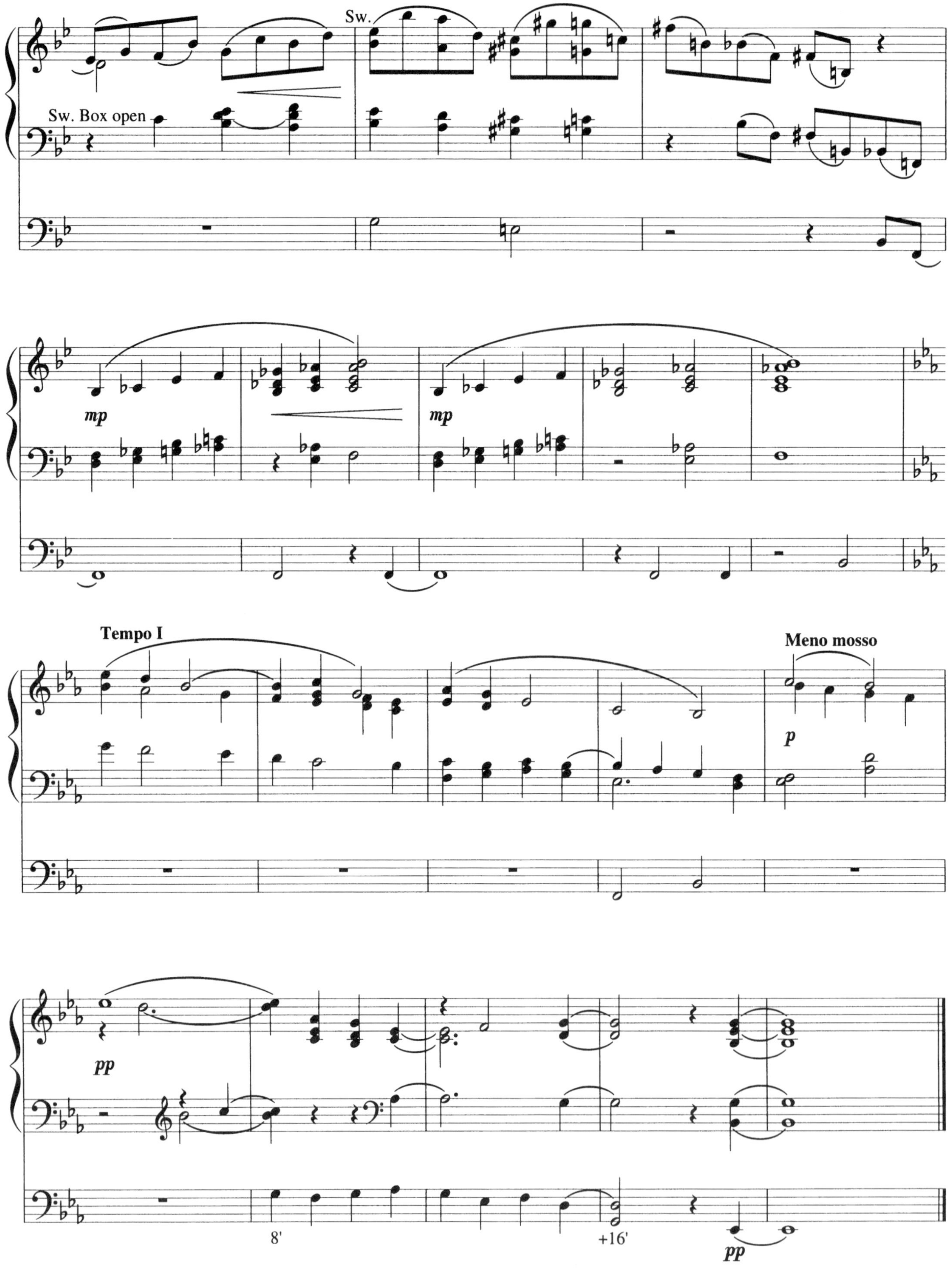
Sw.
Sw. Box open
mp
mp
Tempo I
Meno mosso
p
pp
8'
+16'
pp

CHACONNE FOR GOOD FRIDAY

June Nixon

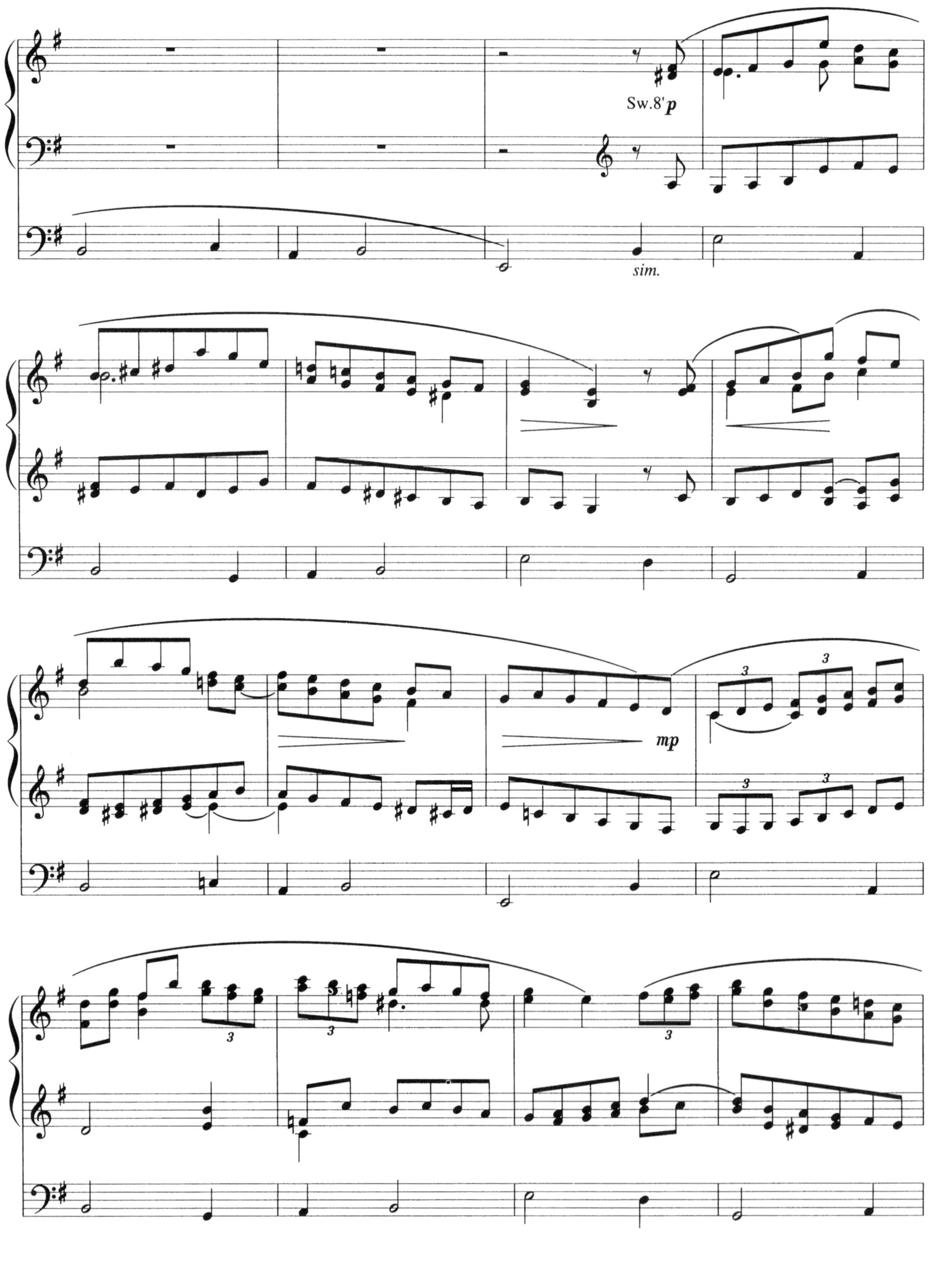
Sw.8' p
sim.
mp

53

FESTIVAL MARCH

Norman Warren

Full
Sw.
poco rall.
a tempo
Gt. to Sw.
ff
poco rall. al fine
Solo Tuba (or Tpt.)
ff

PALACE BEAUTIFUL

Richard Shephard

Con moto (♩ = c.120)

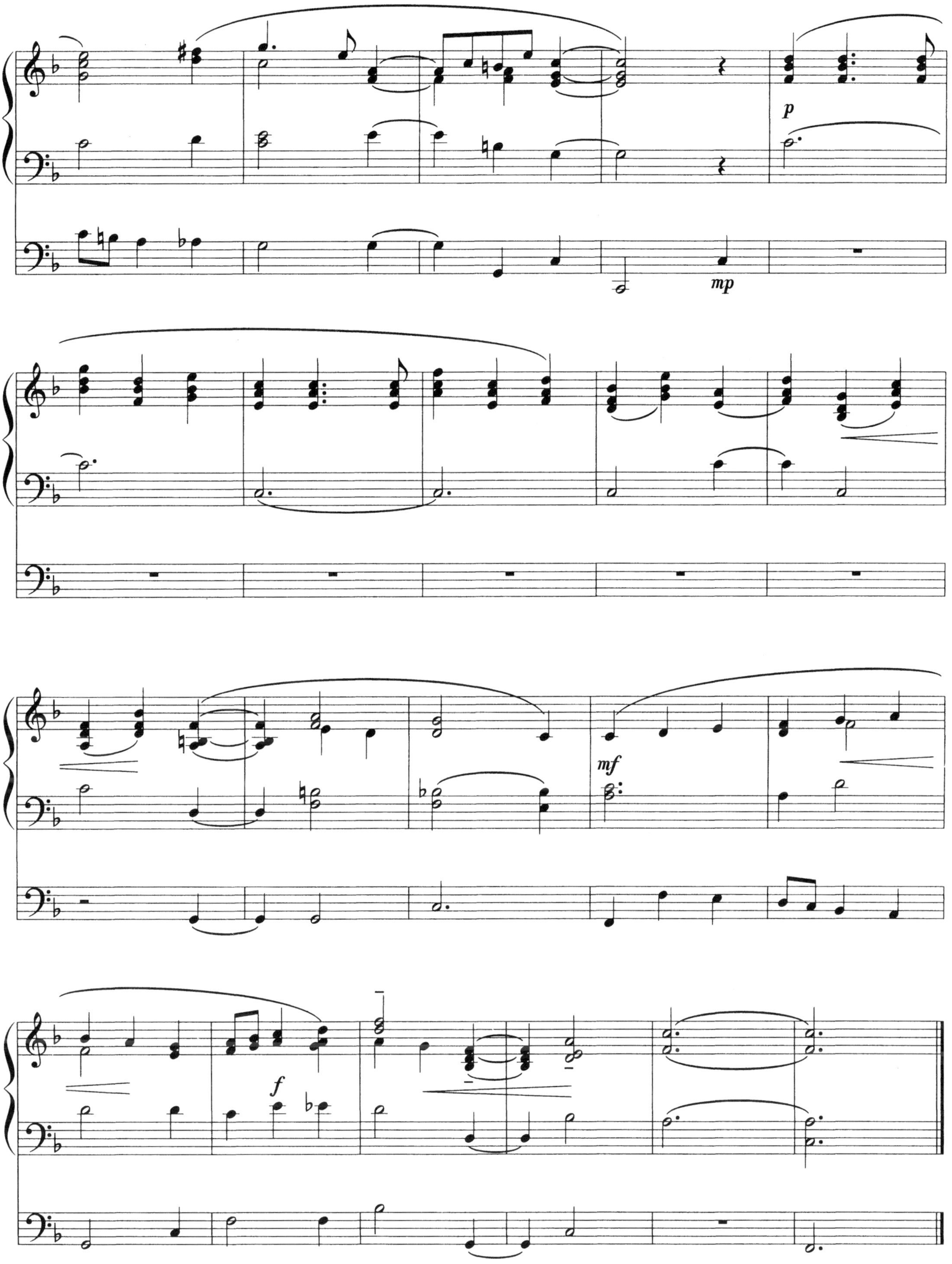
mp
p
mf
f

PAEAN

Colin Hand

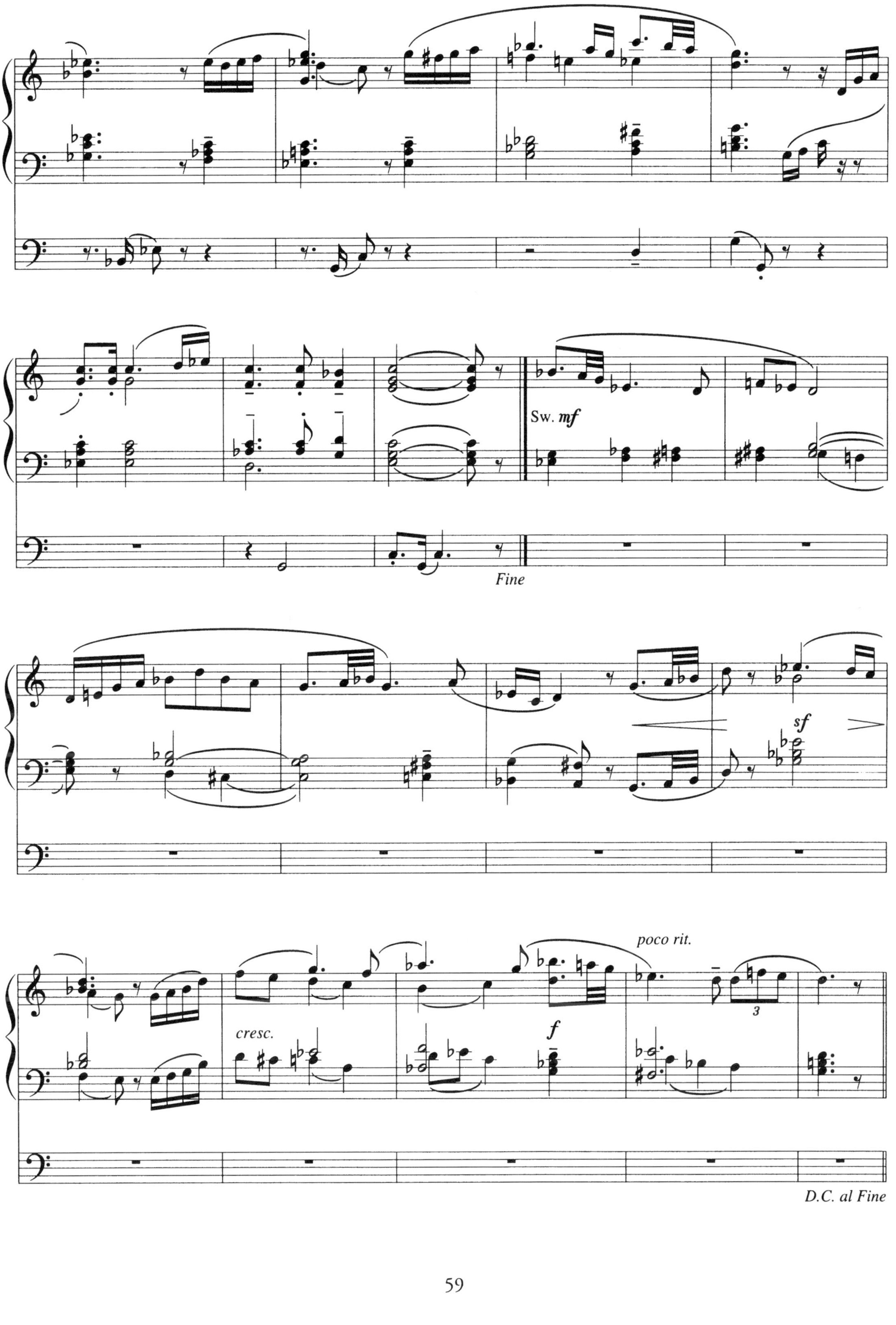
Sw. mf
Fine
sf
cresc.
f
poco rit.
3
D.C. al Fine

for Martin Schellenberg

ALLA MARCIA

Malcolm Archer

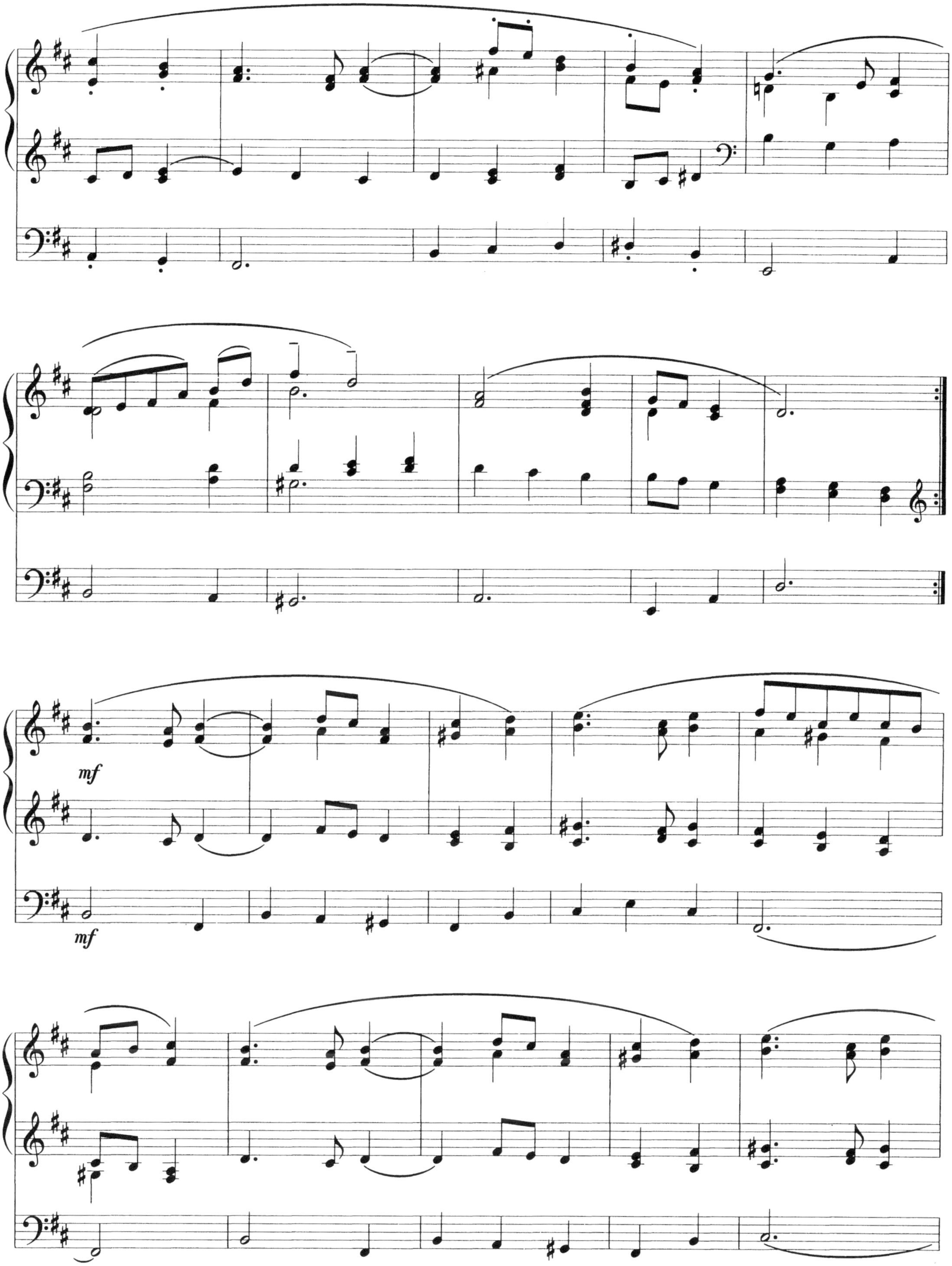
mf
mf

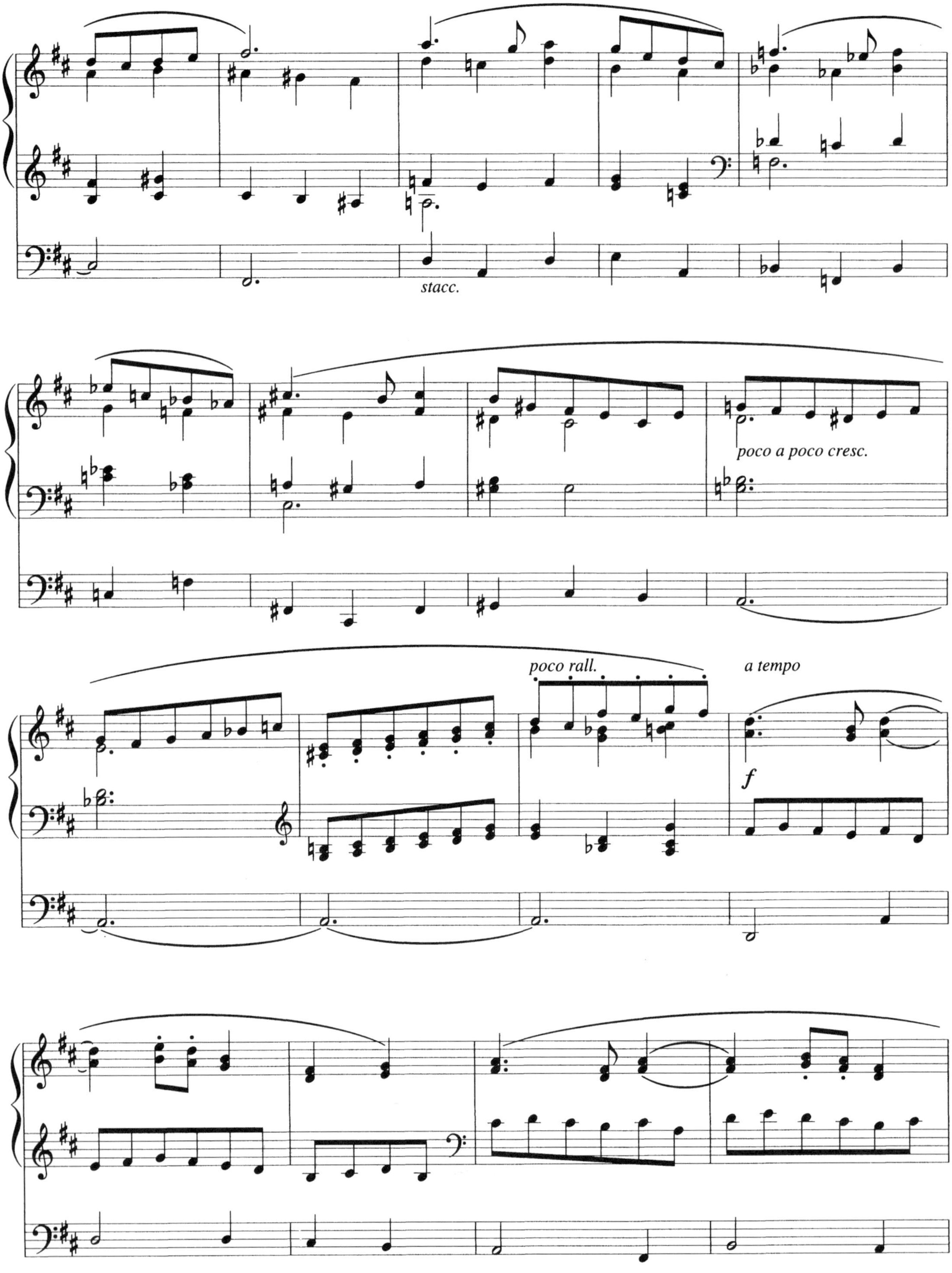
stacc.
poco a poco cresc.
poco rall.
a tempo
f

last time to Coda

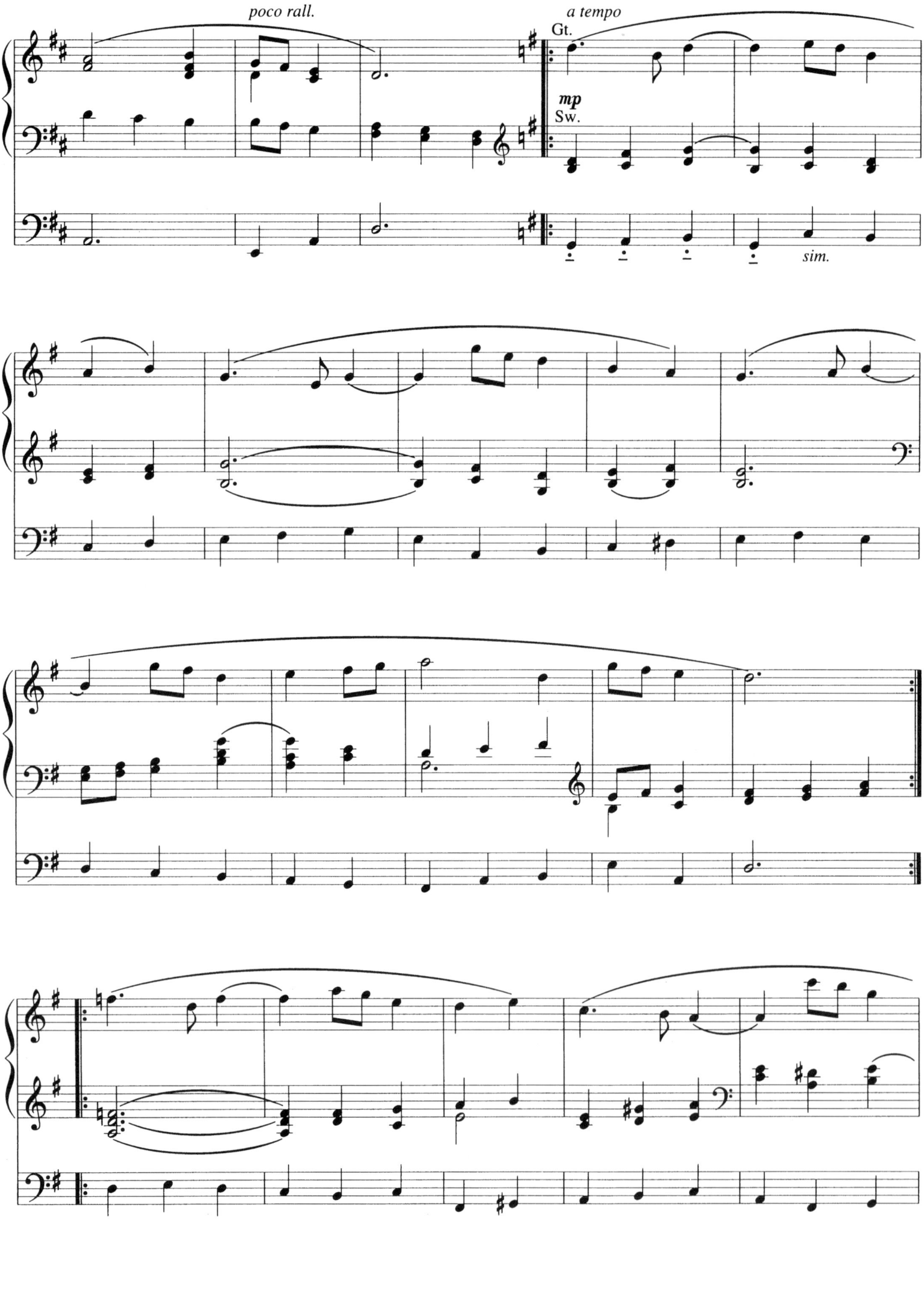
poco rall.
a tempo
Gt.
mp
Sw.
sim.

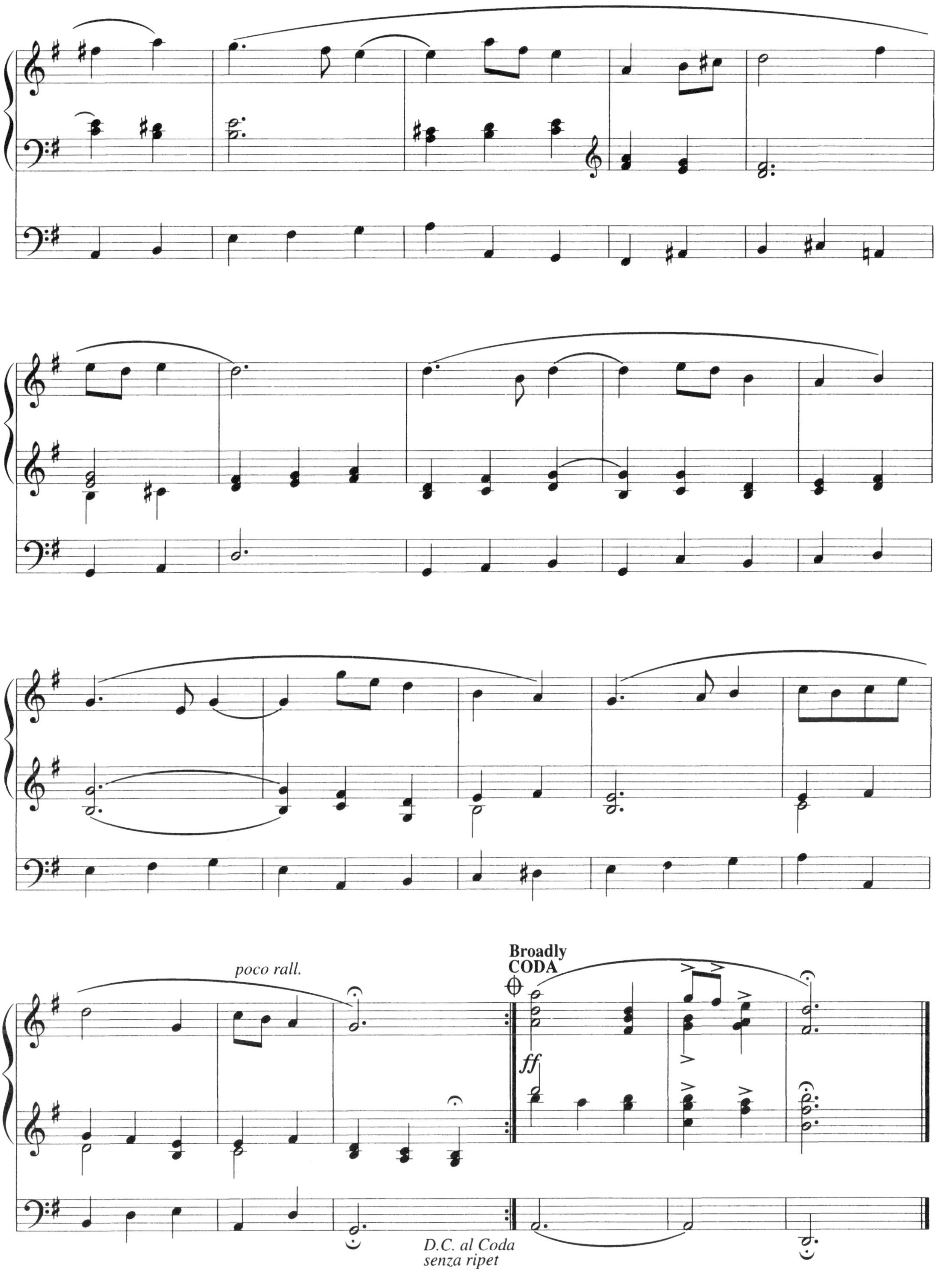
poco rall.
Broadly
CODA
ff
D.C. al Coda
senza ripet

SORTIE

Richard Knight

Maestoso ma con moto

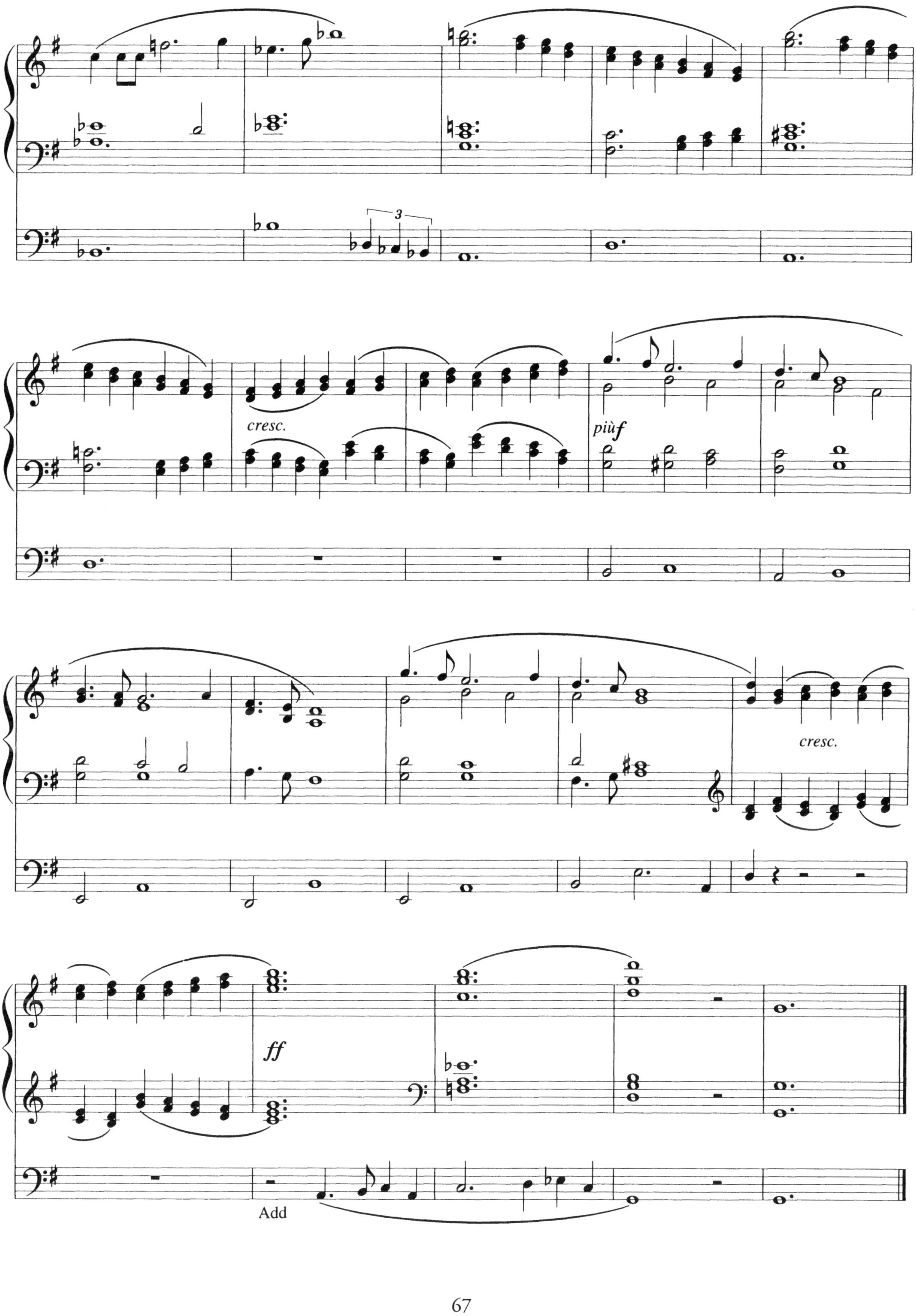

cresc.
più f
cresc.
ff
Add

TRUMPET DOUBLE

Alan Ridout

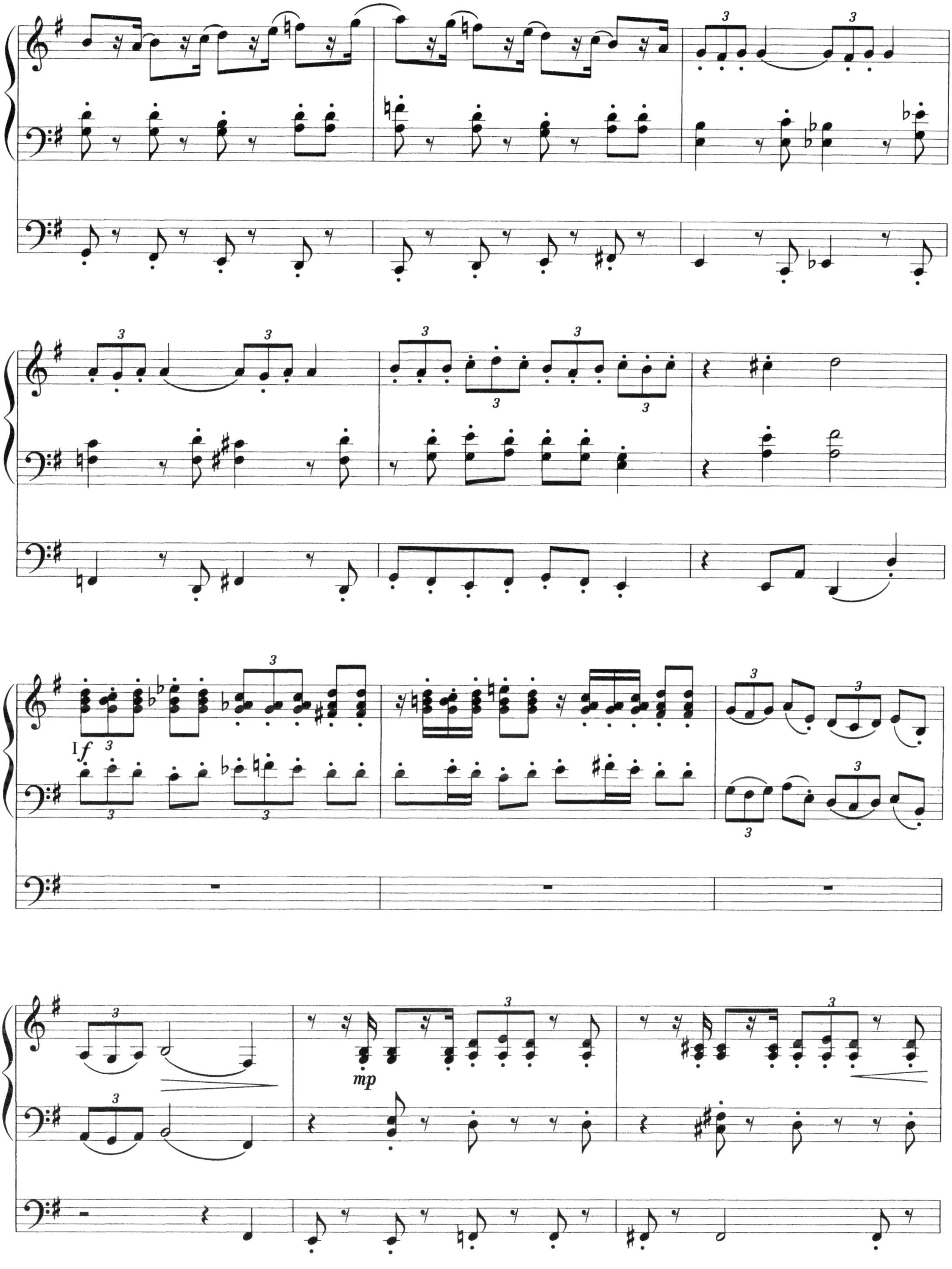
I f
mp

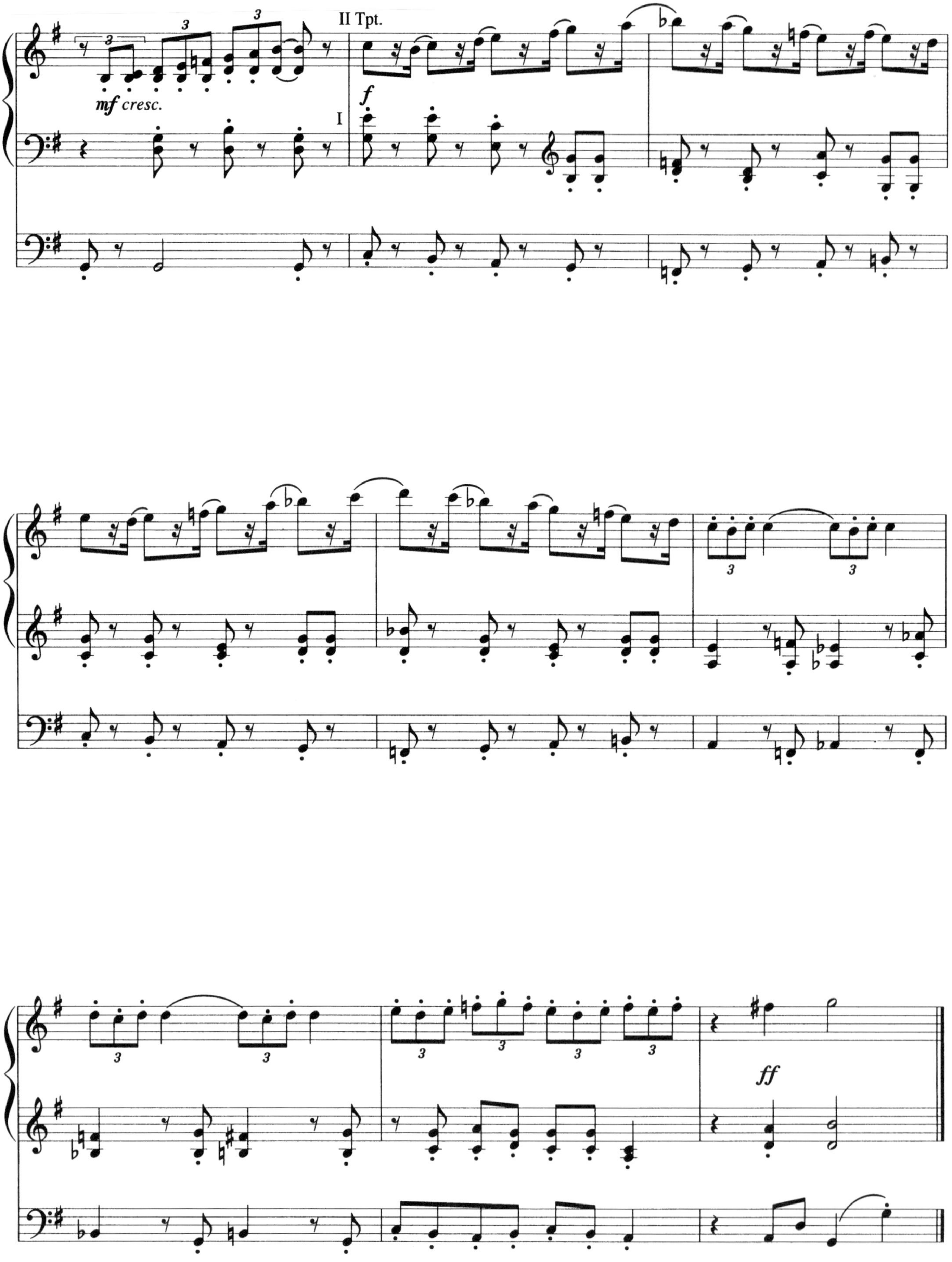
II Tpt.
mf cresc.
f
I
ff

ECCE SACERDOS MAGNUS

Andrew Gant

Allegretto alla marcia

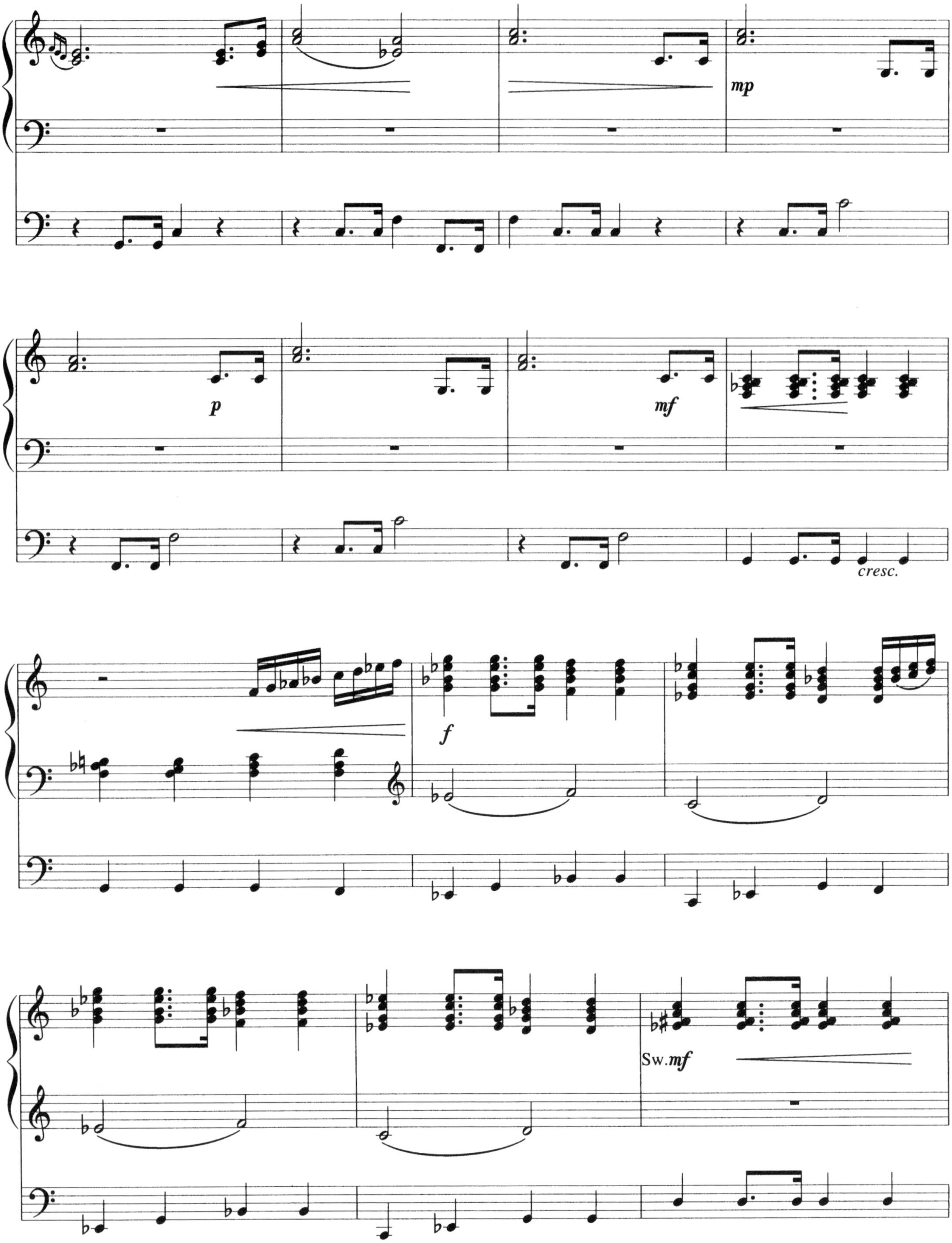
mp
p
mf
cresc.
f
Sw.mf

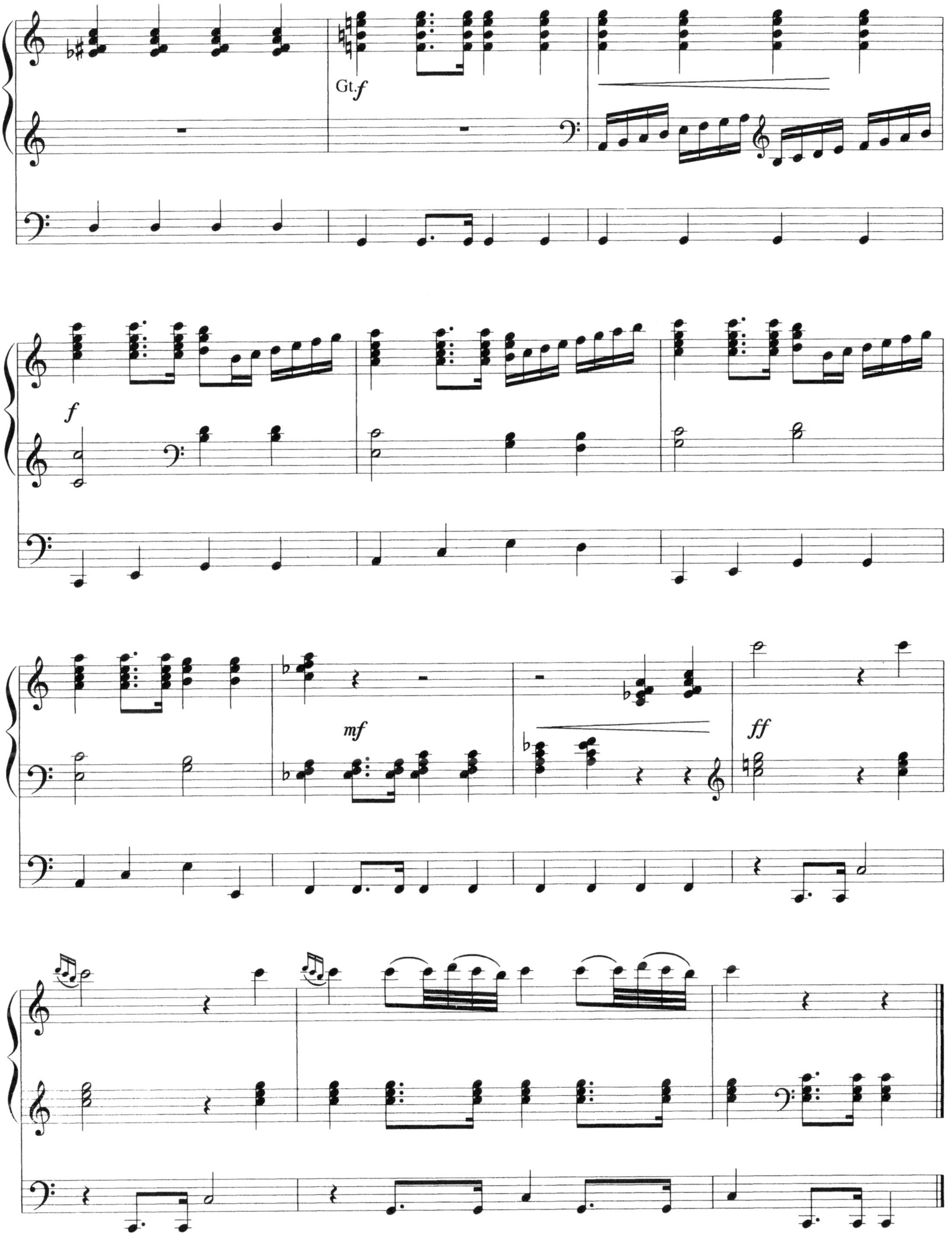
Gt. f
f
mf
ff

'Floreat Glenalmond'

CARILLON

Christopher Tambling

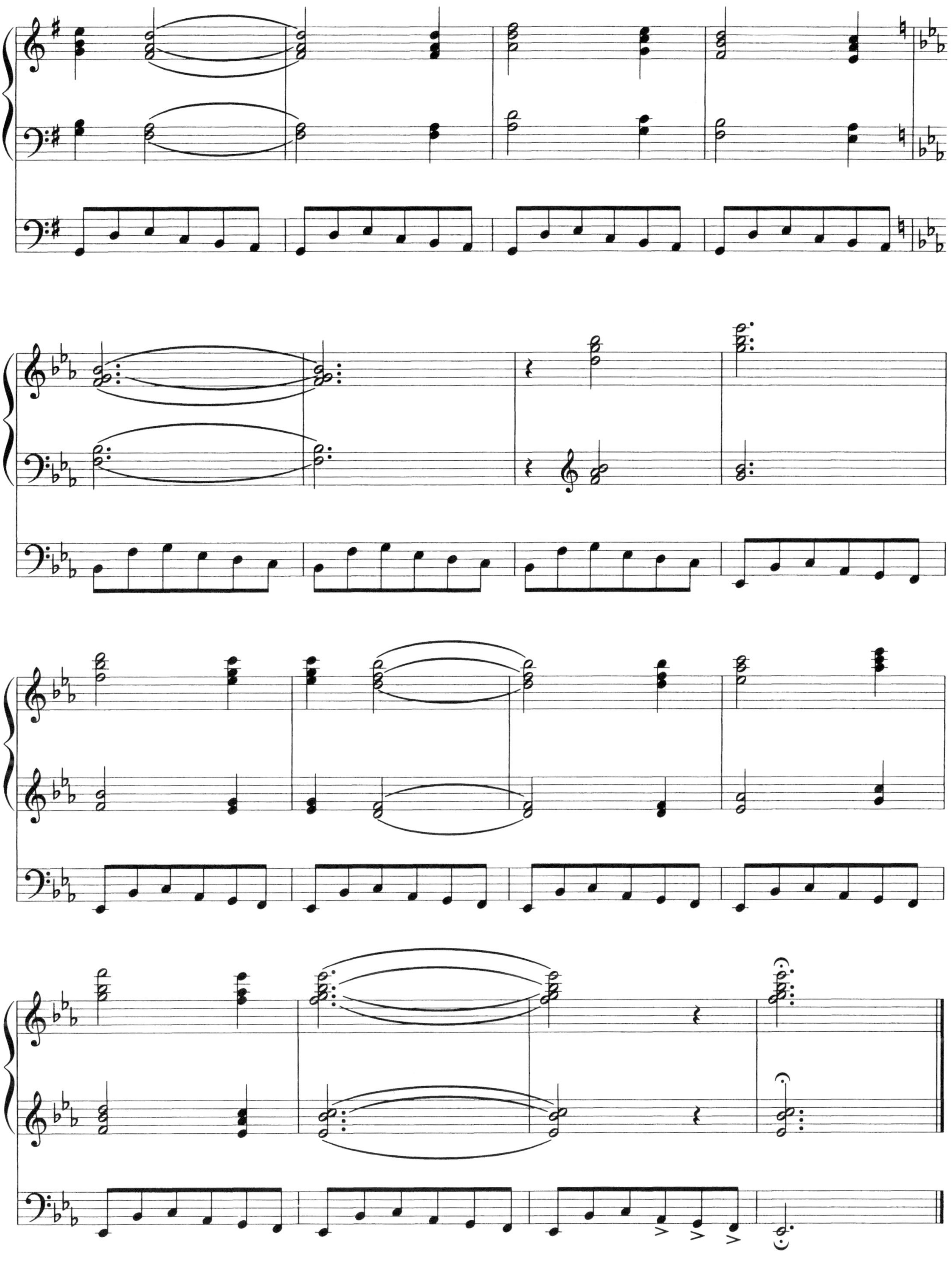

EXEUNT OMNES

Richard Lloyd

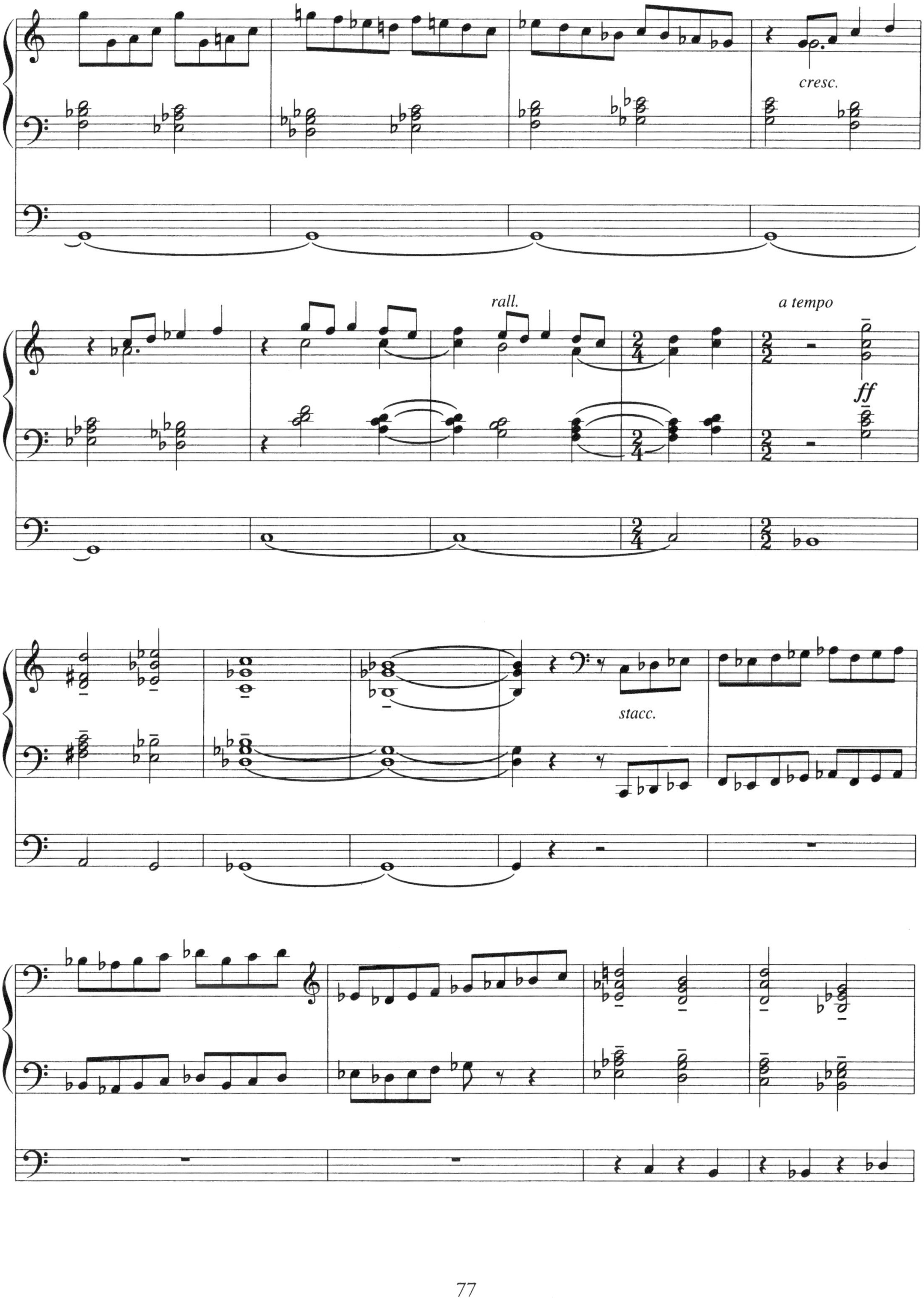
cresc.
rall.
a tempo
ff
stacc.

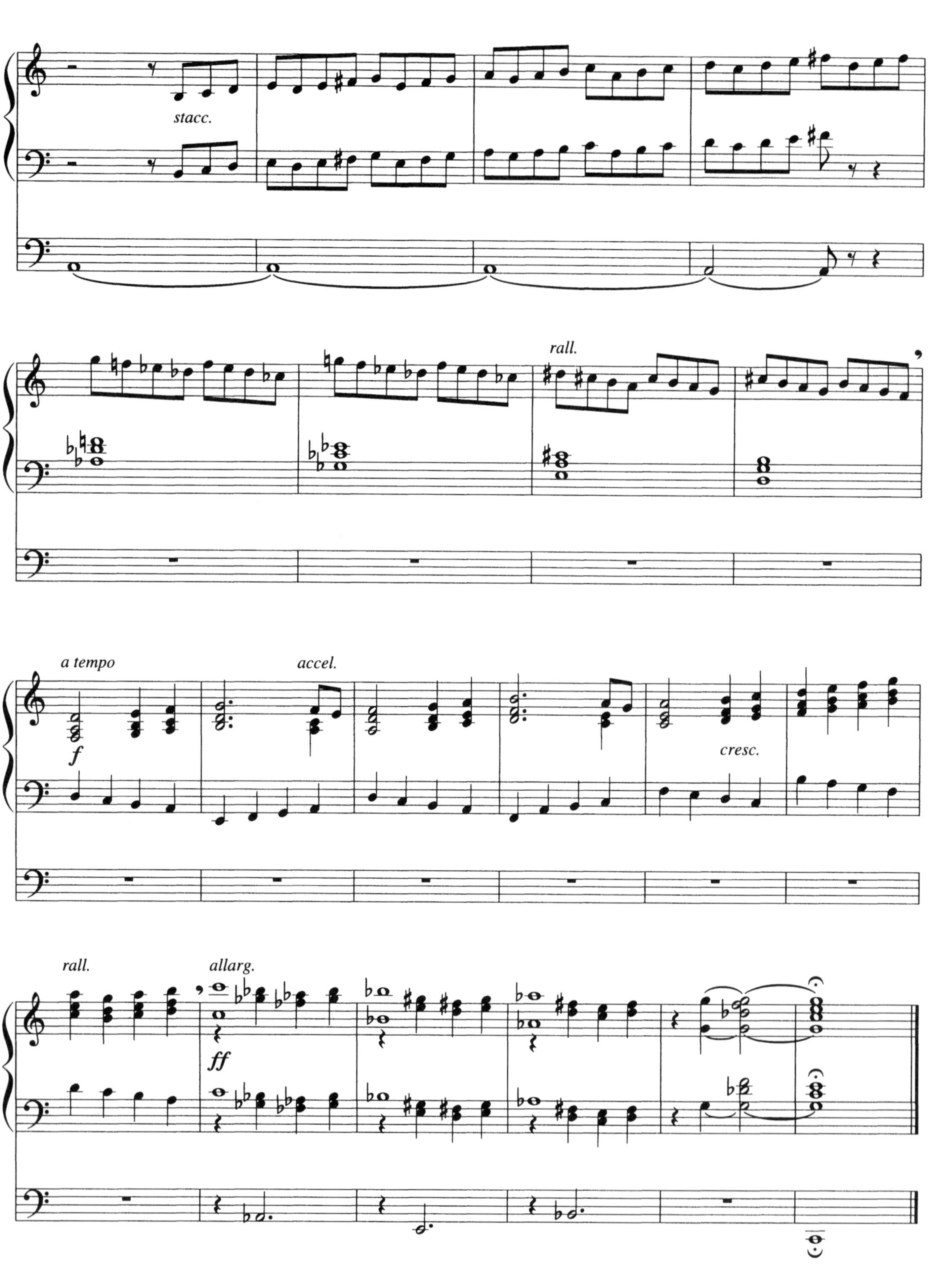
stacc.
rall.
a tempo
accel.
f
cresc.
rall.
allarg.
ff

to Summer

LARGO

Betty Roe

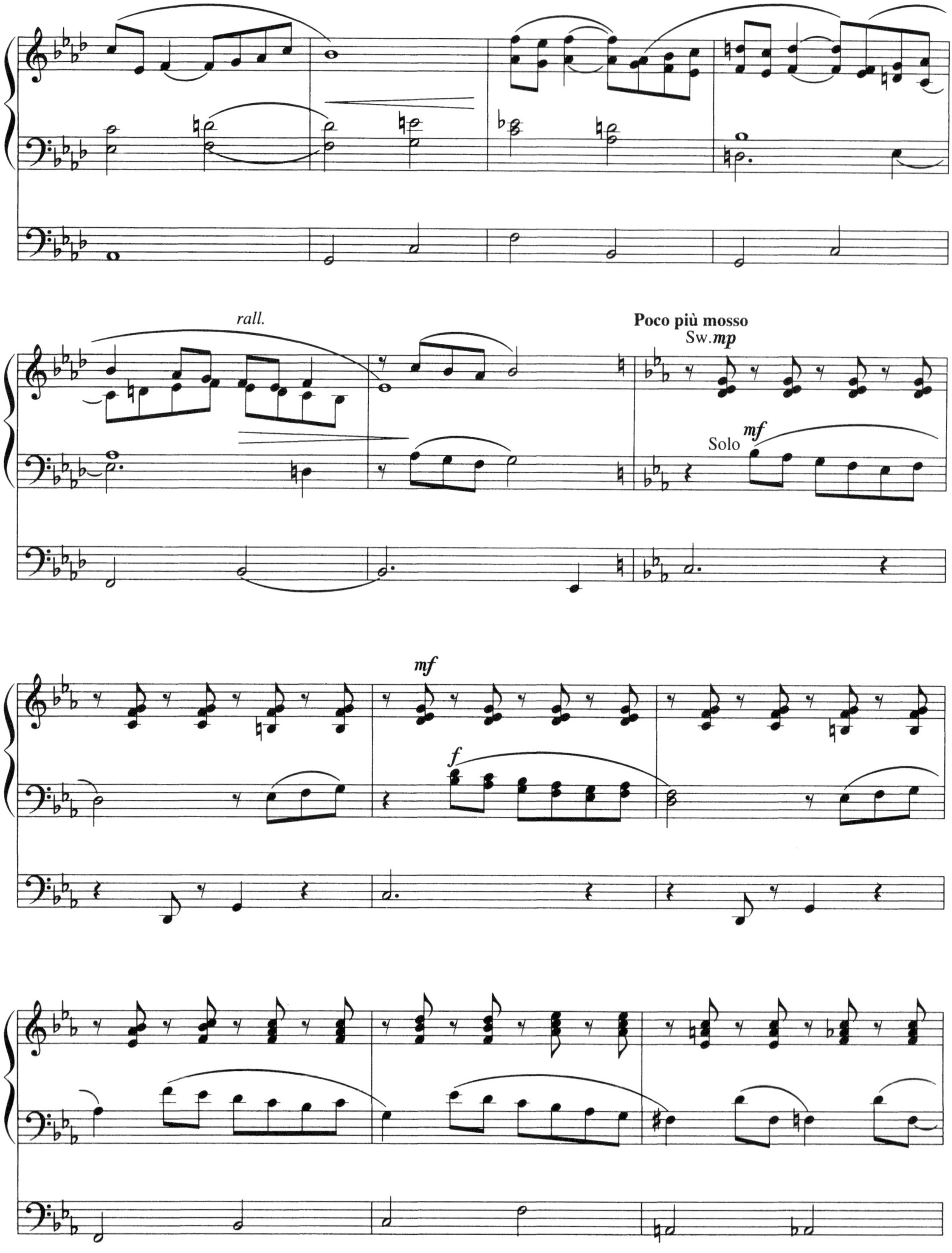
rall.
Poco più mosso
Sw. mp
Solo mf
mf
f

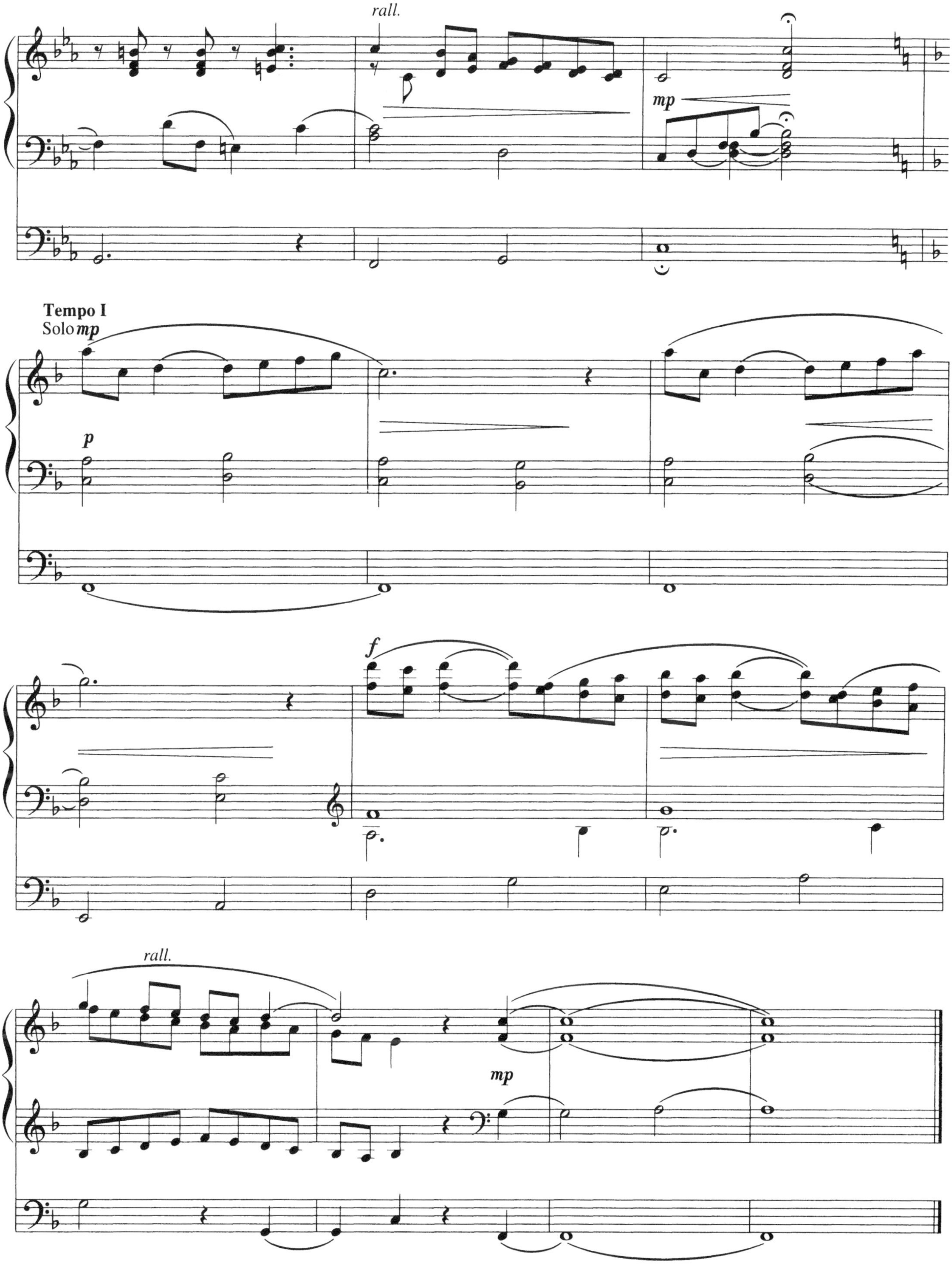
rall.
mp
Tempo I
Solo mp
p
f
rall.
mp

for Elizabeth Stodola

FLOURISH AND SARABANDE

Stephen Kemp

Lento tranquillo alla sarabande

83

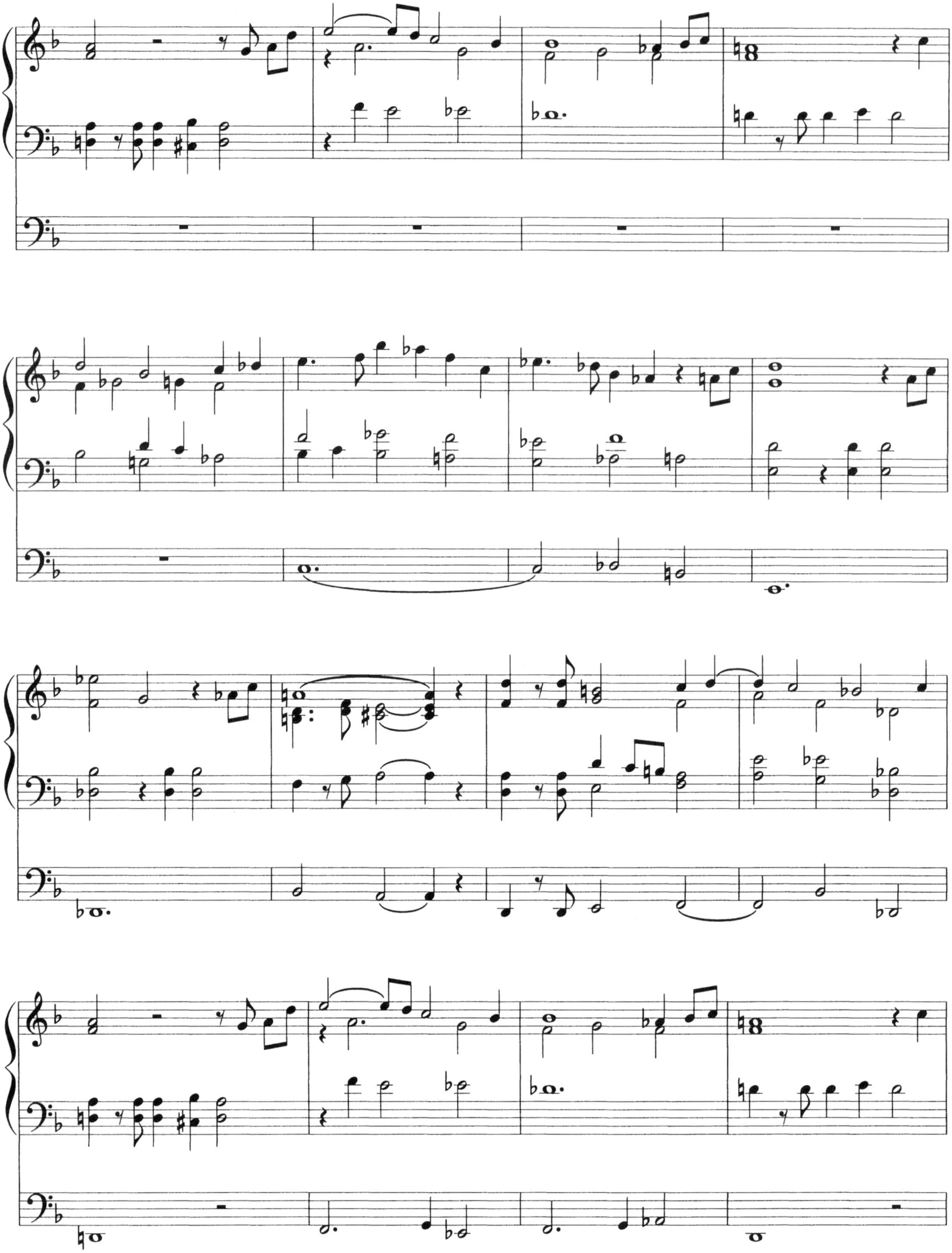

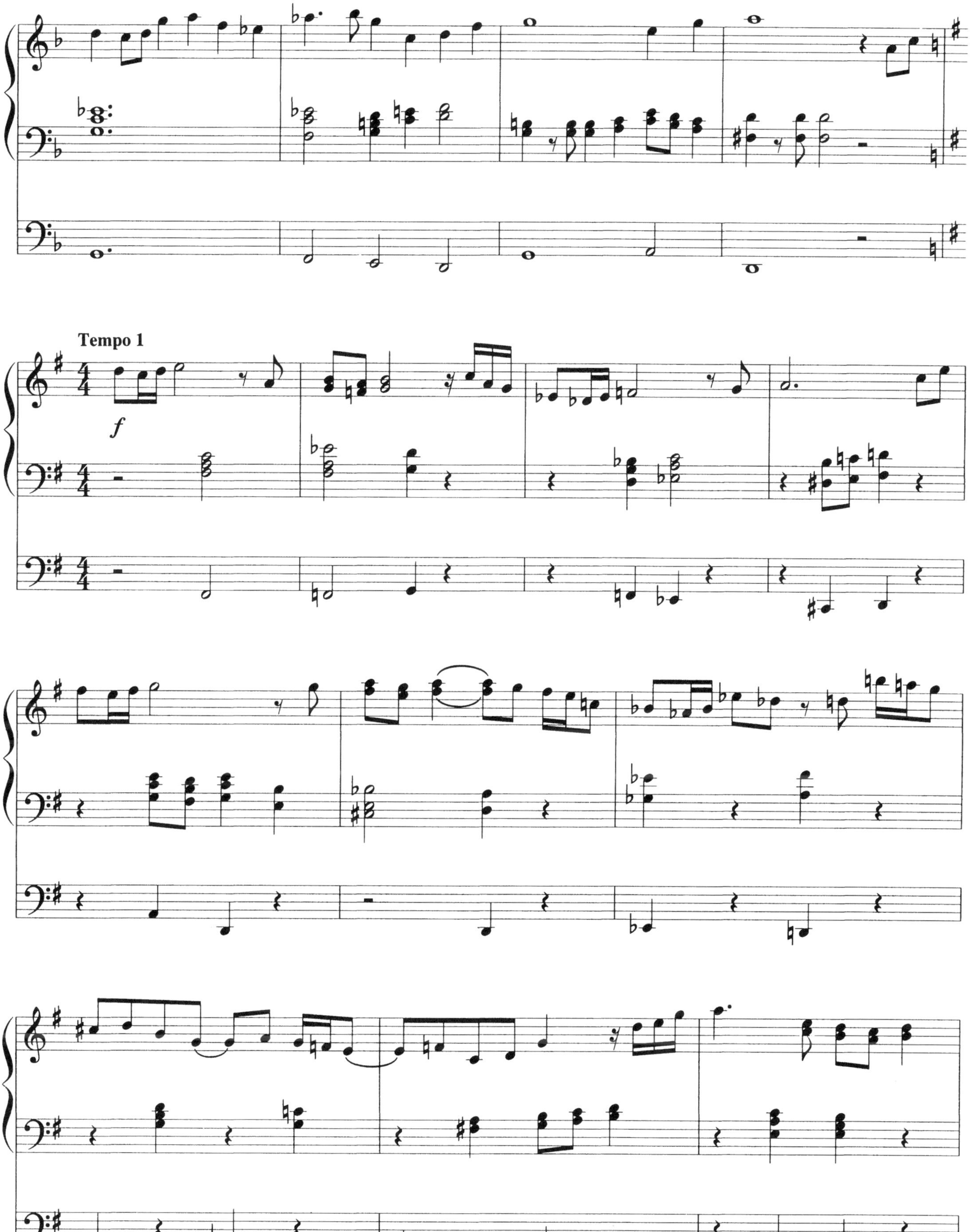
Tempo 1
f

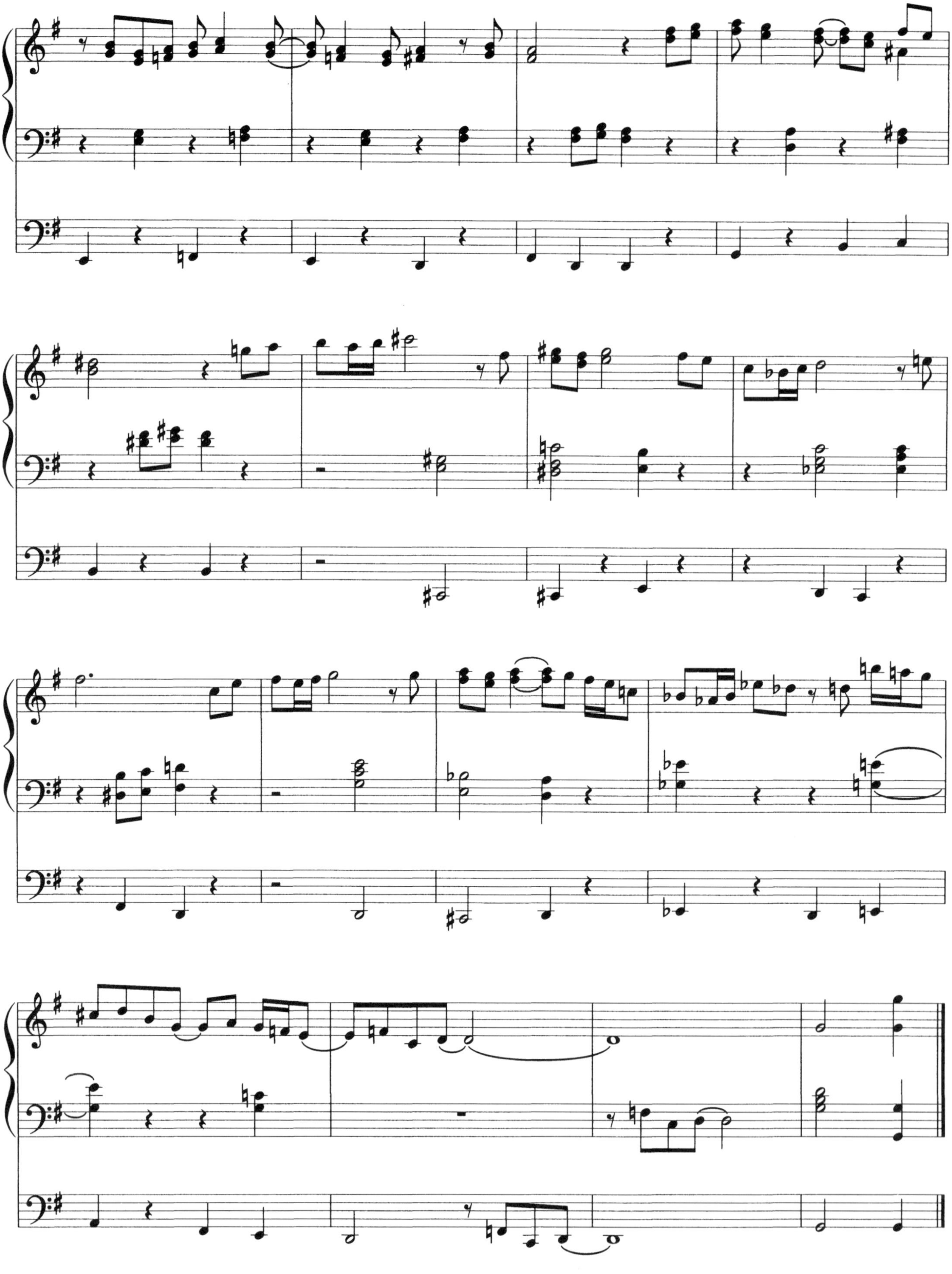

SOLEMN RECESSIONAL

Colin Mawby

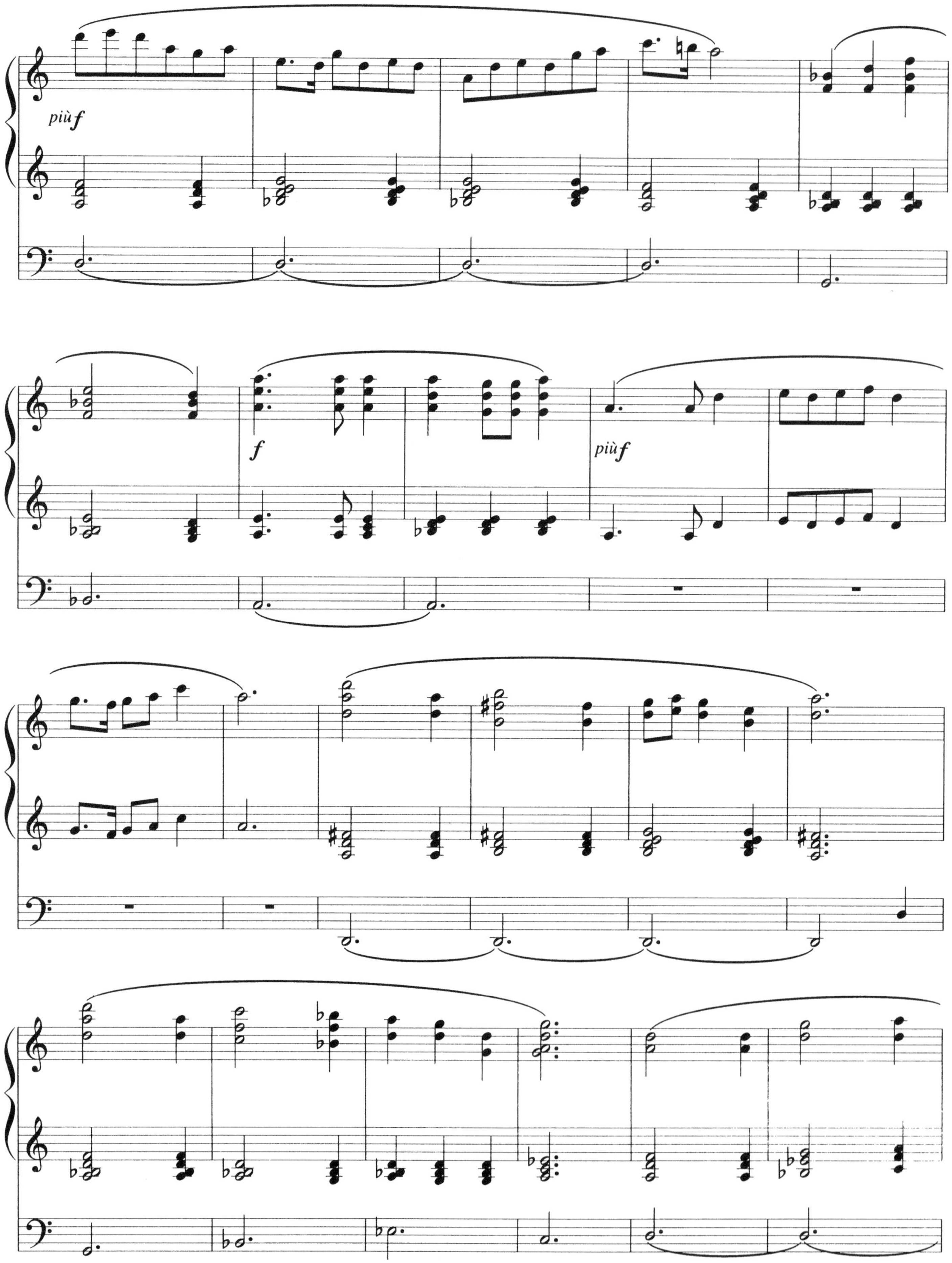
più f
f
più f

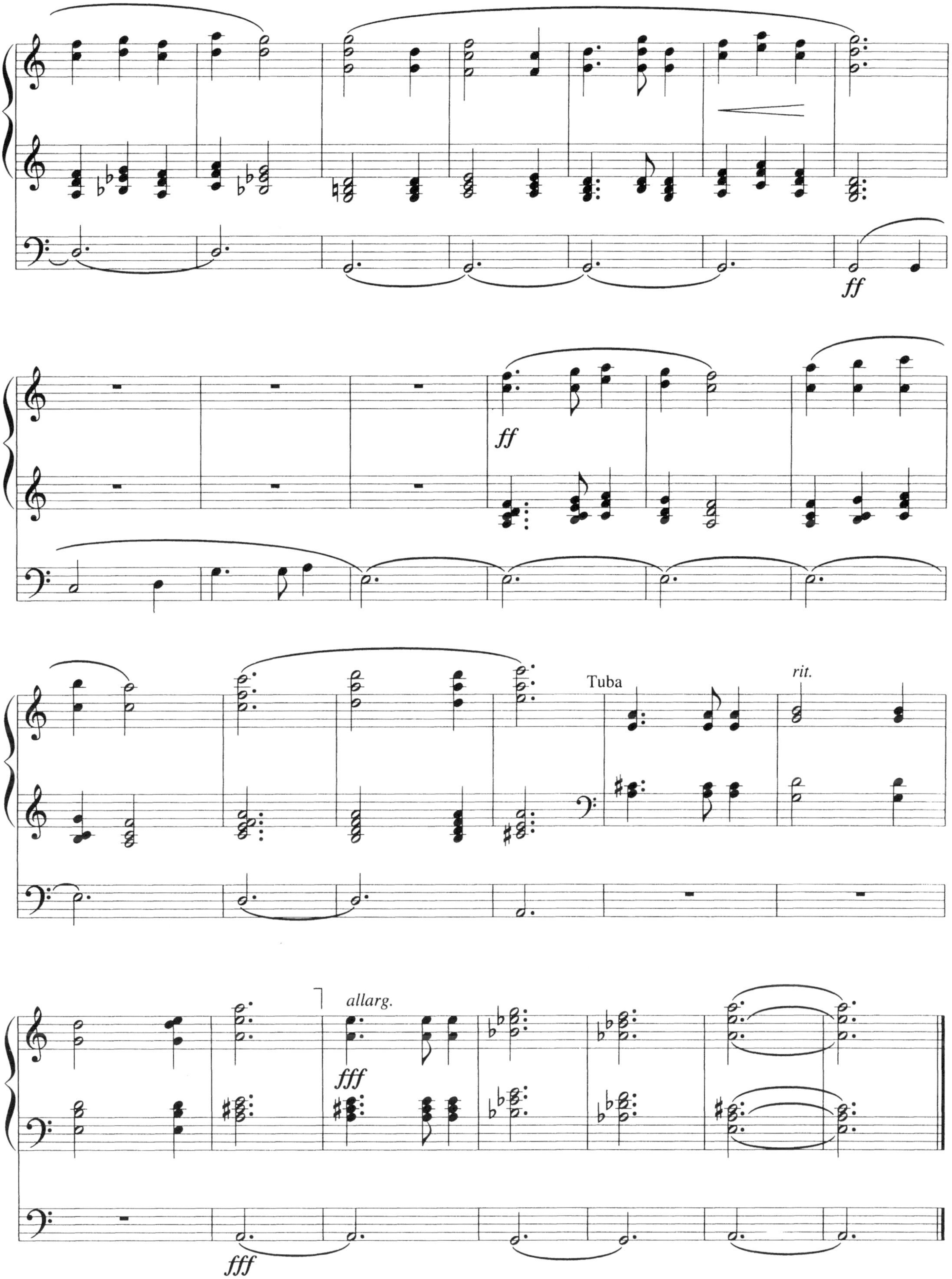
ff
ff
Tuba
rit.
allarg.
fff
fff

ALLA MARCIA

John Marsh

Maestoso ma con moto

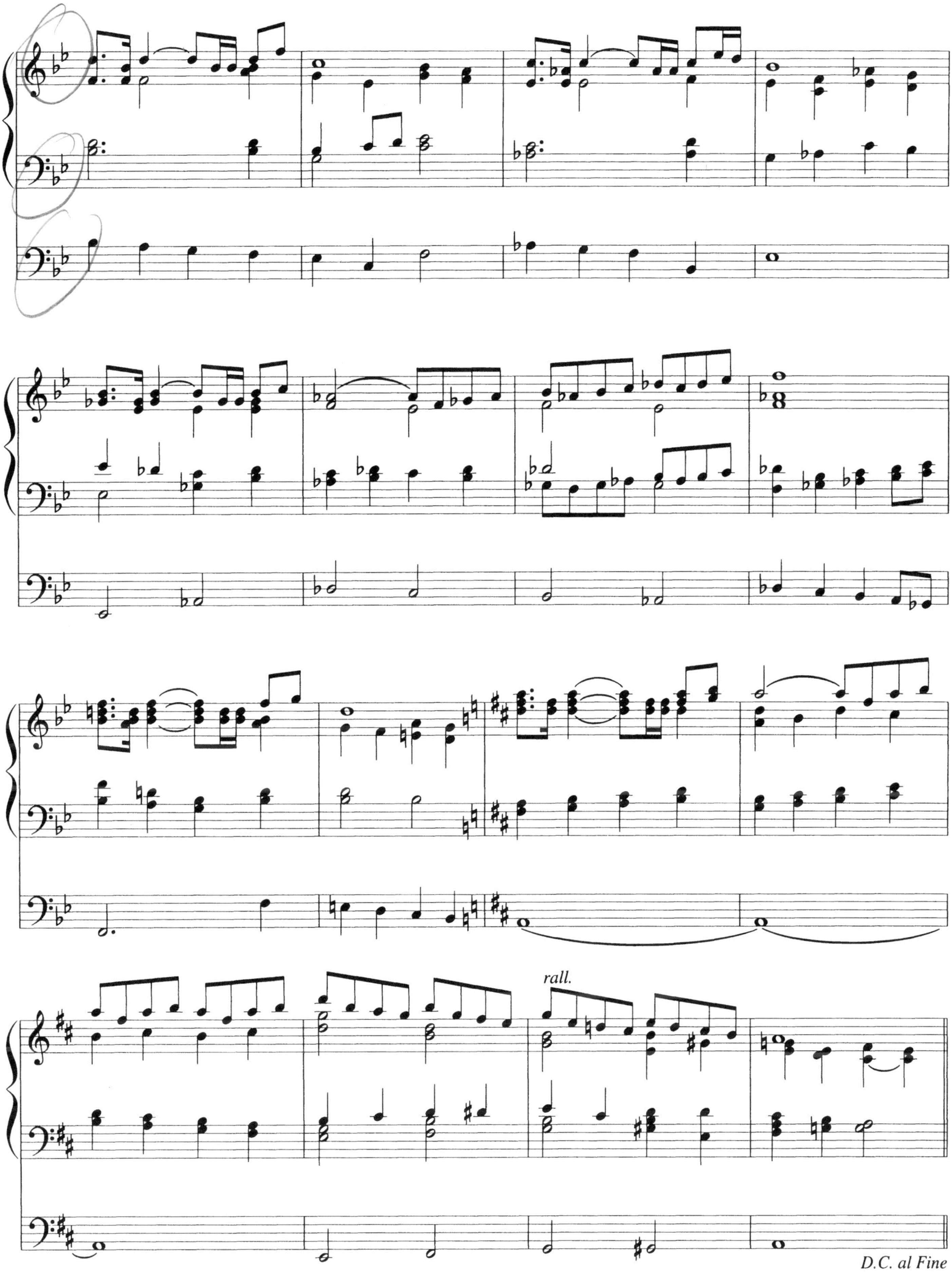
rall.
D.C. al Fine

TOCCATA AND MELODY

Andrew Gant

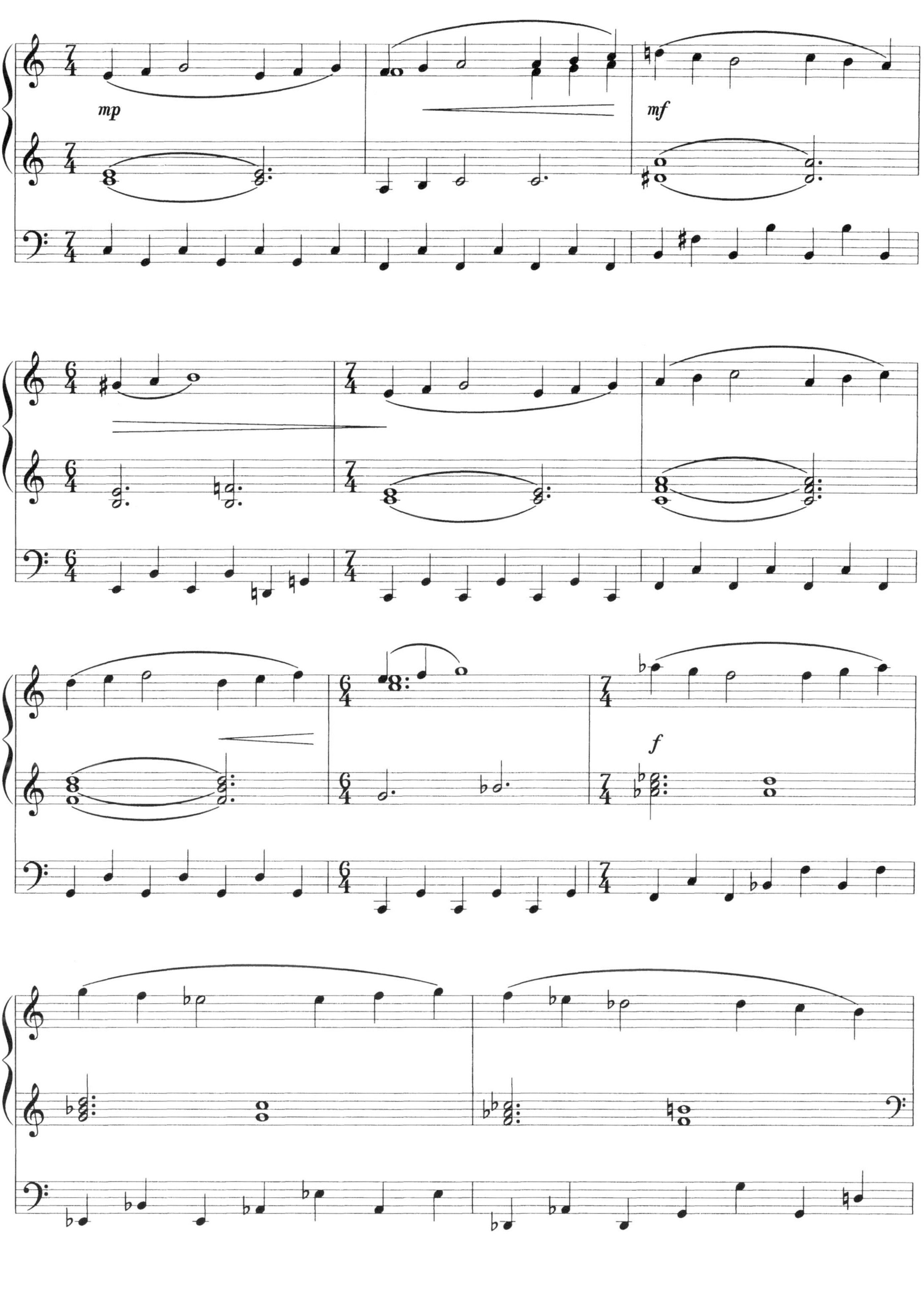
mp
mf
f

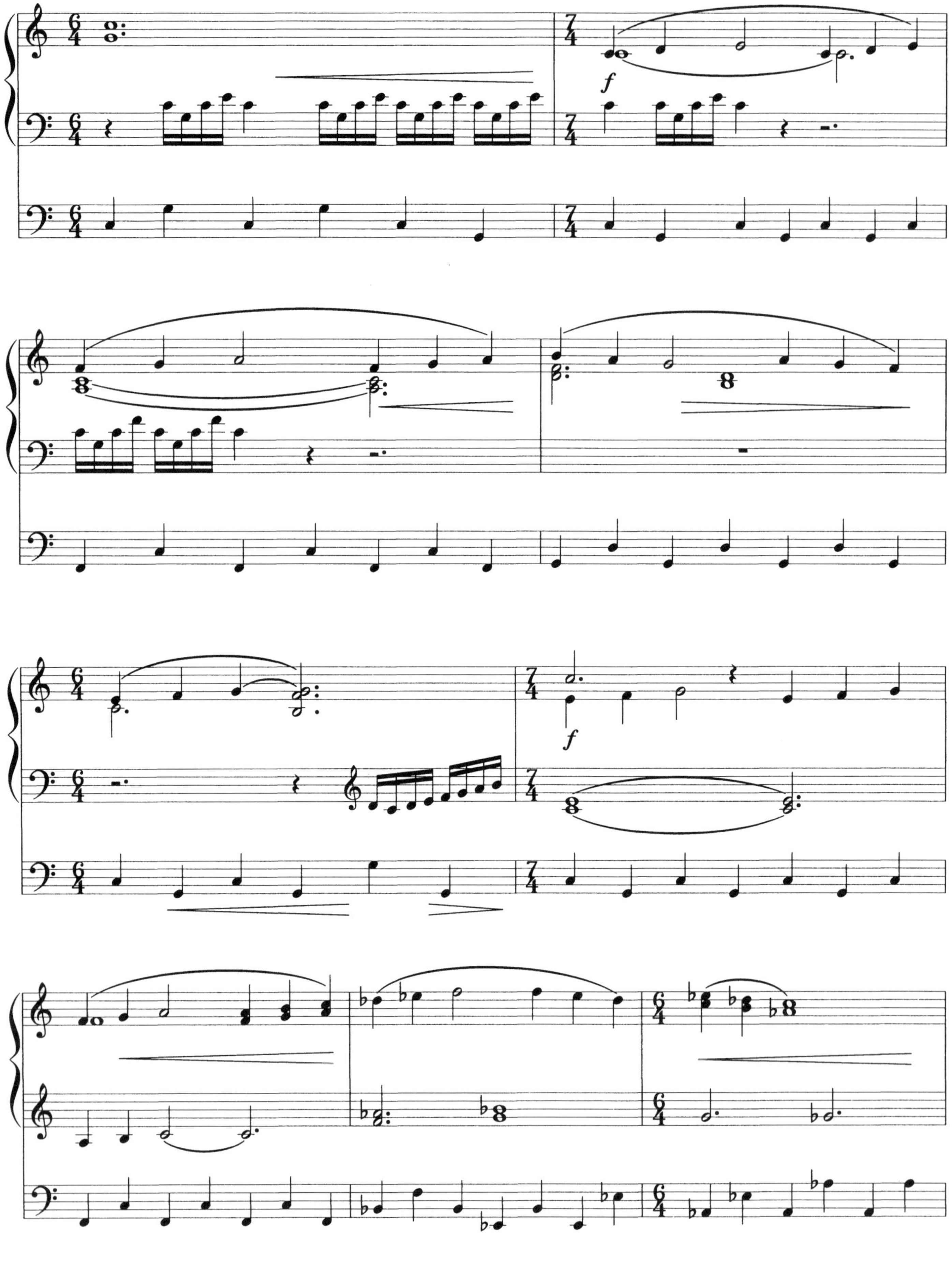
f
f

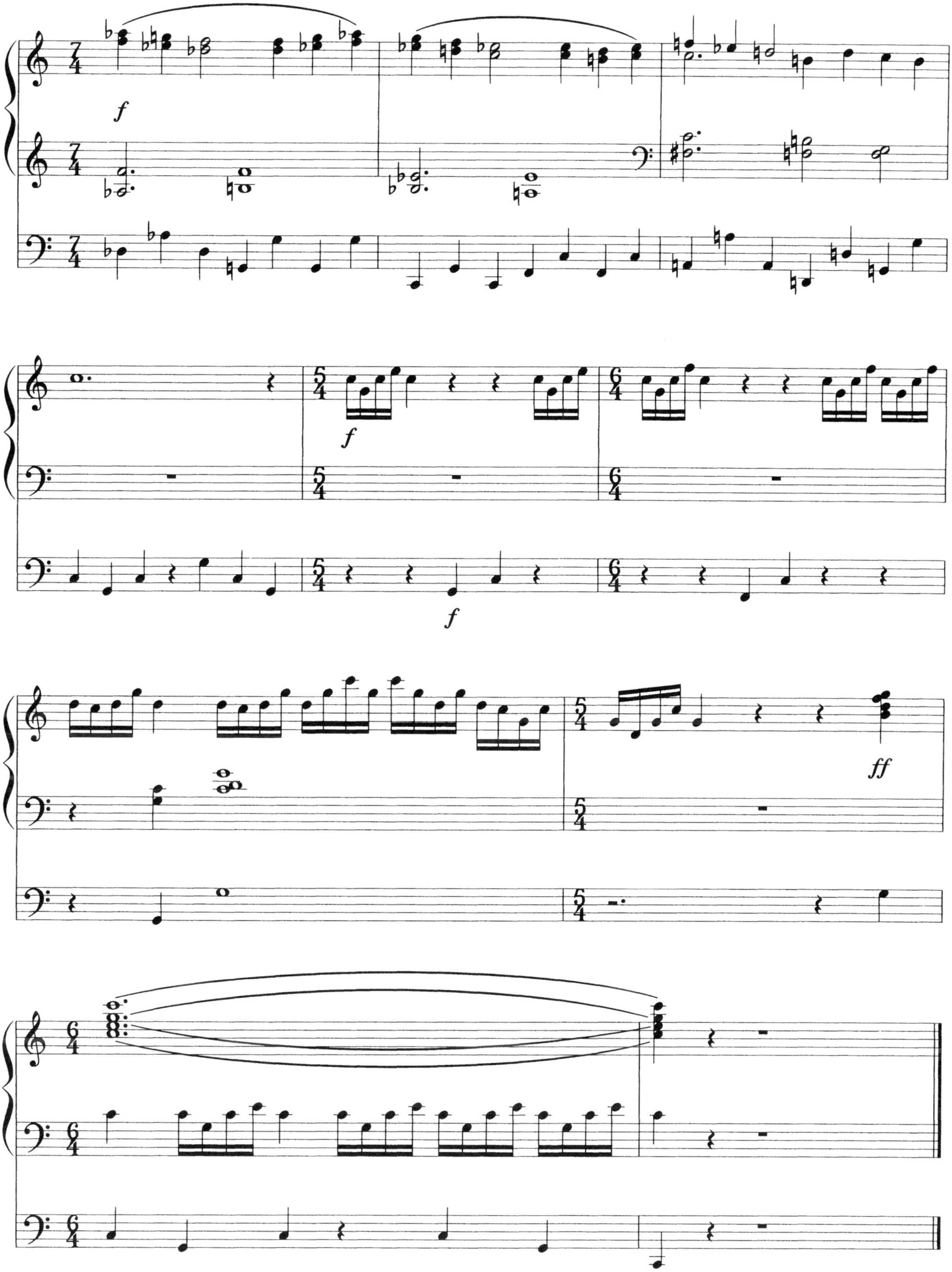
f
f
f
ff

for Marika Kelsey
PROCESSION INTO LIGHT
Richard Pantcheff

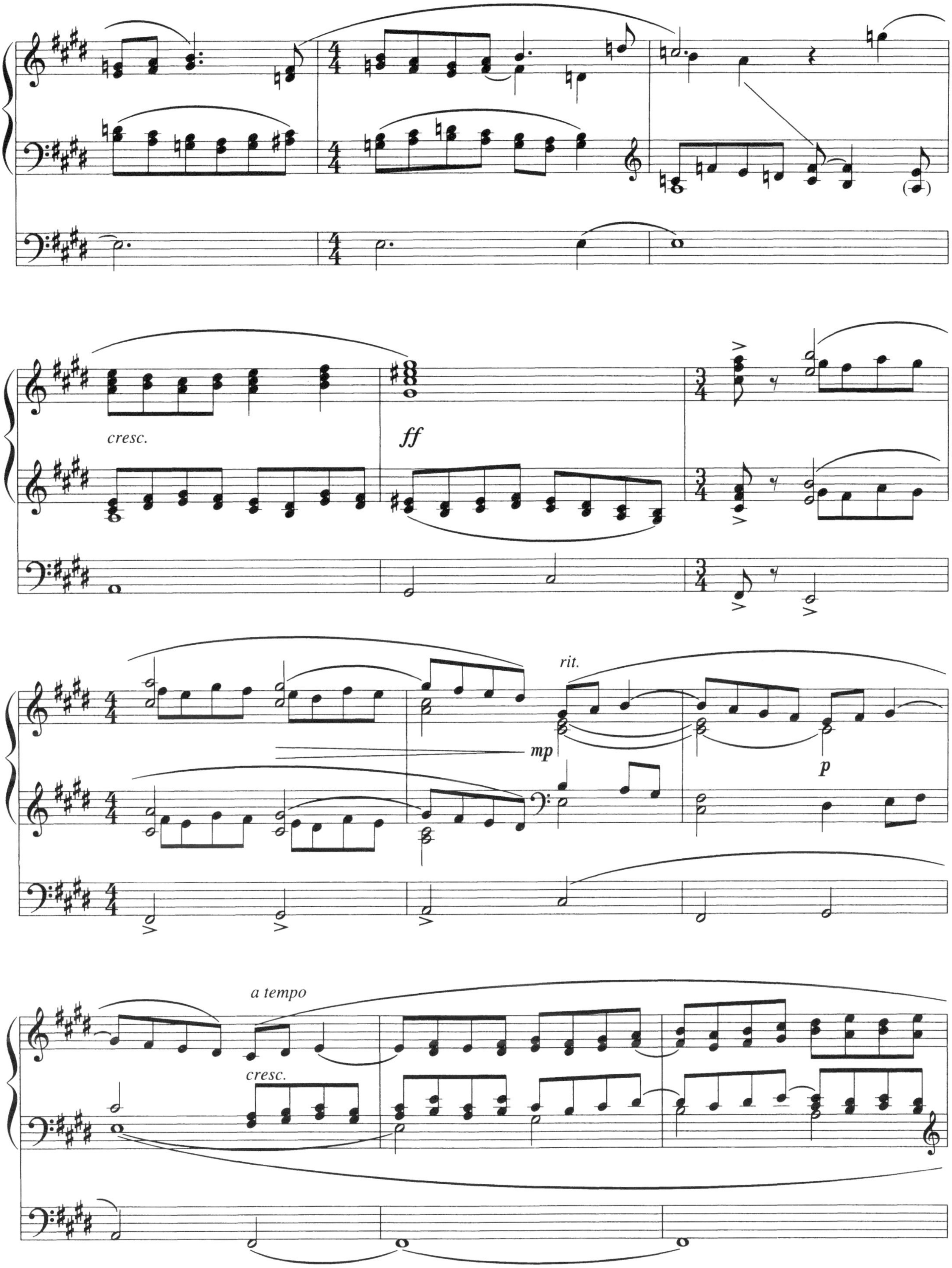
cresc.
ff
mp
rit.
p
a tempo
cresc.

Slightly faster
ff
Full
ff poco a poco dim.
f
mf
a tempo
II p
rit. al fine
mp
II
pp

SARABANDE

Philip Moore

Con moto, alla sarabande ($\quad$ = c.80)

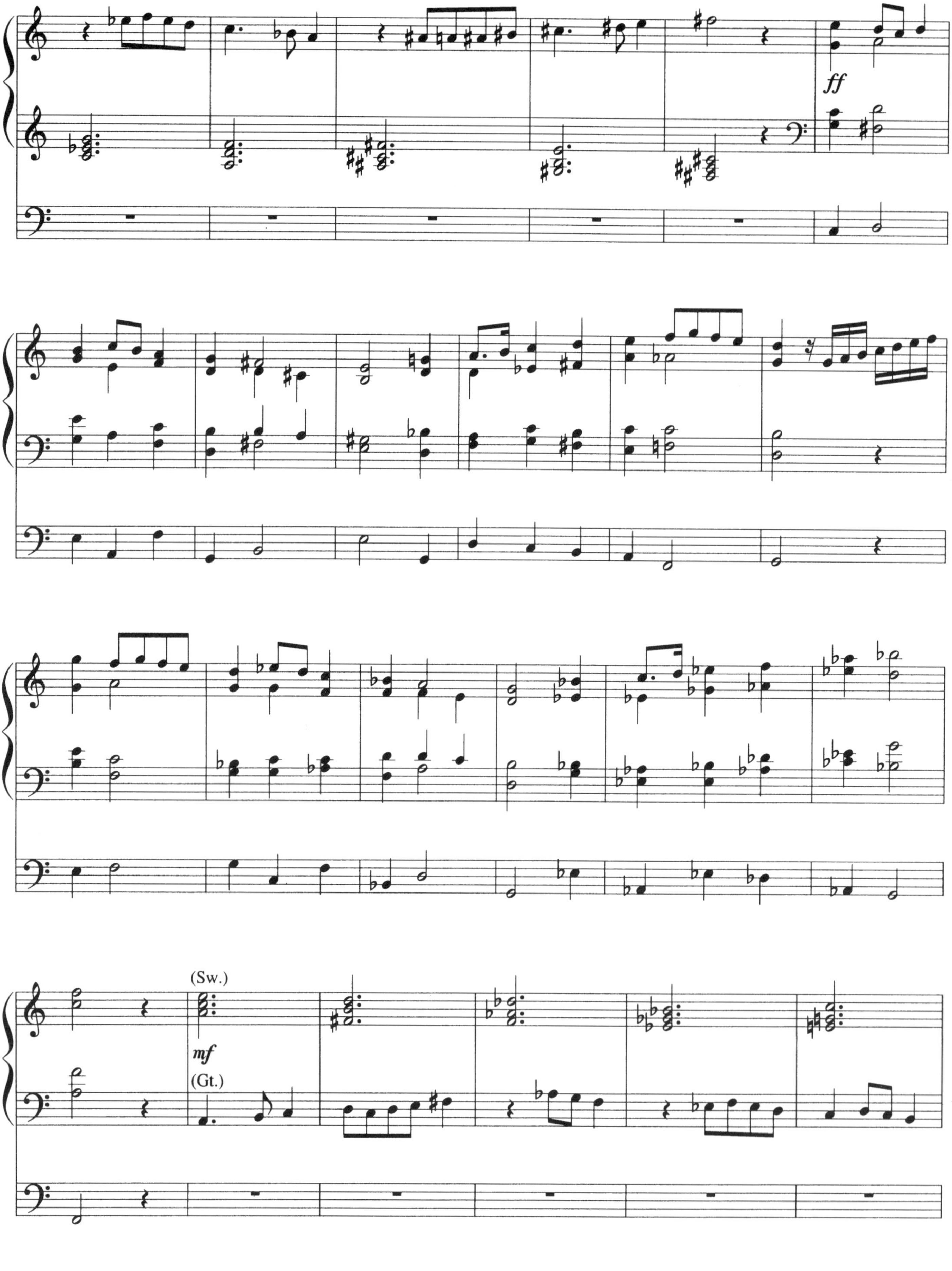
ff
(Sw.)
mf
(Gt.)

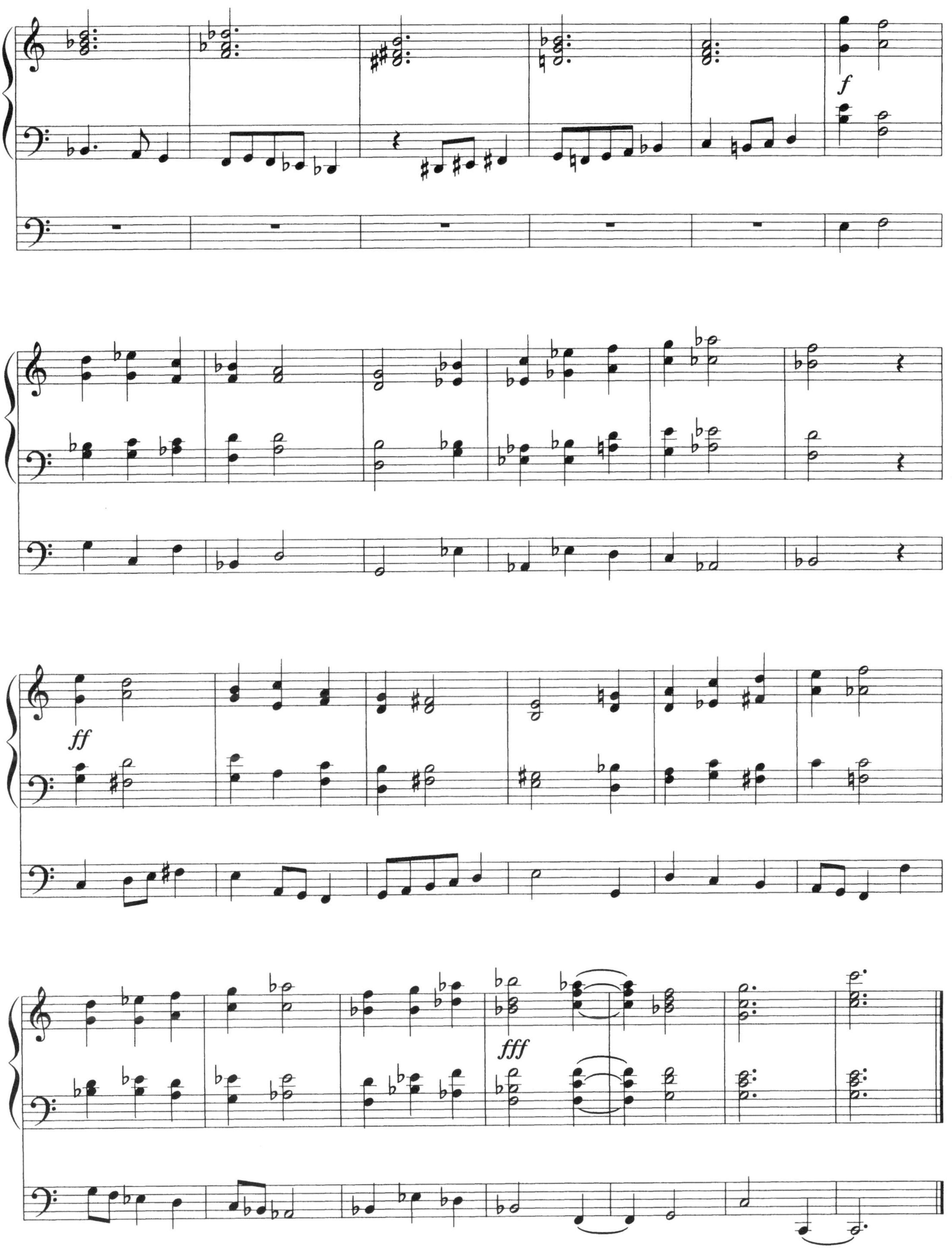
f
ff
fff

TRIUMPHANT PROCESSIONAL

Owain Edwards

D.C.

⊕ TRIO

Sw. mf

Sw. to Ped.

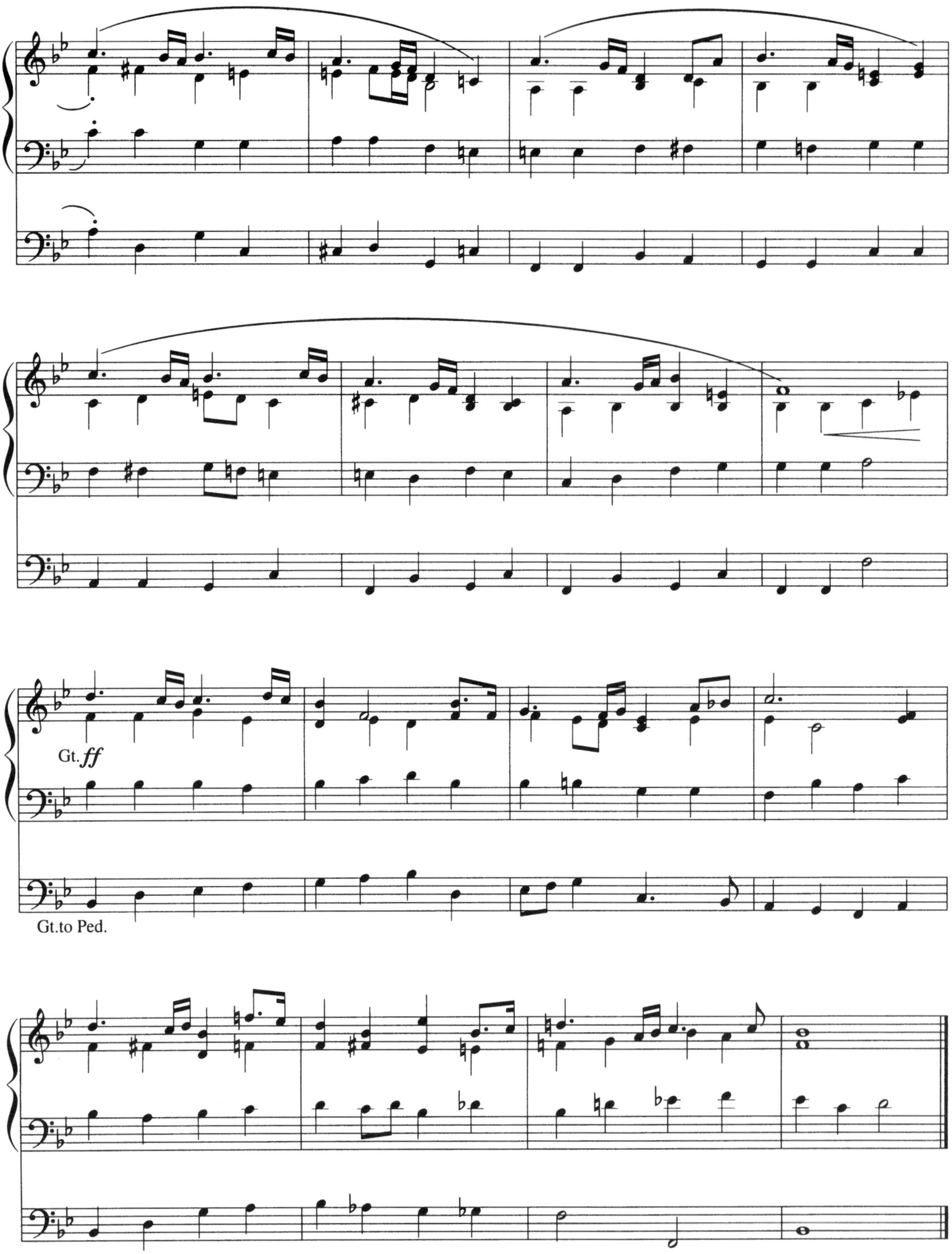
Gt. ff
Gt.to Ped.

CORTÈGE

Malcolm Archer

With dignity ($\bd = 58$)

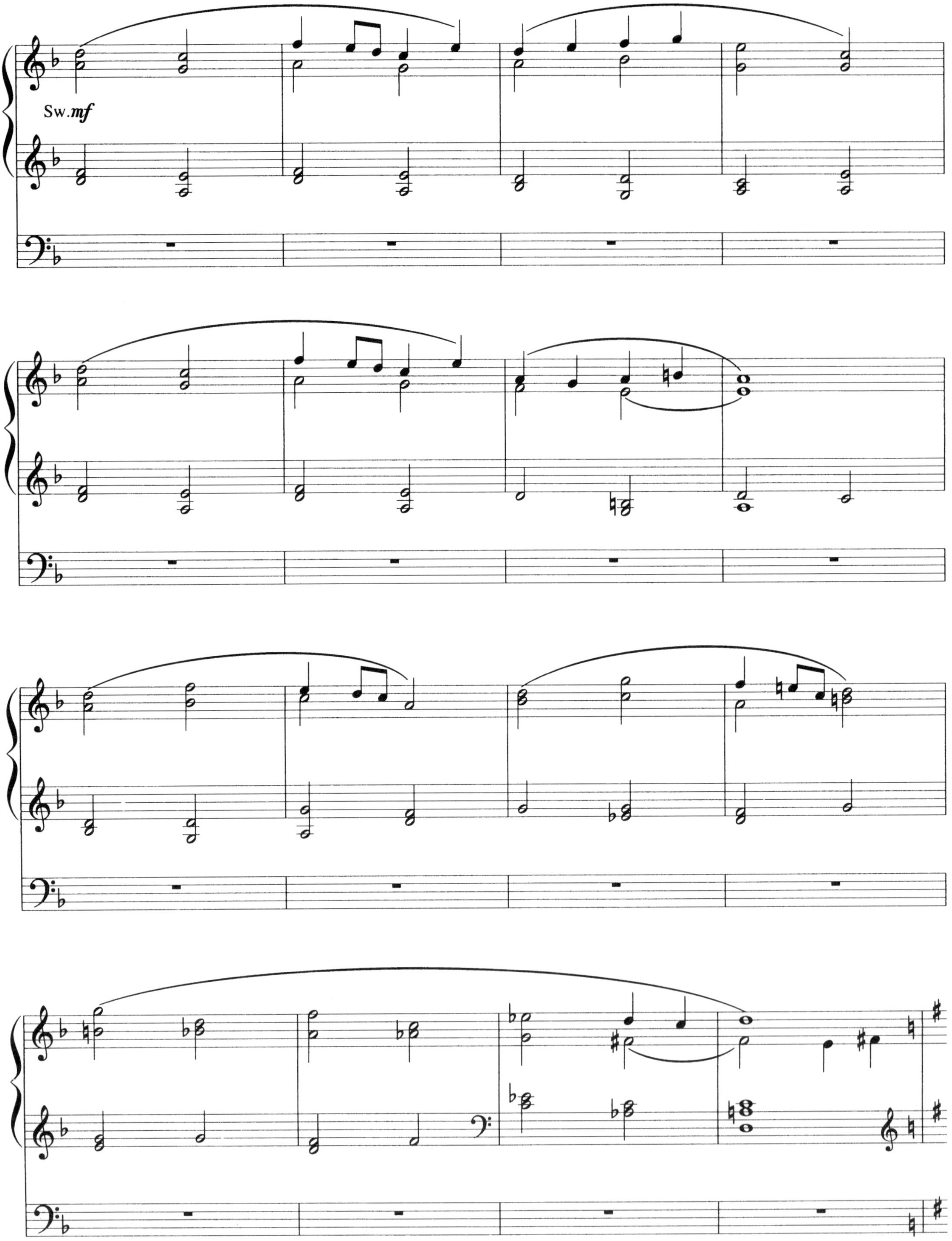
Sw. mf

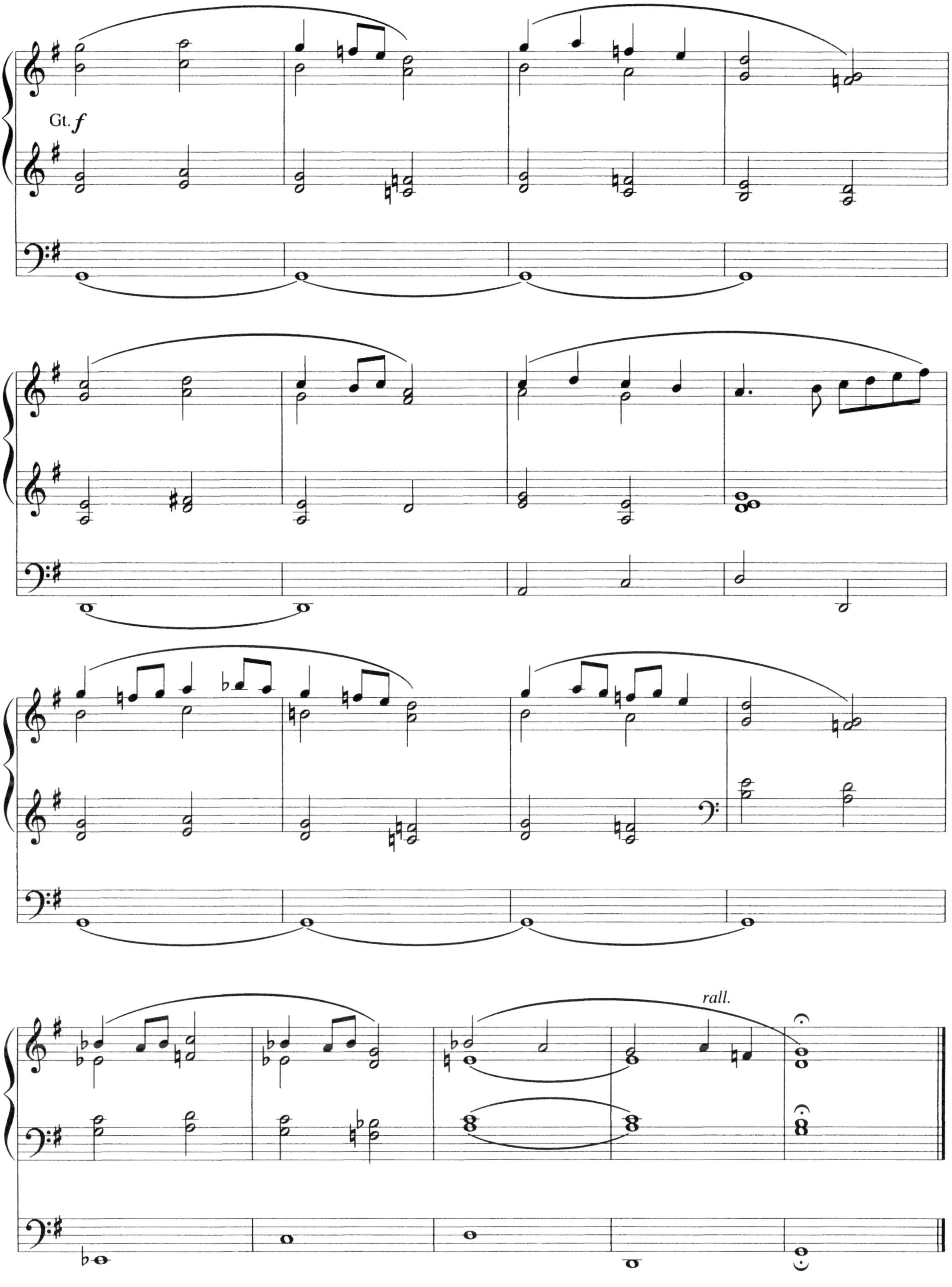
Gt. f
rall.

TOCCATA

Norman Warren

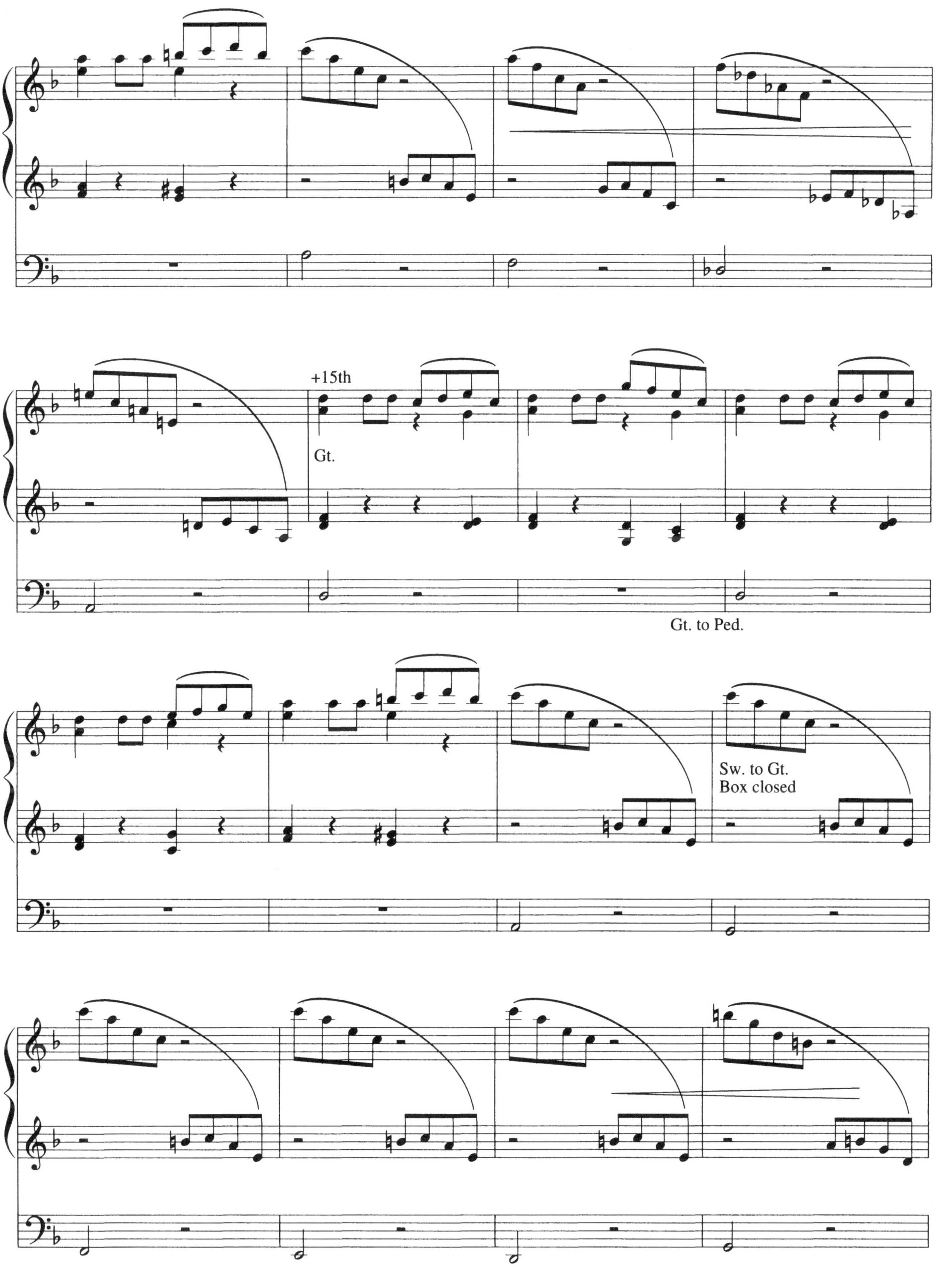
+15th
Gt.
Gt. to Ped.
Sw. to Gt.
Box closed

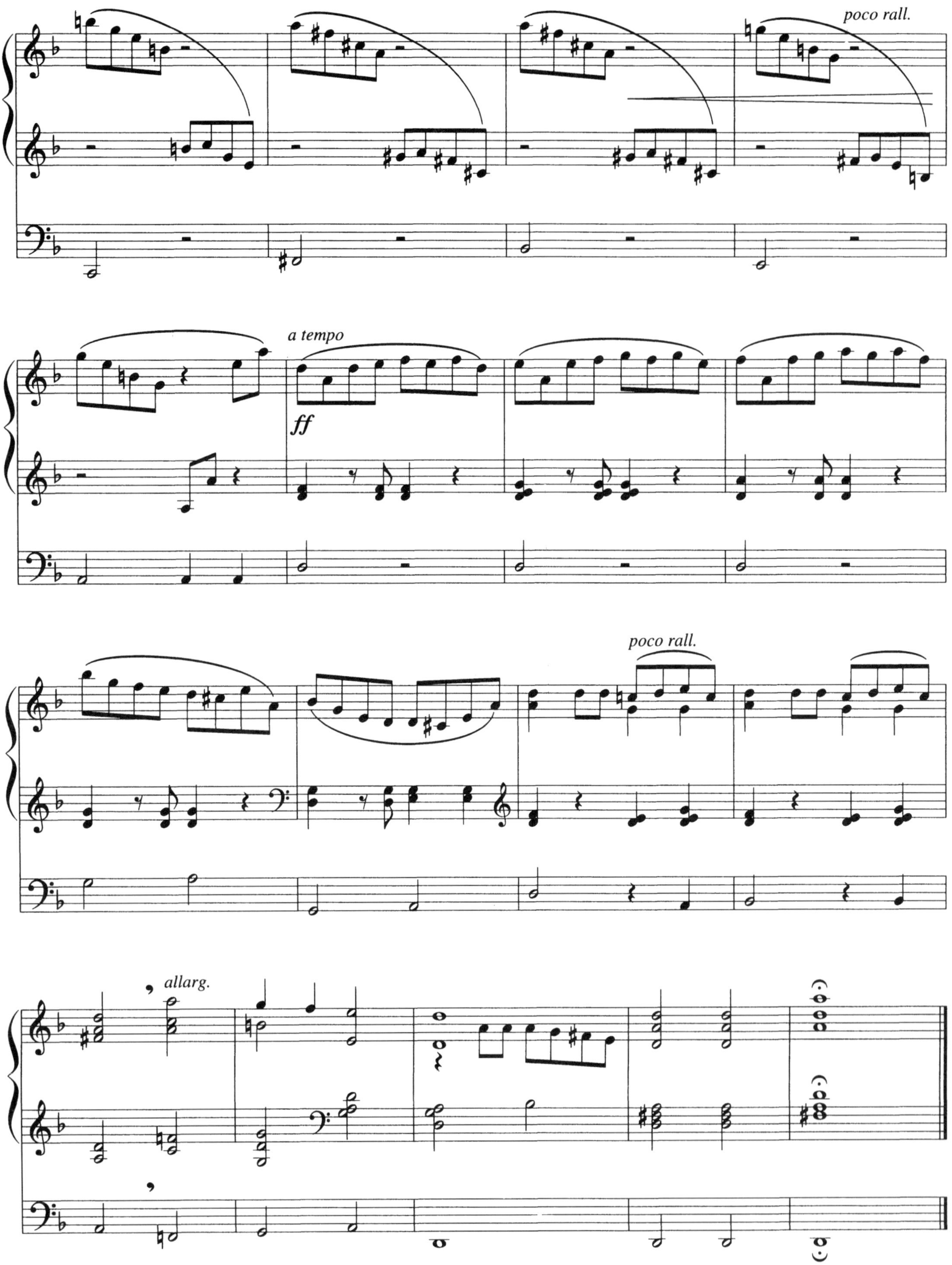
poco rall.
a tempo
ff
poco rall.
allarg.

GRAND SORTIE

Andrew Fletcher

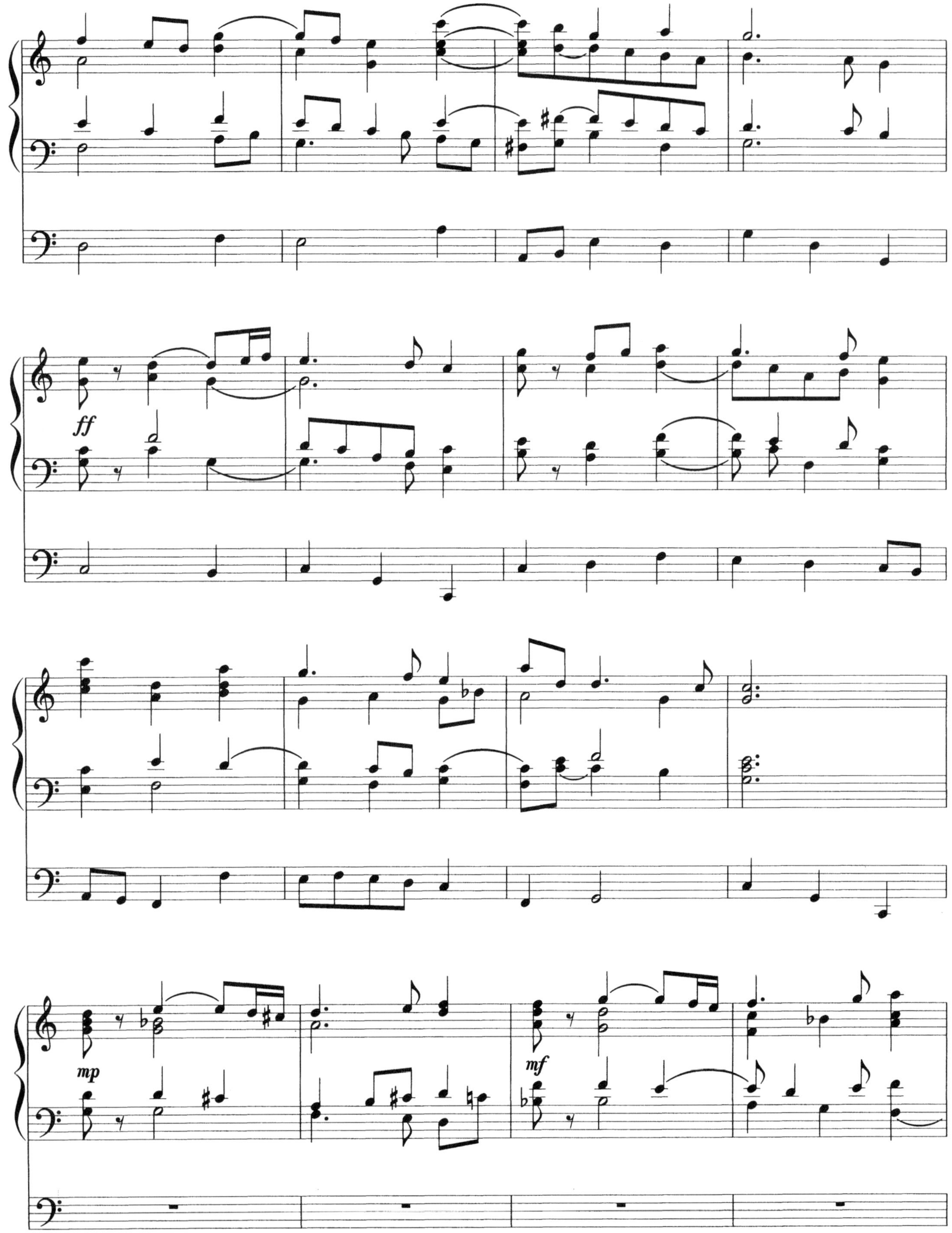
ff
mp
mf

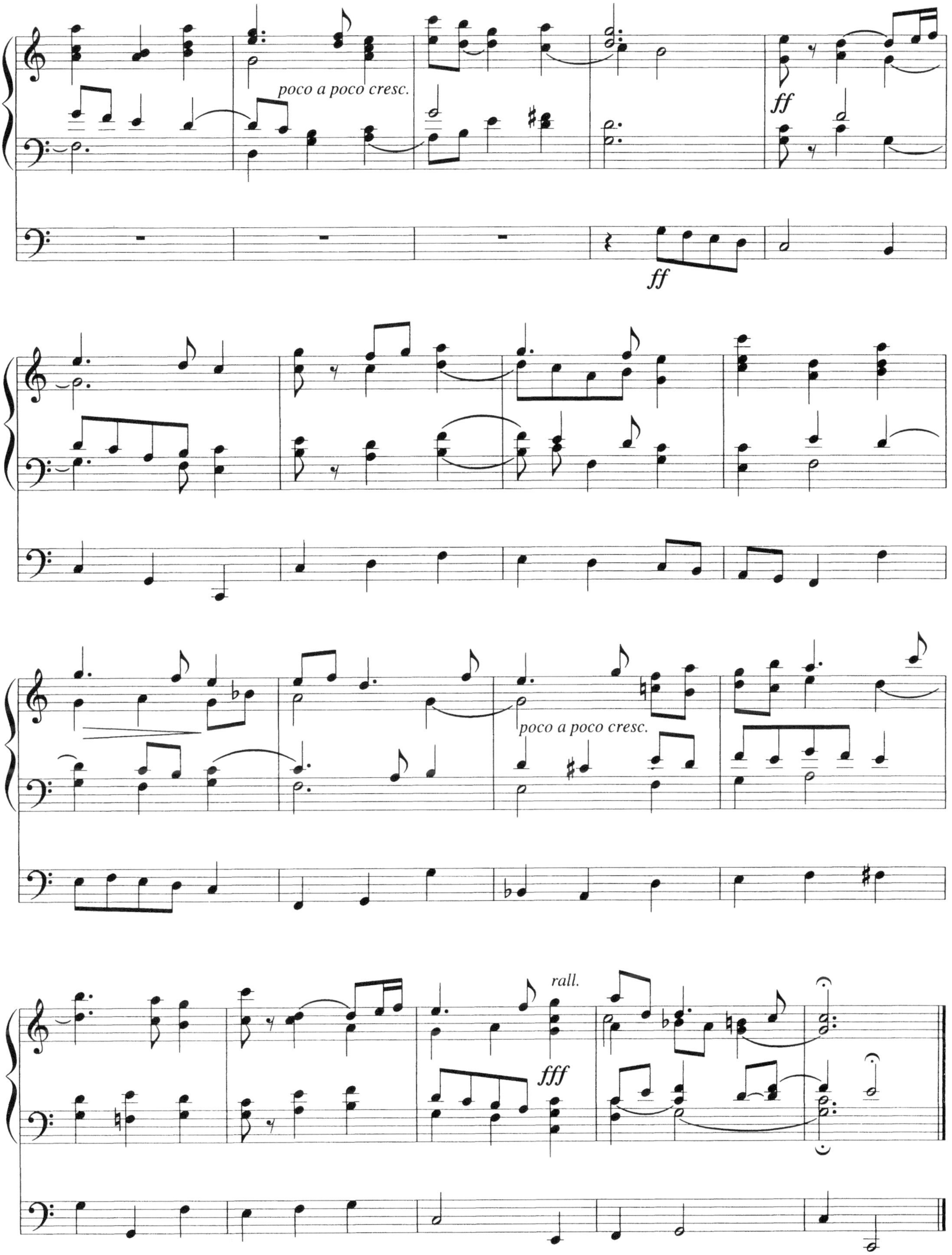
poco a poco cresc.
ff
ff
poco a poco cresc.
rall.
fff

INTRADA

John Marsh

Maestoso ma con moto

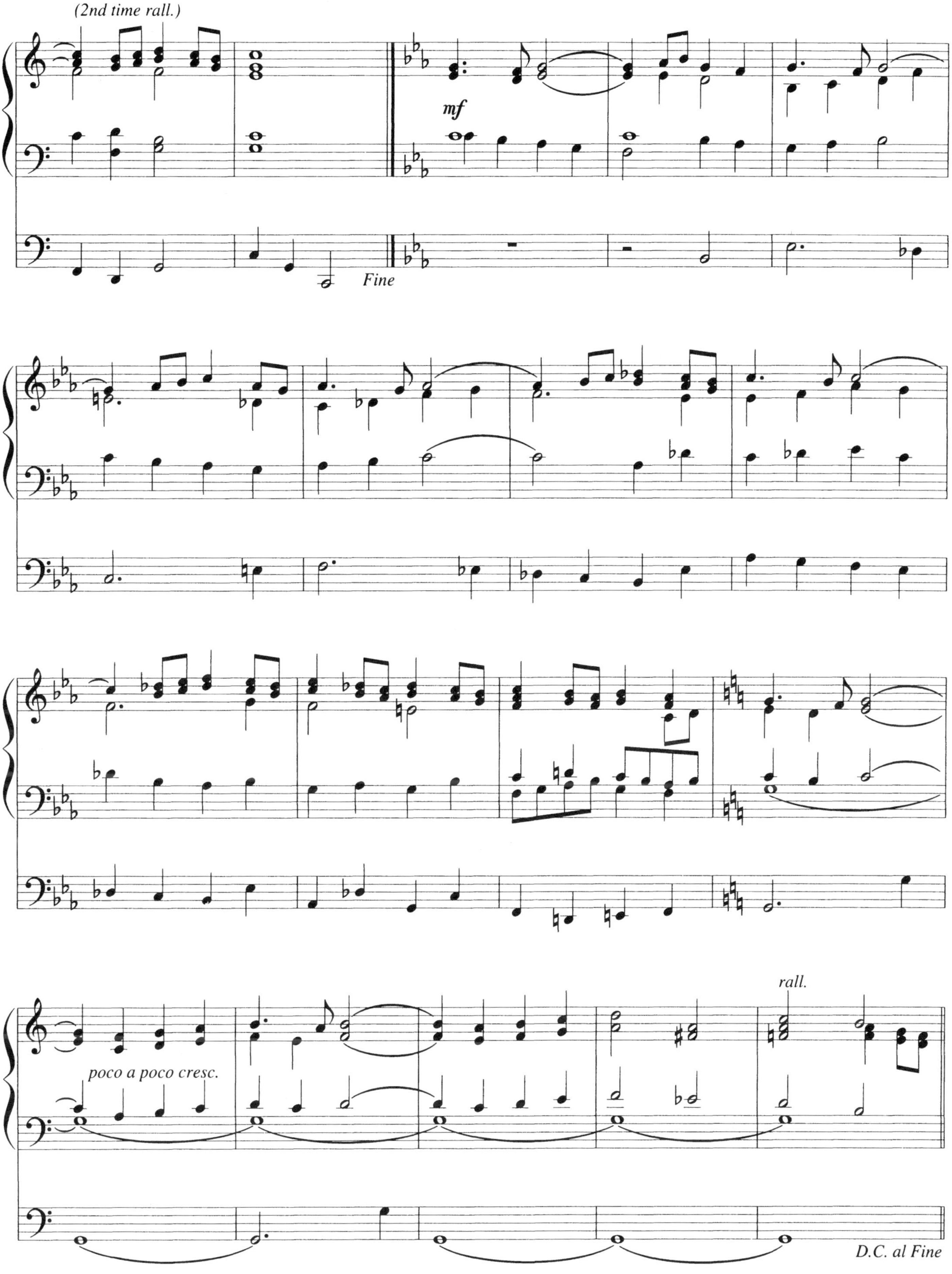

(2nd time rall.)
mf
Fine
poco a poco cresc.
rall.
D.C. al Fine

SLOW MARCH

Richard Shephard

Moderato (♩ = 116)

mp

mf

mp

116

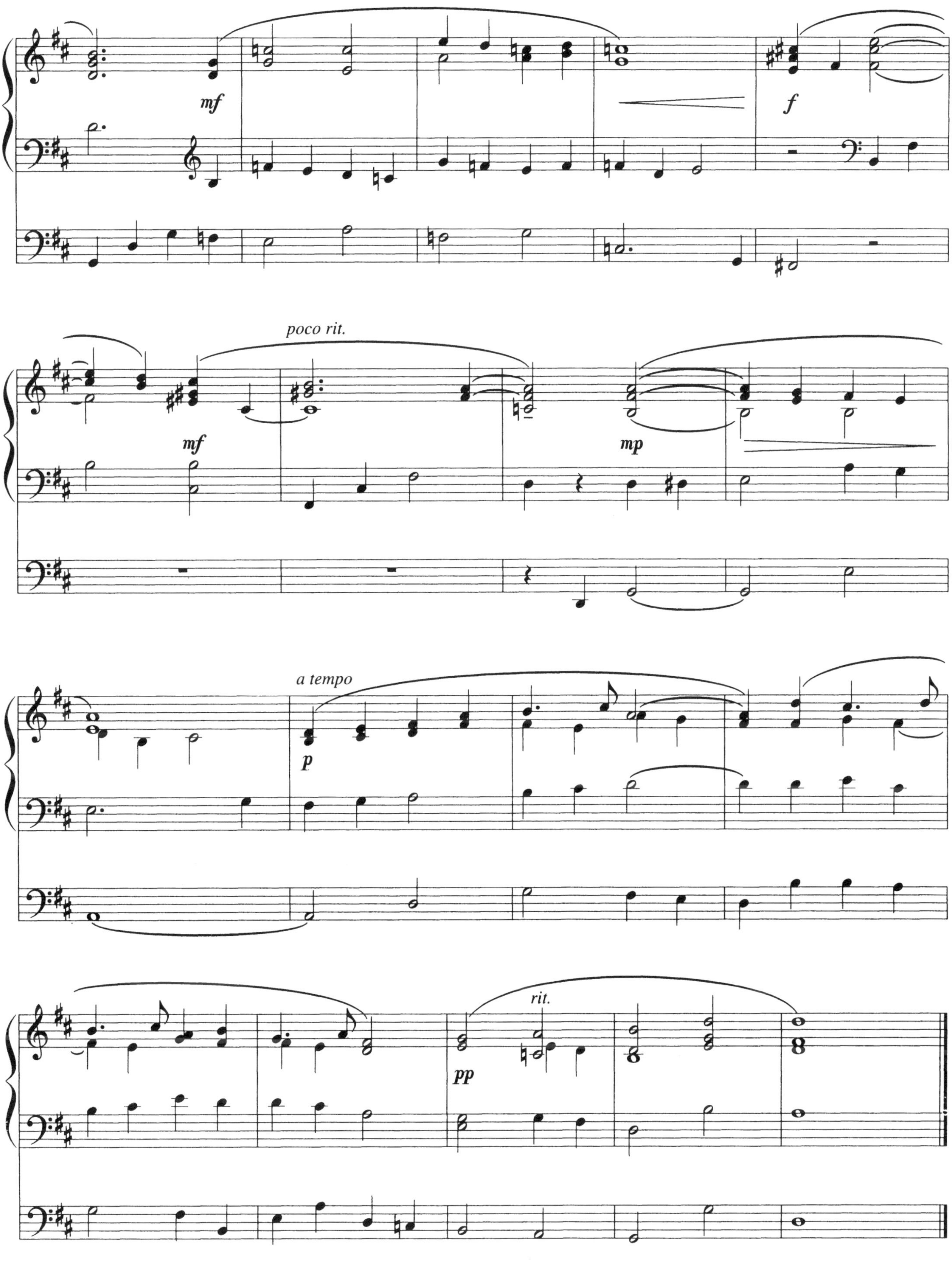
mf
f
poco rit.
mf
mp
a tempo
p
rit.
pp

ARIETTA

Alan Viner

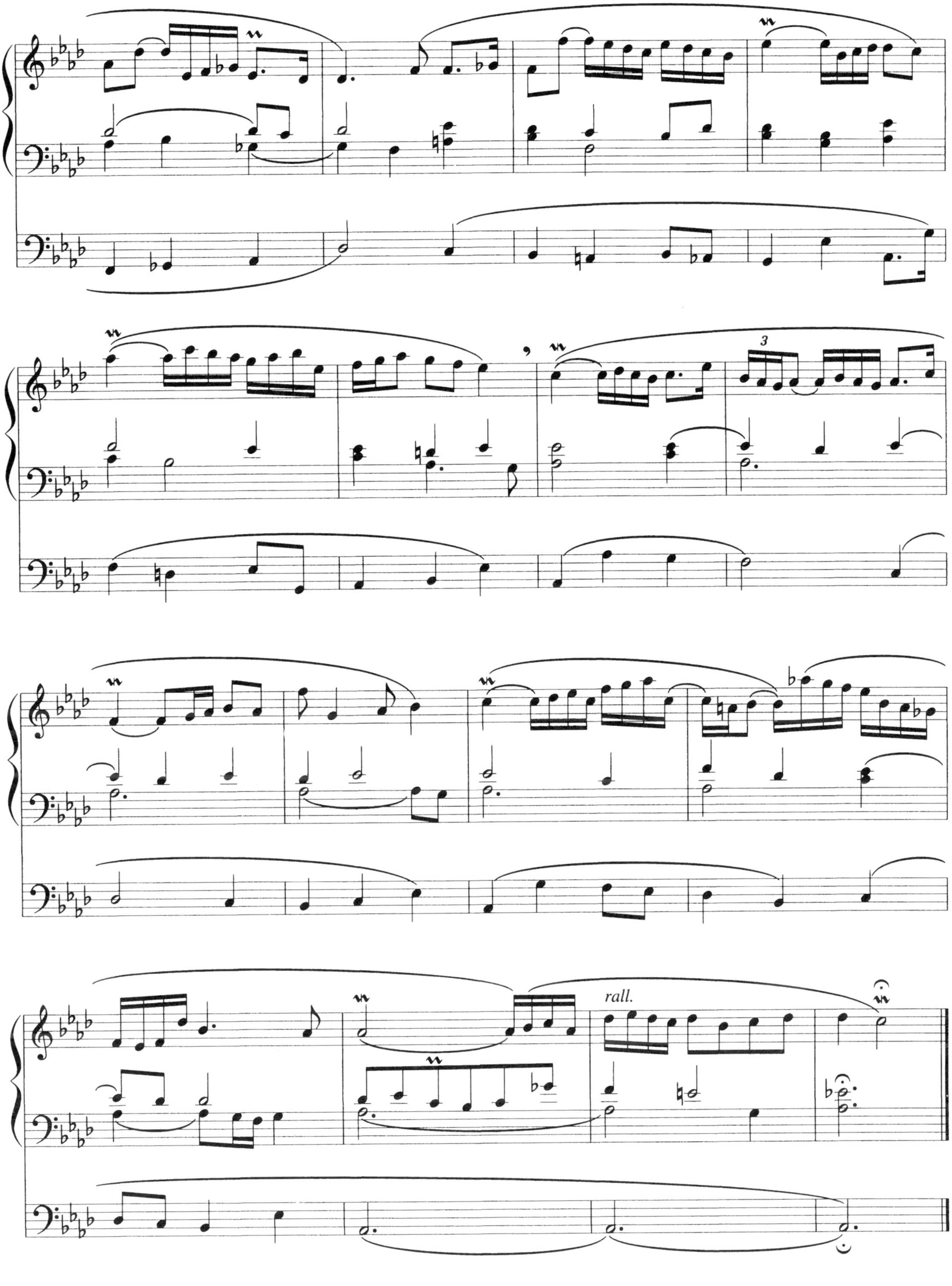
rall.

CARILLON

Malcolm Archer

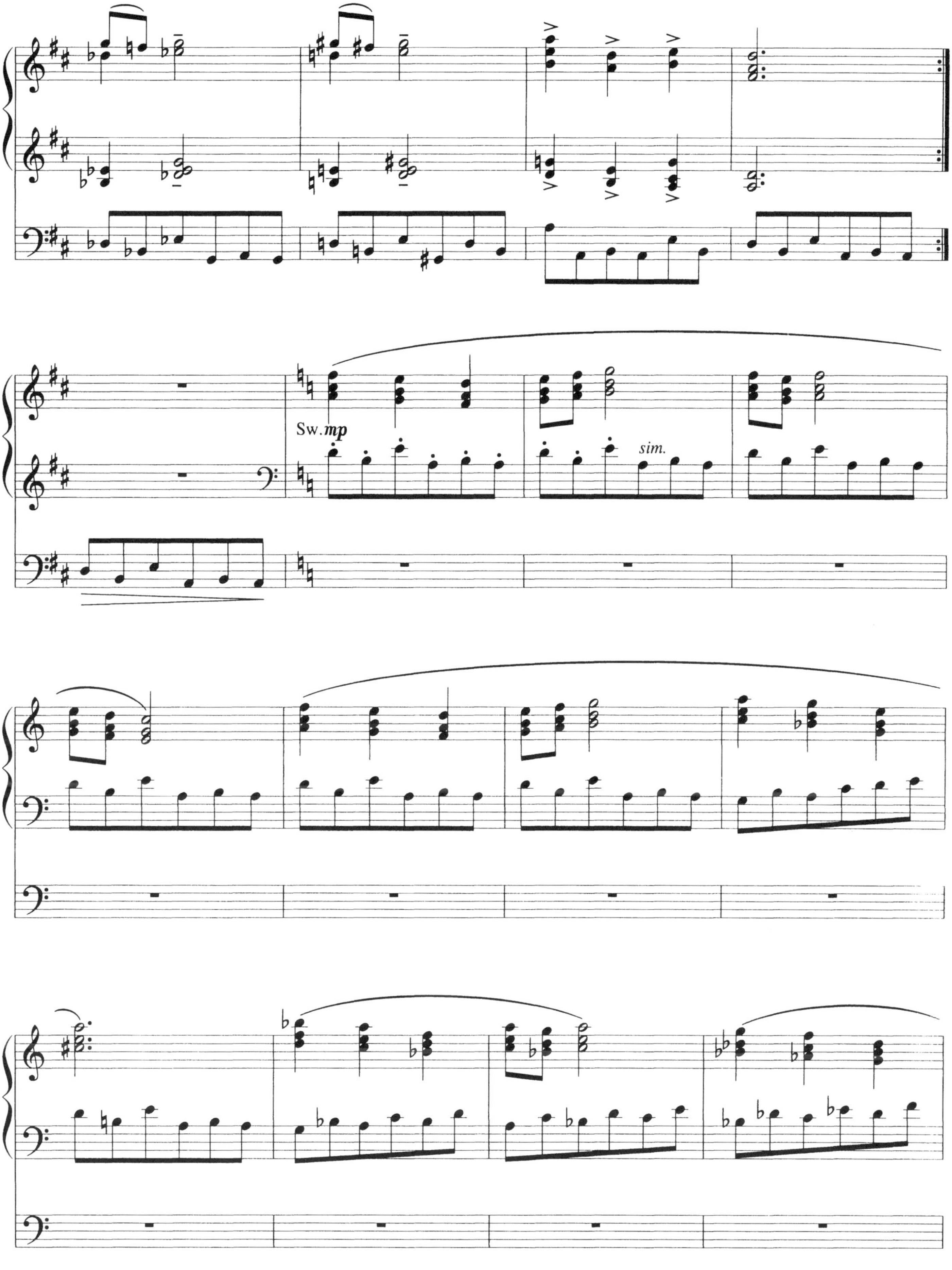
Sw. mp
sim.

poco a poco cresc.

stacc.

Gt.*ff*

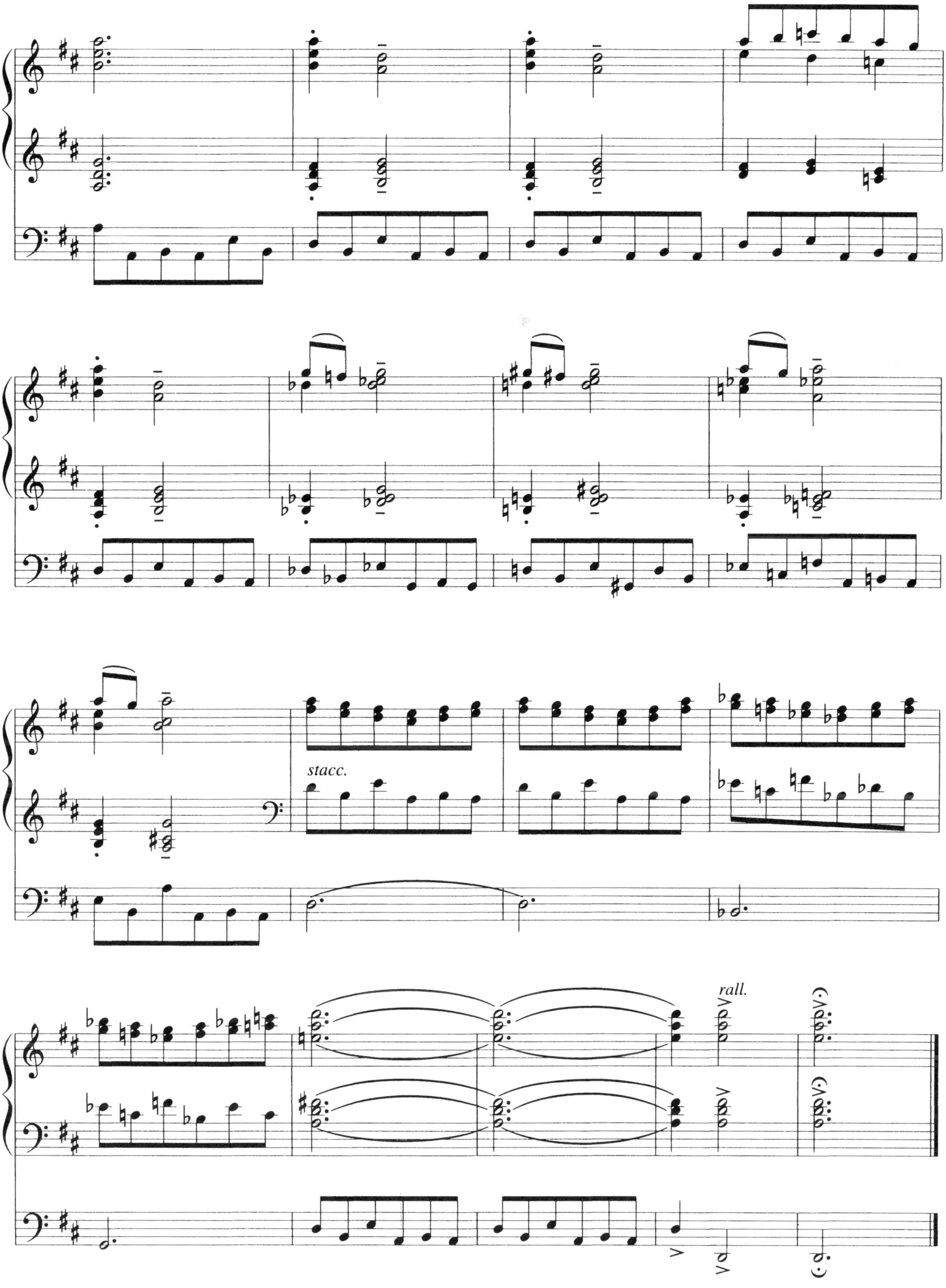
stacc.
rall.

GO FORTH WITH JOY

Colin Hand

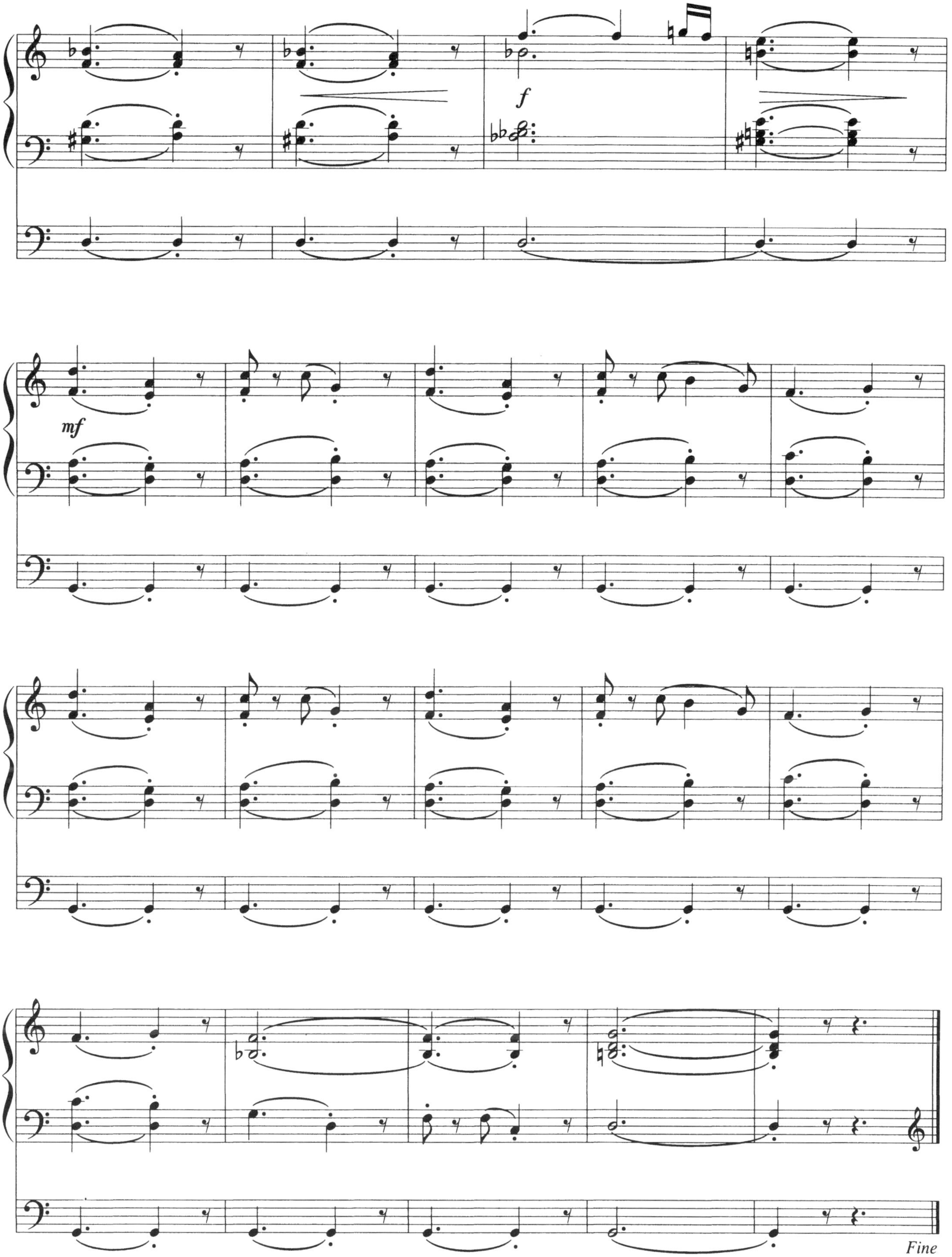

f
mf
Fine

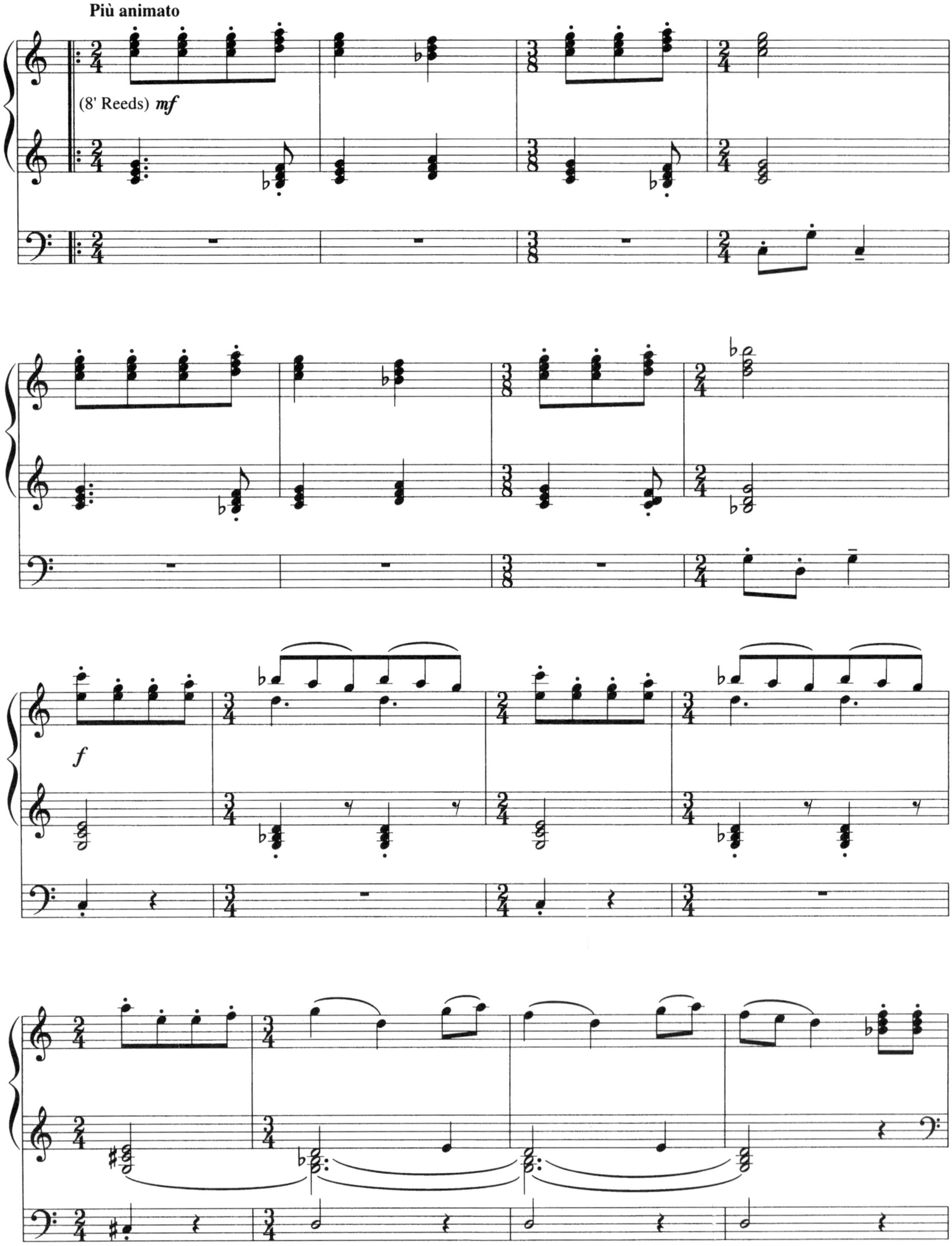

Più animato
(8' Reeds) mf
f

D.S. al Fine
con ripet

SOLEMN INTRODUCTION

Christopher Tambling

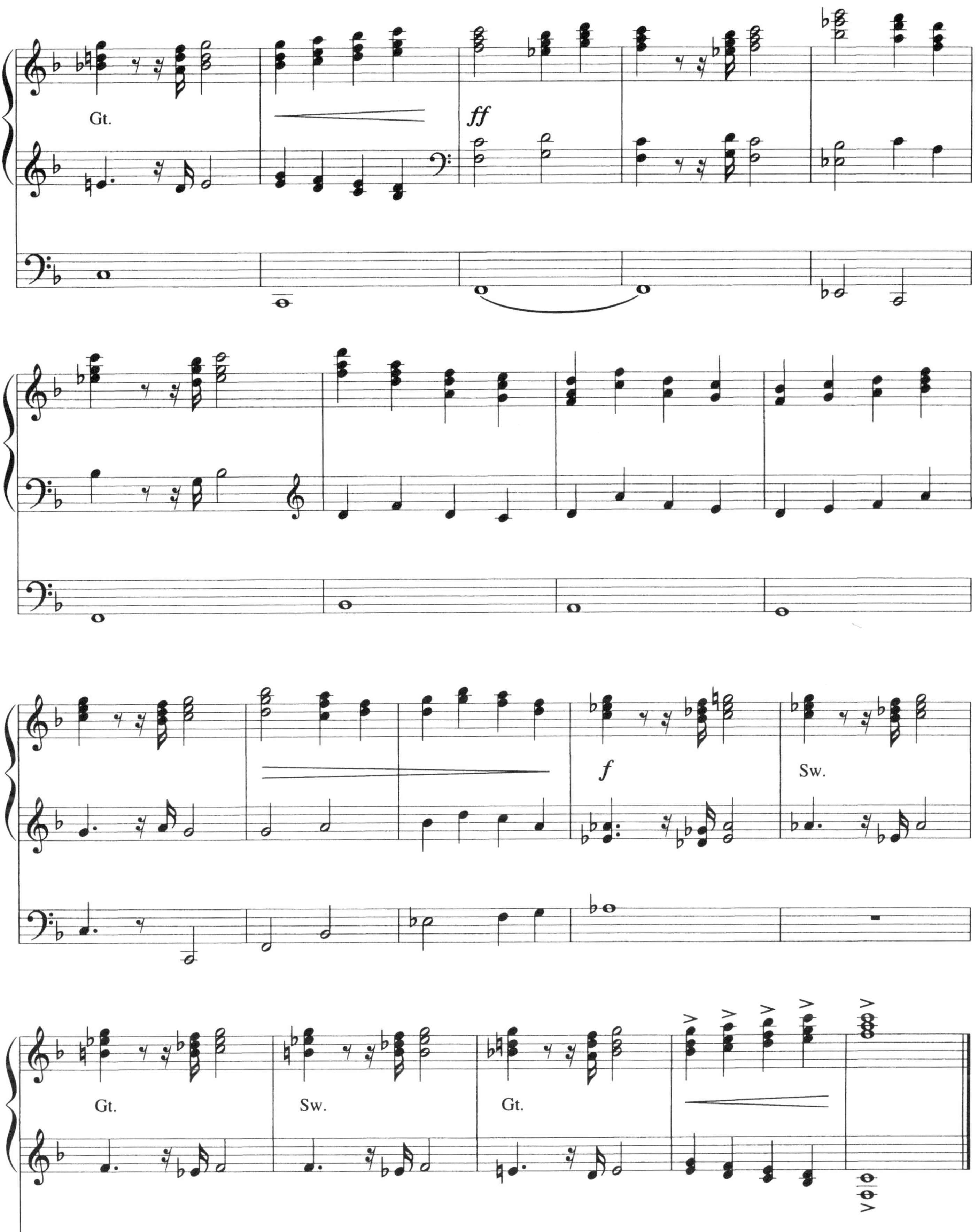
Gt.
ff
f
Sw.
Gt.
Sw.
Gt.

FESTIVAL

Richard Pantcheff

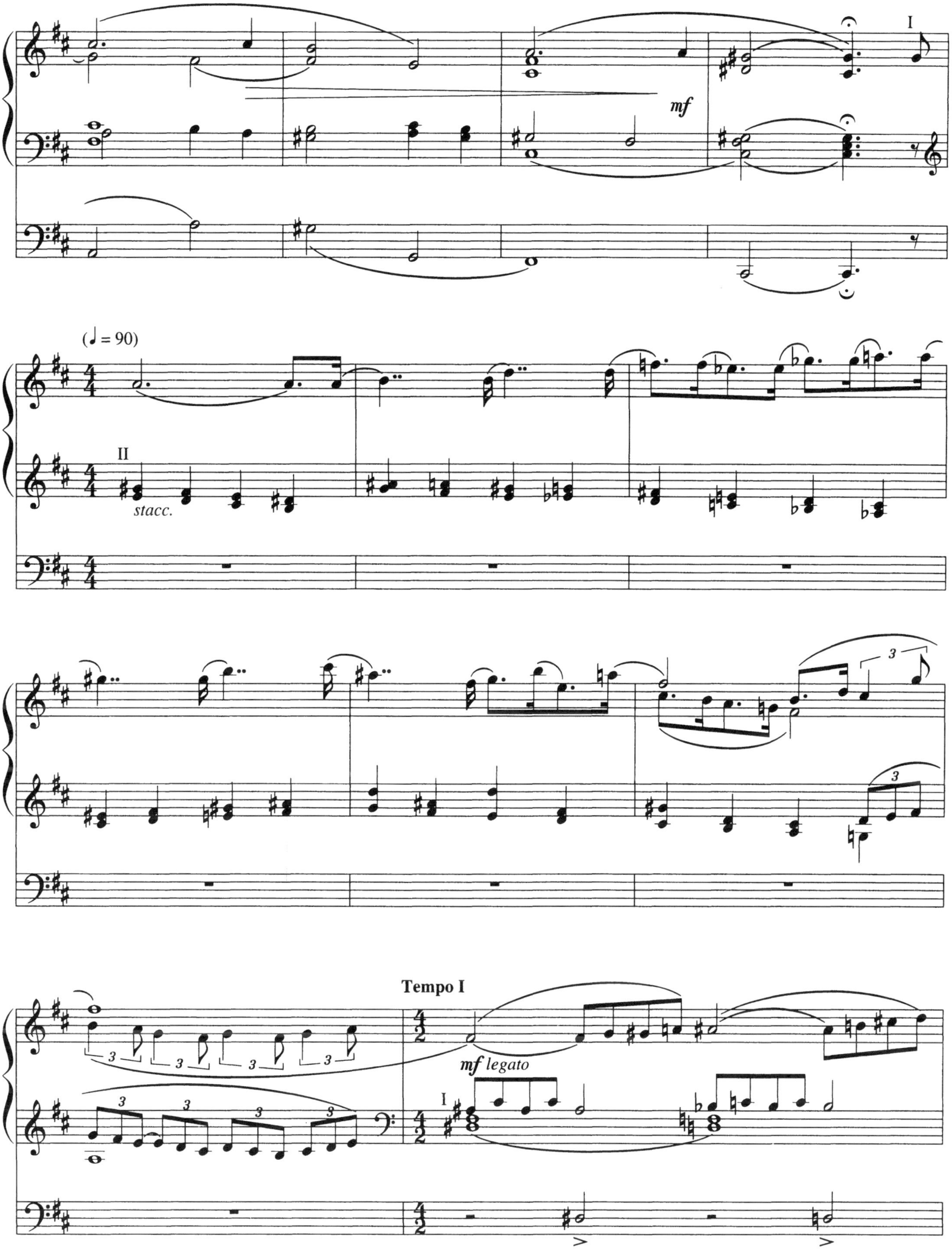
I
mf
(♩ = 90)
II
stacc.
Tempo I
mf legato
I

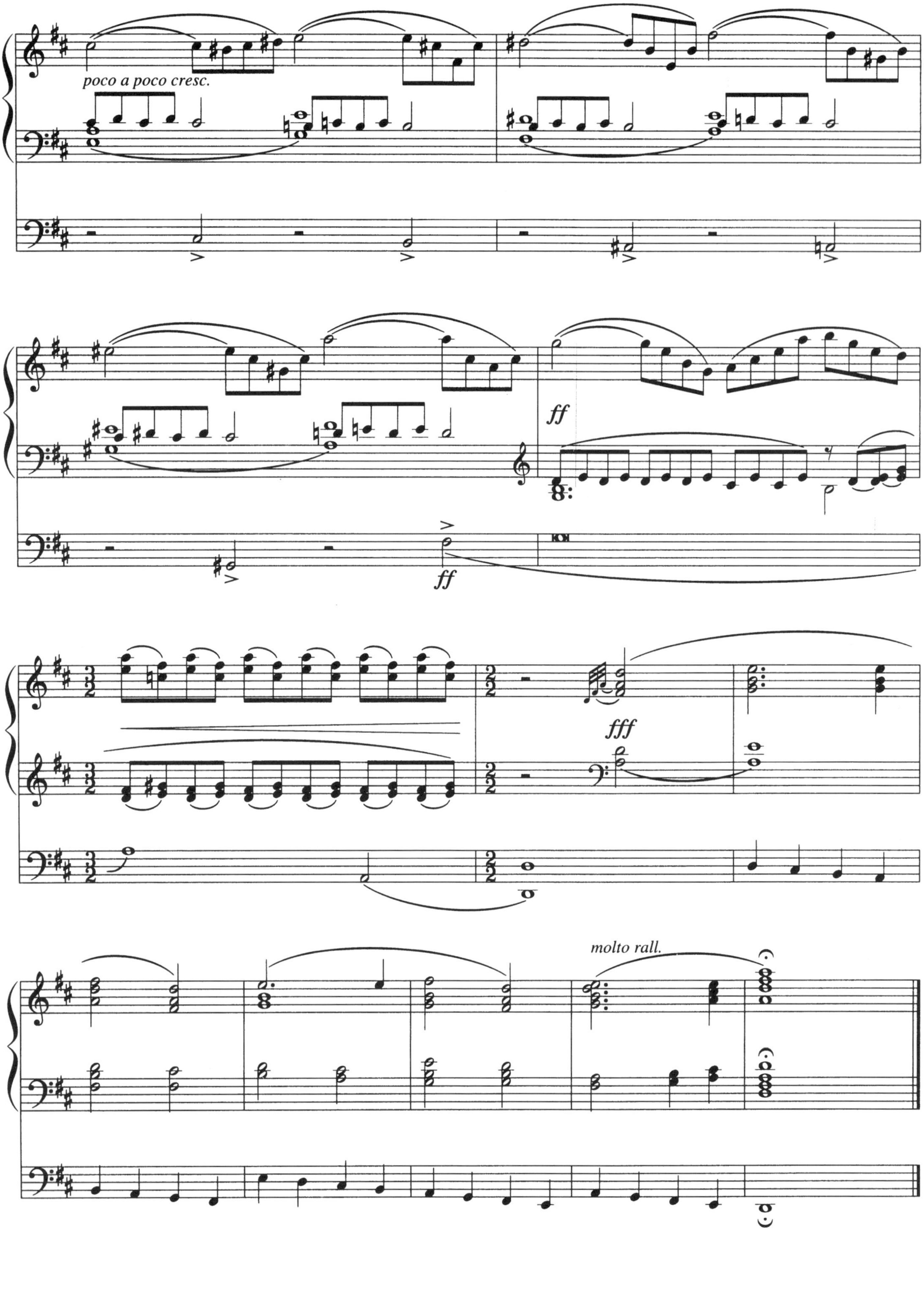
poco a poco cresc.
ff
ff
fff
molto rall.

à mon ami Joseph Baugniet

ORGANUM

Alan Ridout

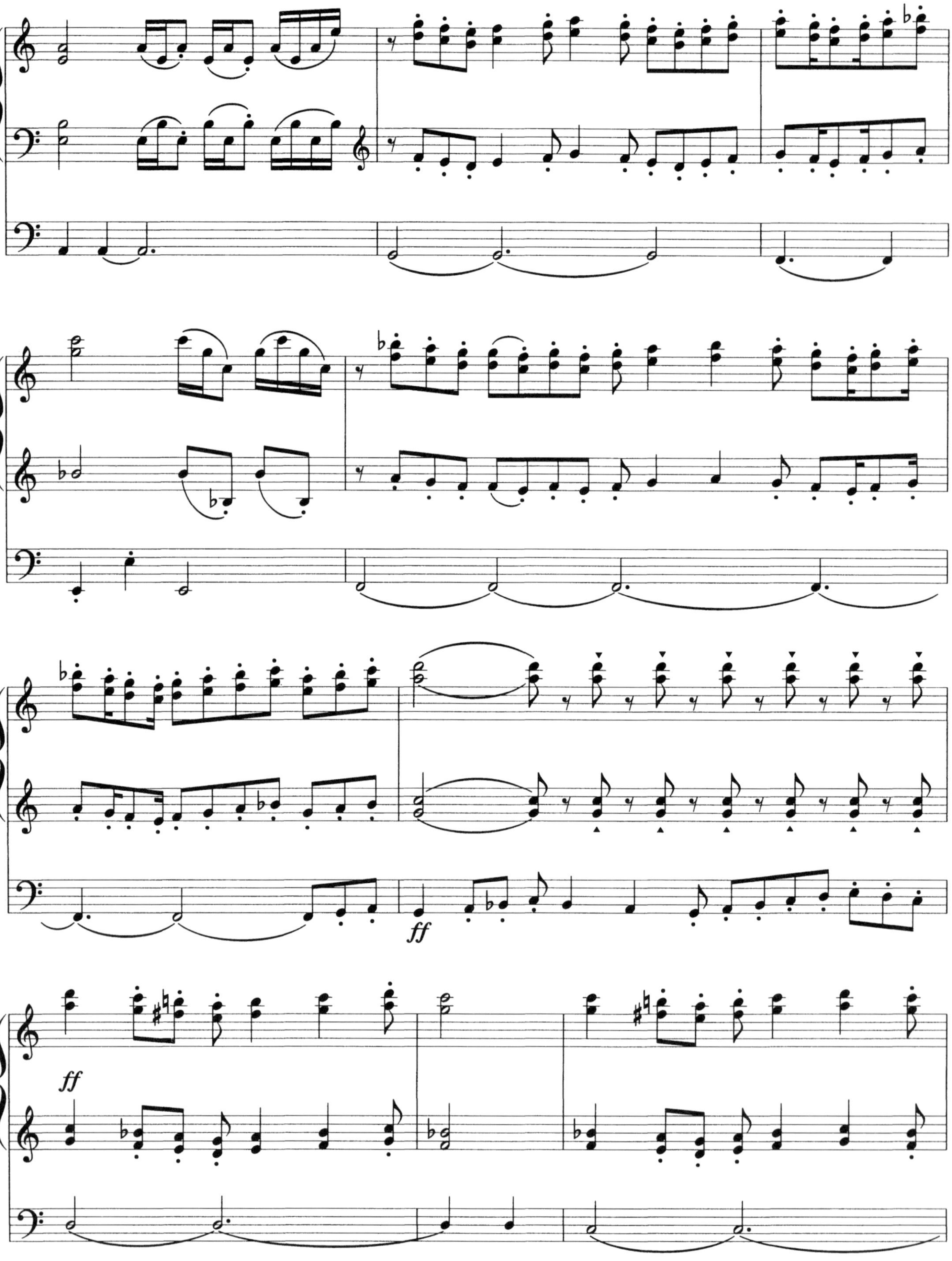
ff
ff

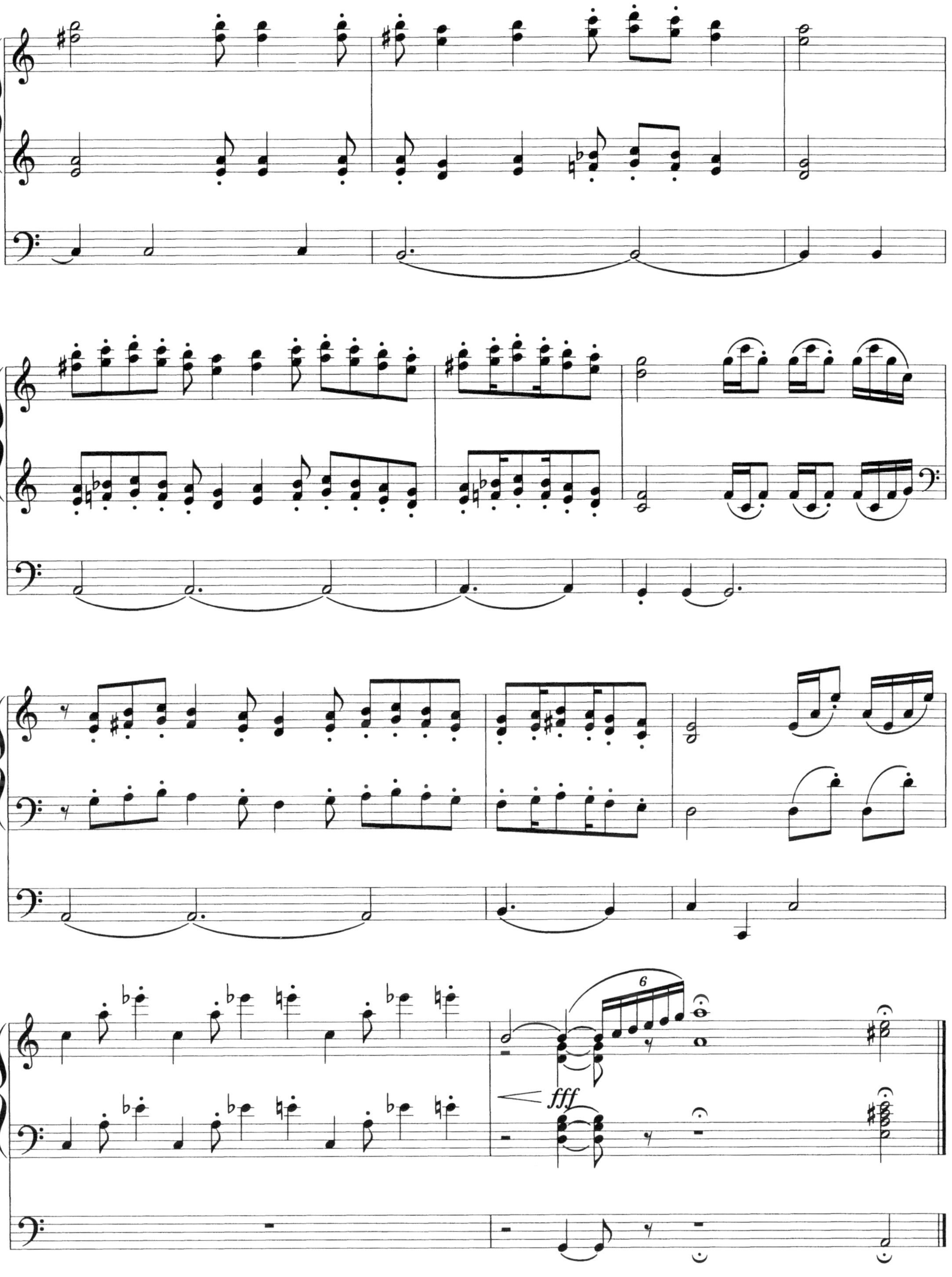
6
fff

TRUMPET AIR AND INTERLUDE

Stanley Vann

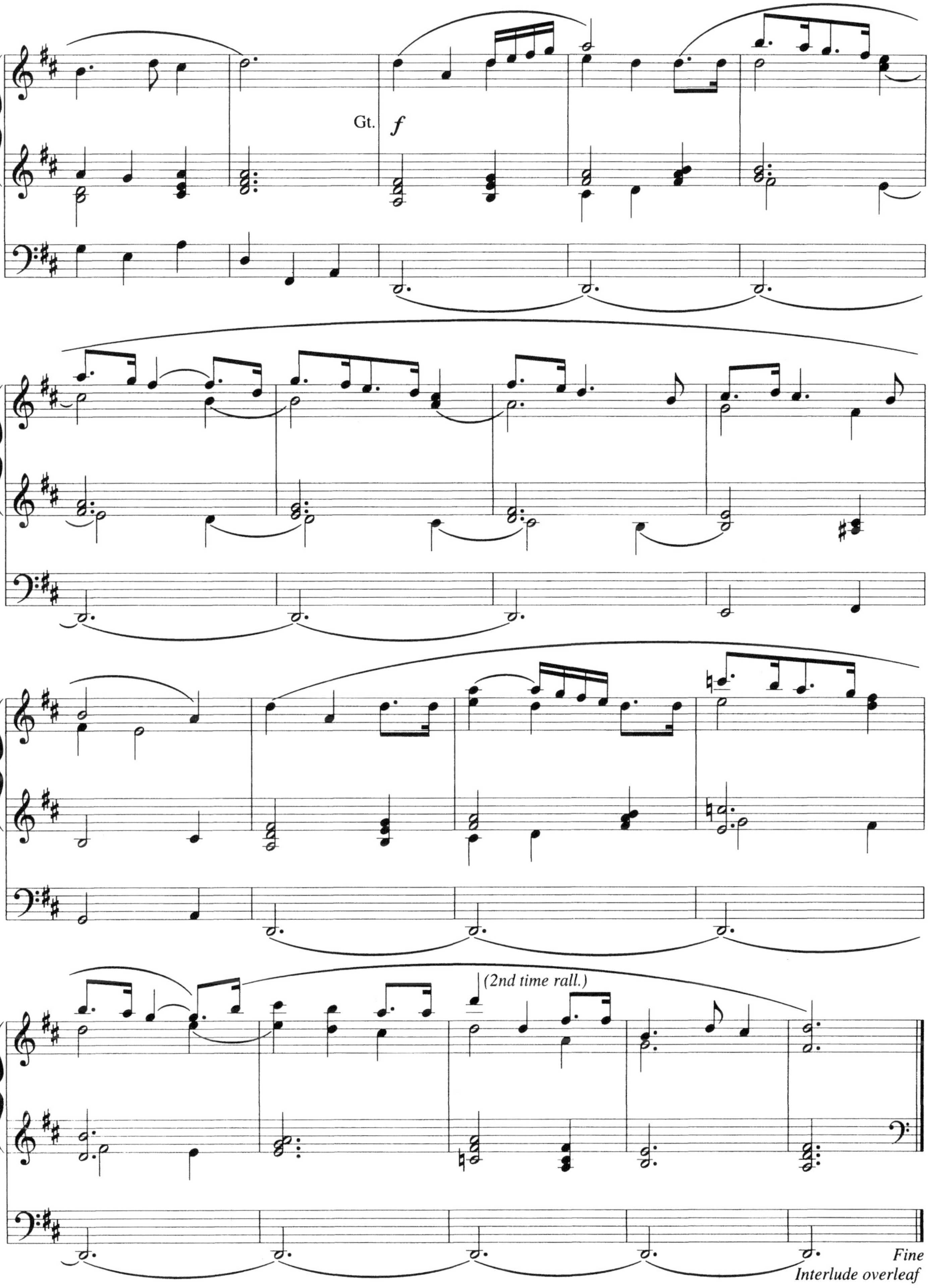
Gt.
f
(2nd time rall.)
Fine
Interlude overleaf

D.C. al Fine

138

for Revd Mary Brotherston: Ordination to the Priesthood (23 April, 1994)

MARCH FOR AN OCCASION

Alan Viner

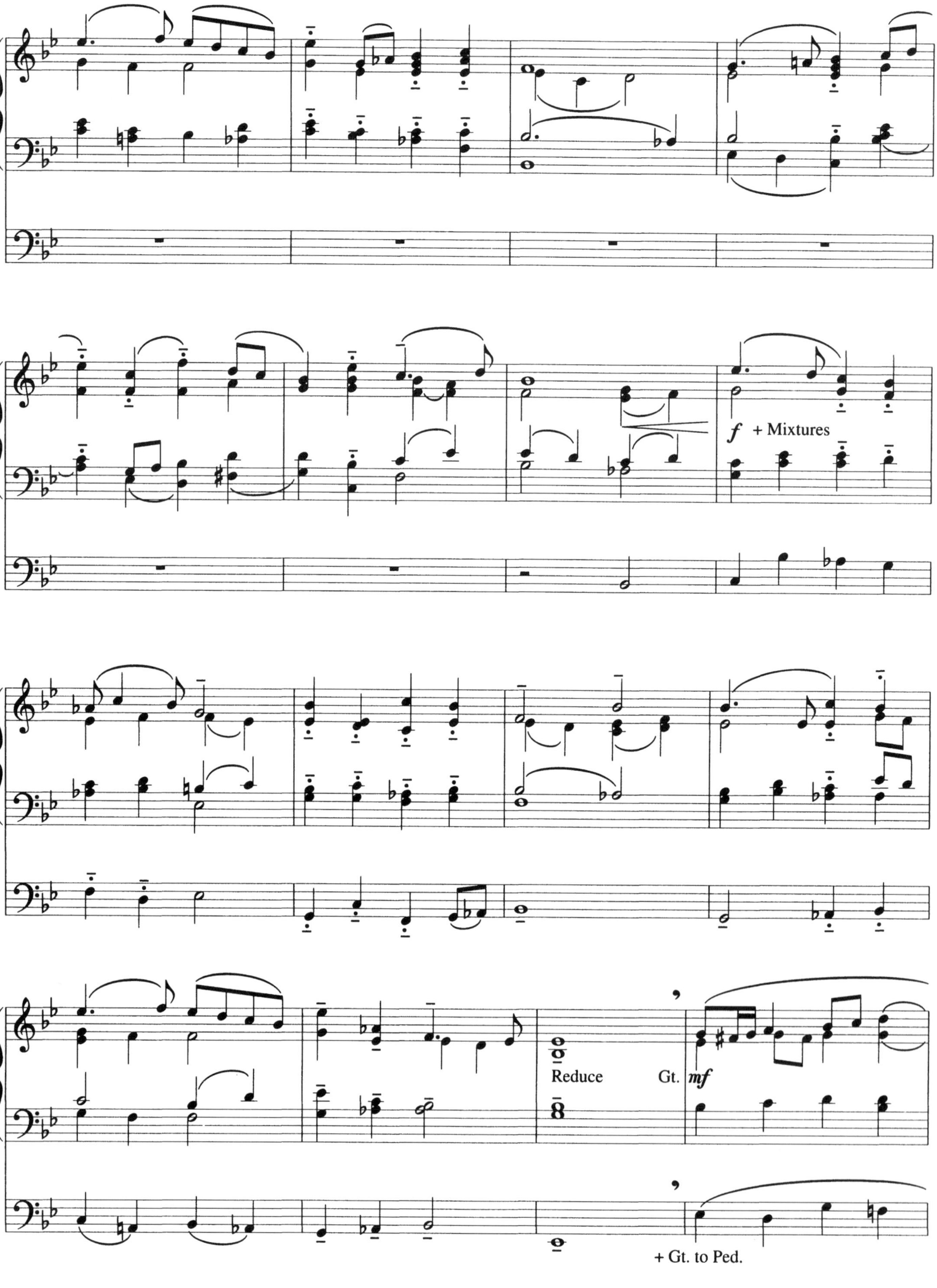
f + Mixtures
Reduce
Gt.
mf
+ Gt. to Ped.

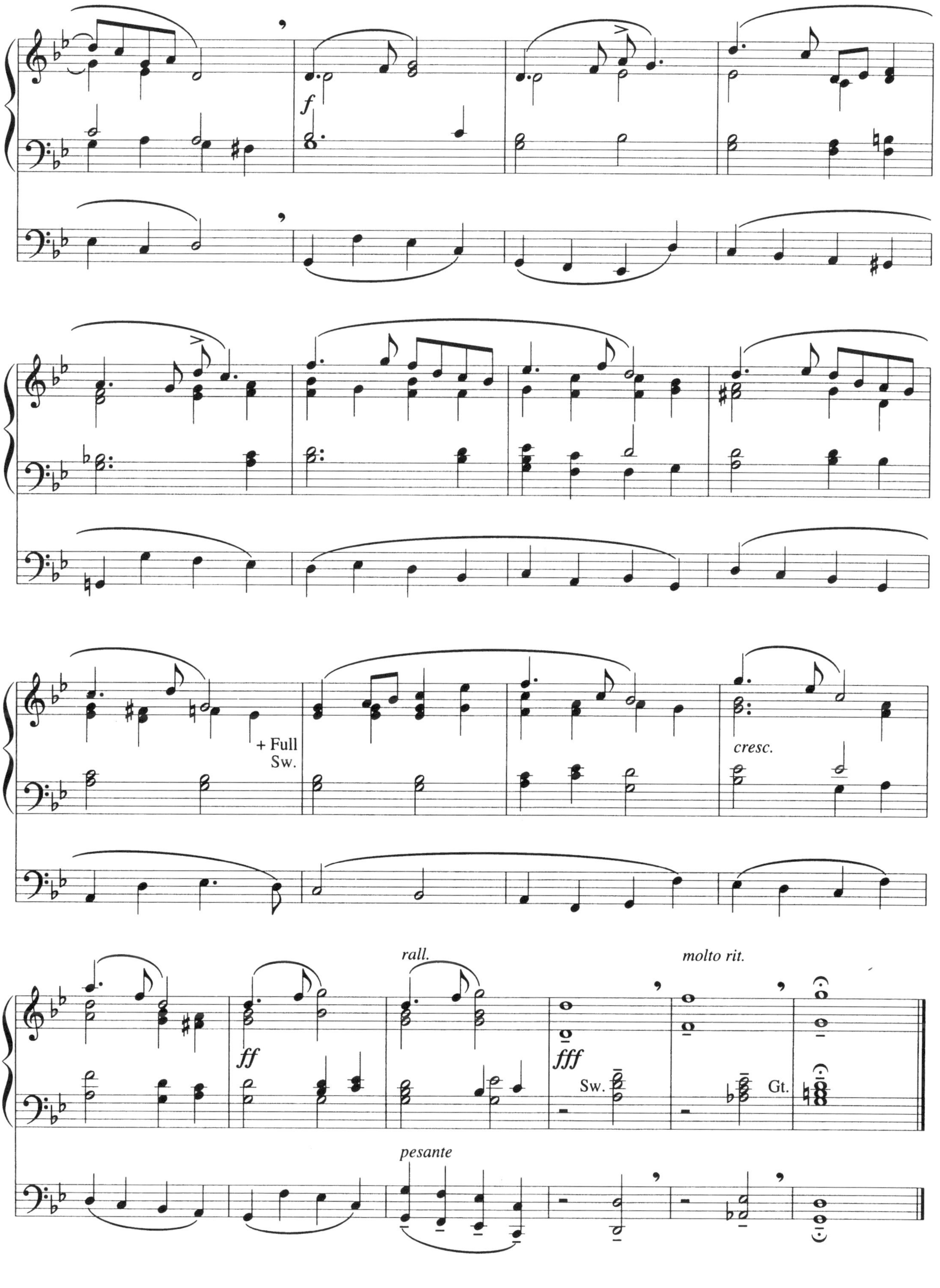
f
+ Full Sw.
cresc.
rall.
molto rit.
ff
fff
Sw.
Gt.
pesante

SOLEMN PRELUDE

John Marsh

D.C. al Coda

⊕ CODA

rall.

TRIUMPHAL MARCH

Andrew Fletcher

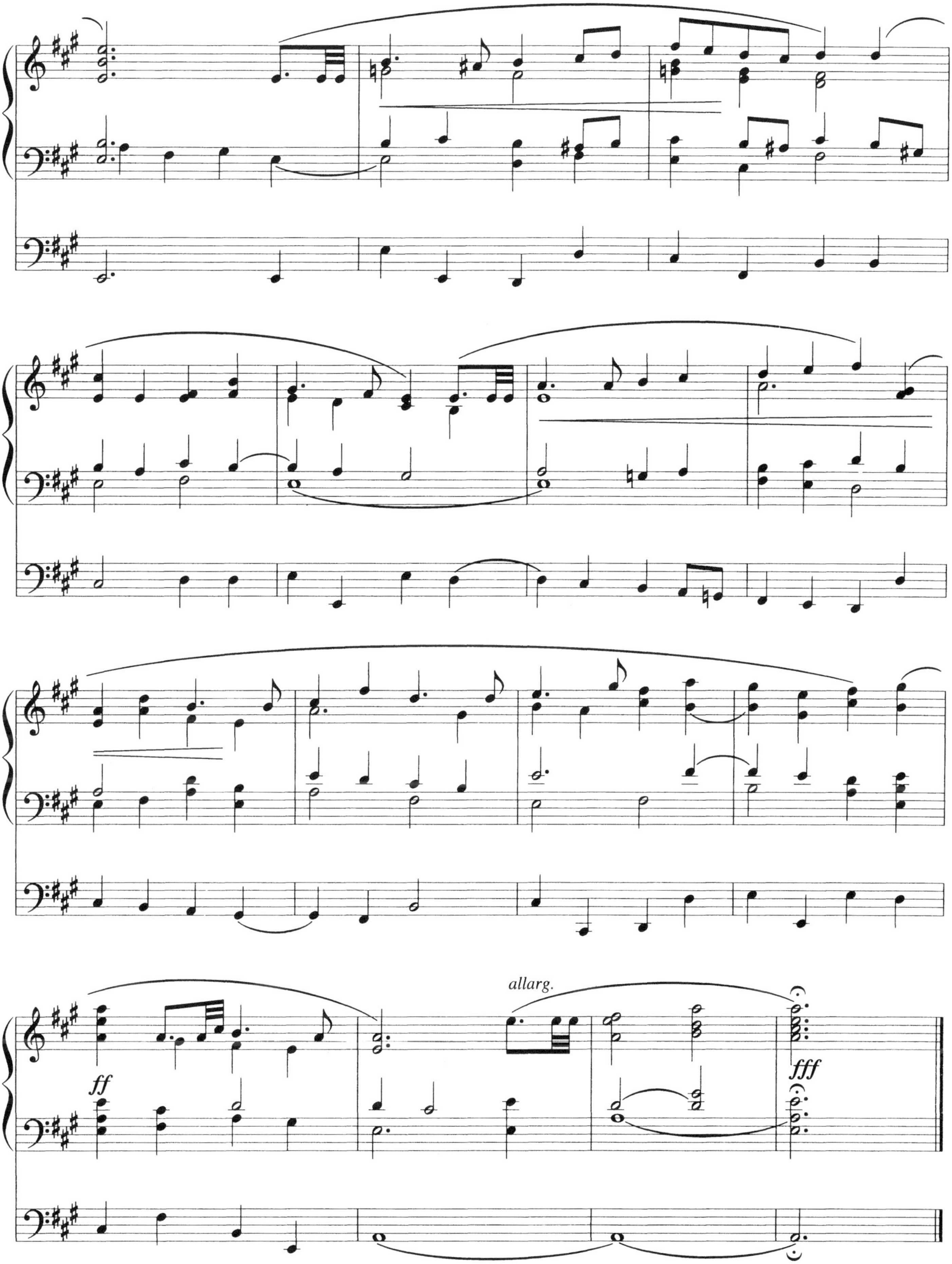

allarg.
ff
fff

GLORIA IN EXCELSIS

Philip Moore

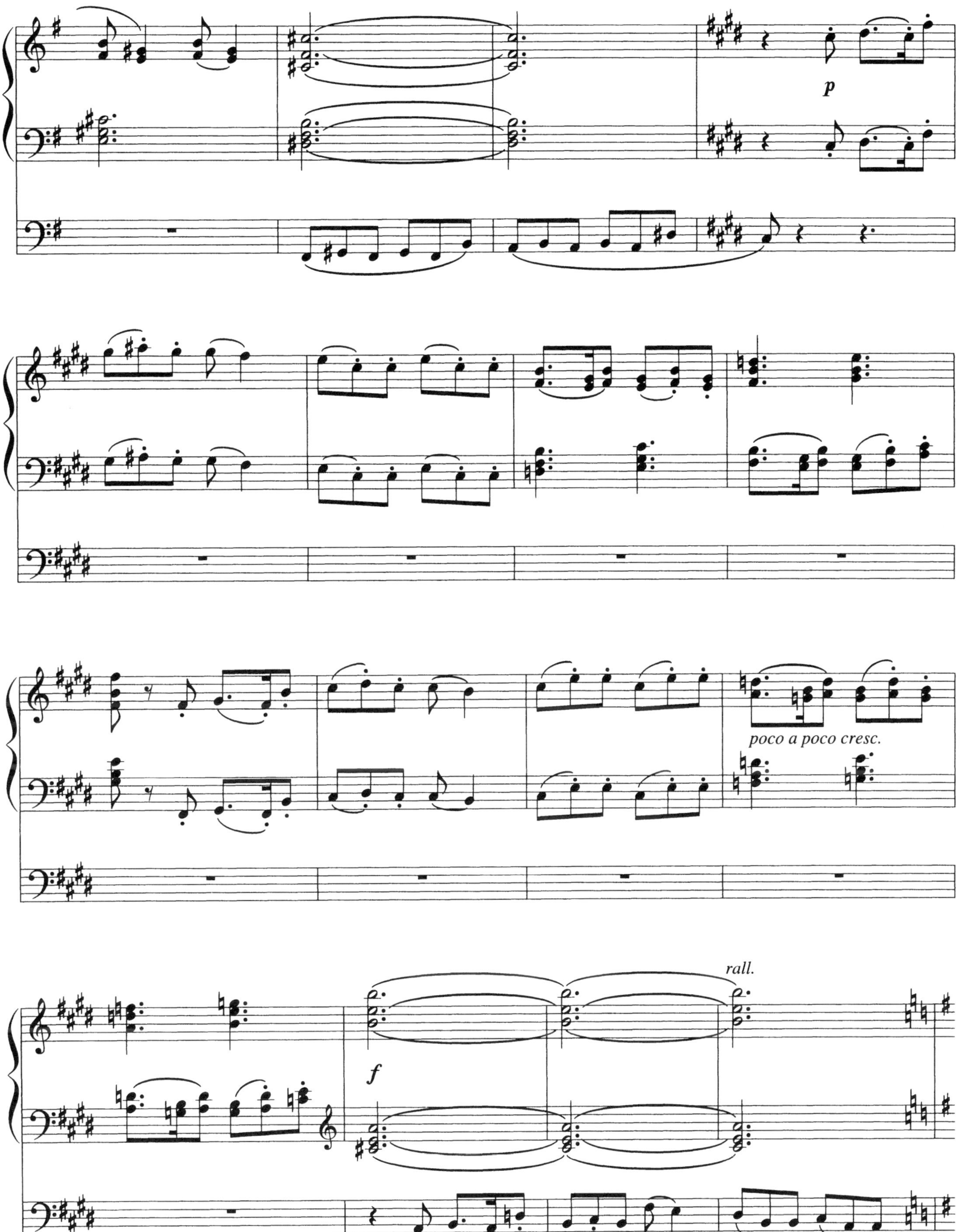

p
poco a poco cresc.
f
rall.

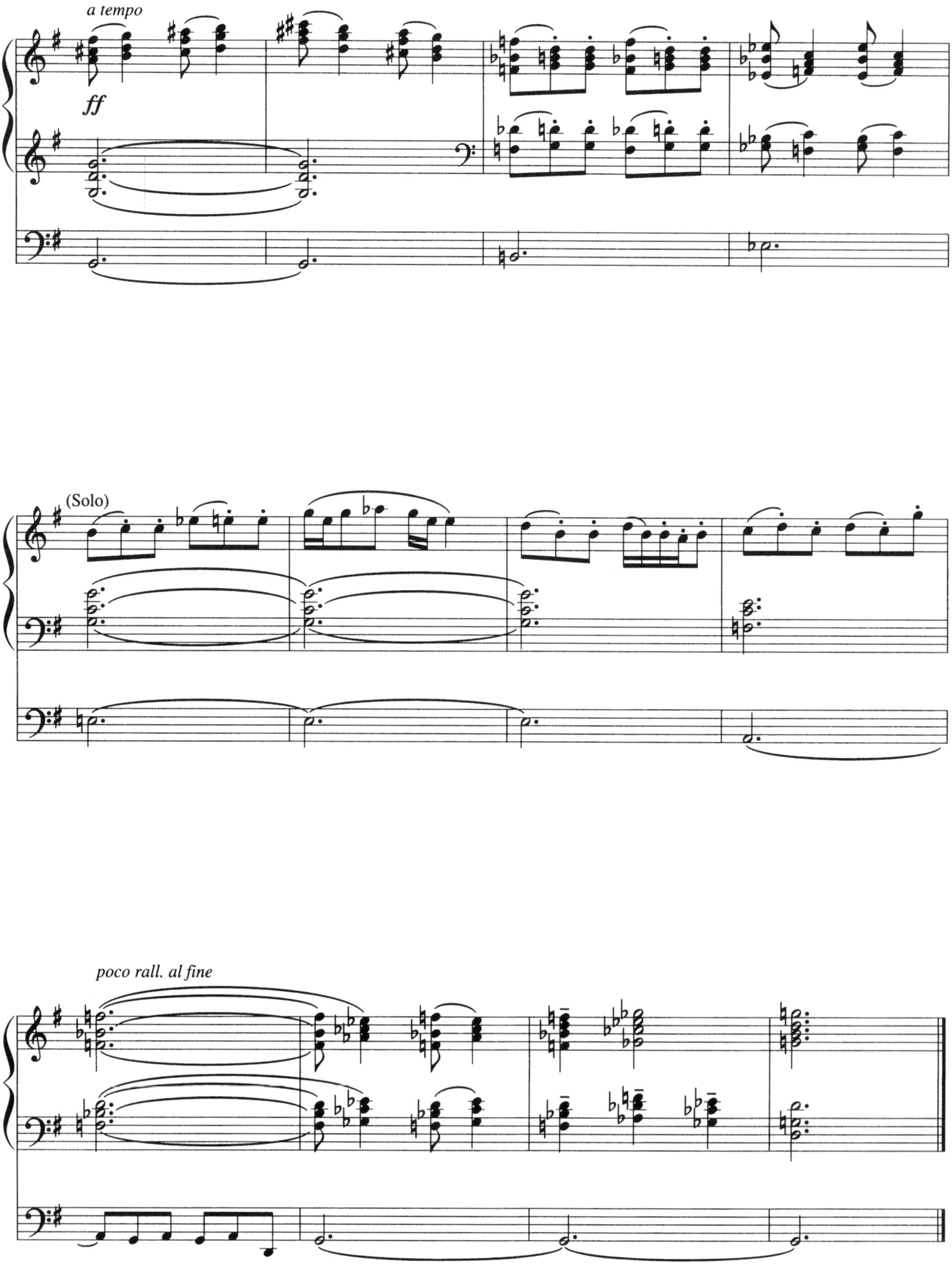
a tempo
ff
(Solo)
poco rall. al fine

FESTAL RECESSIONAL

Colin Mawby

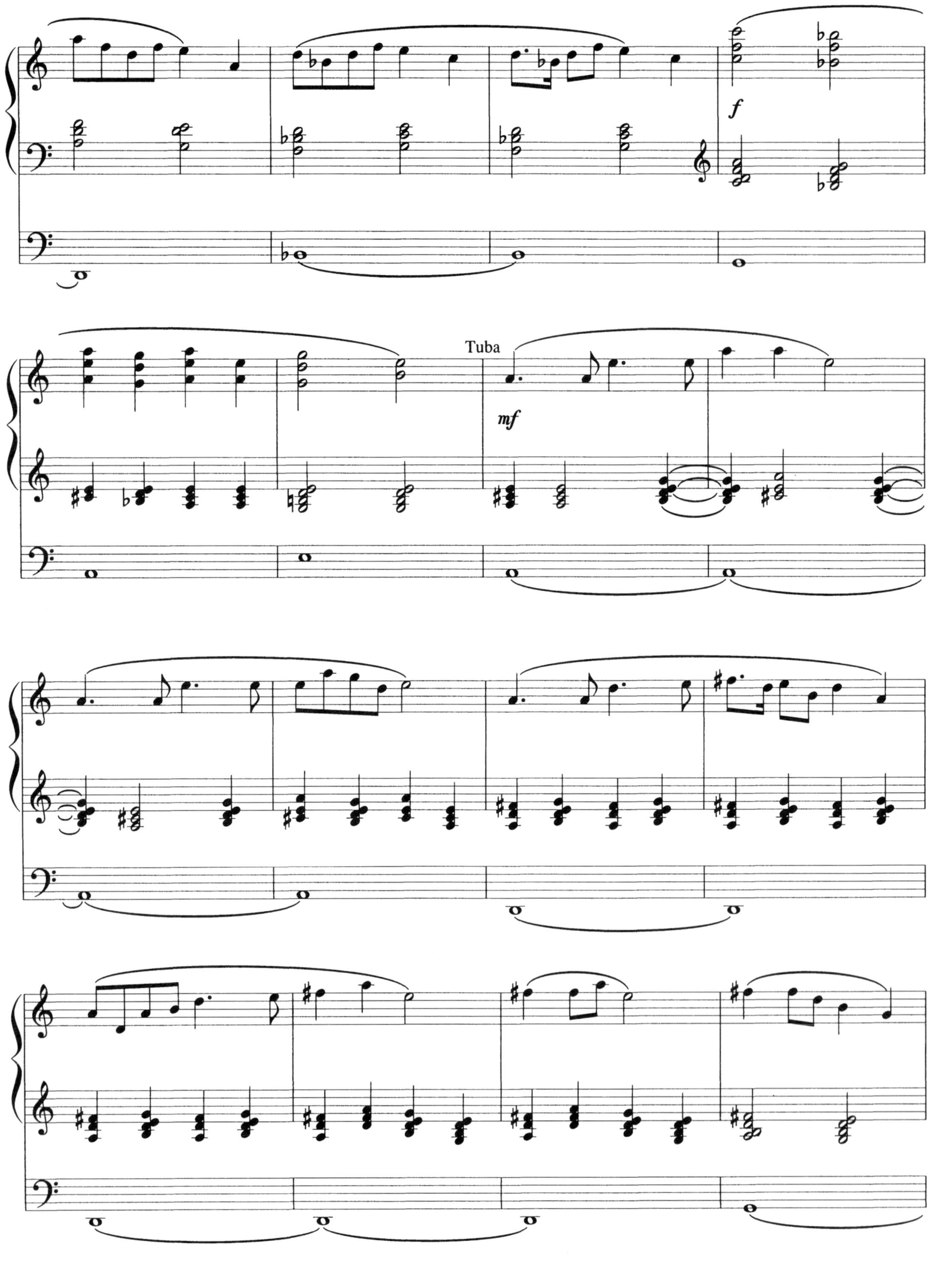
f
Tuba
mf

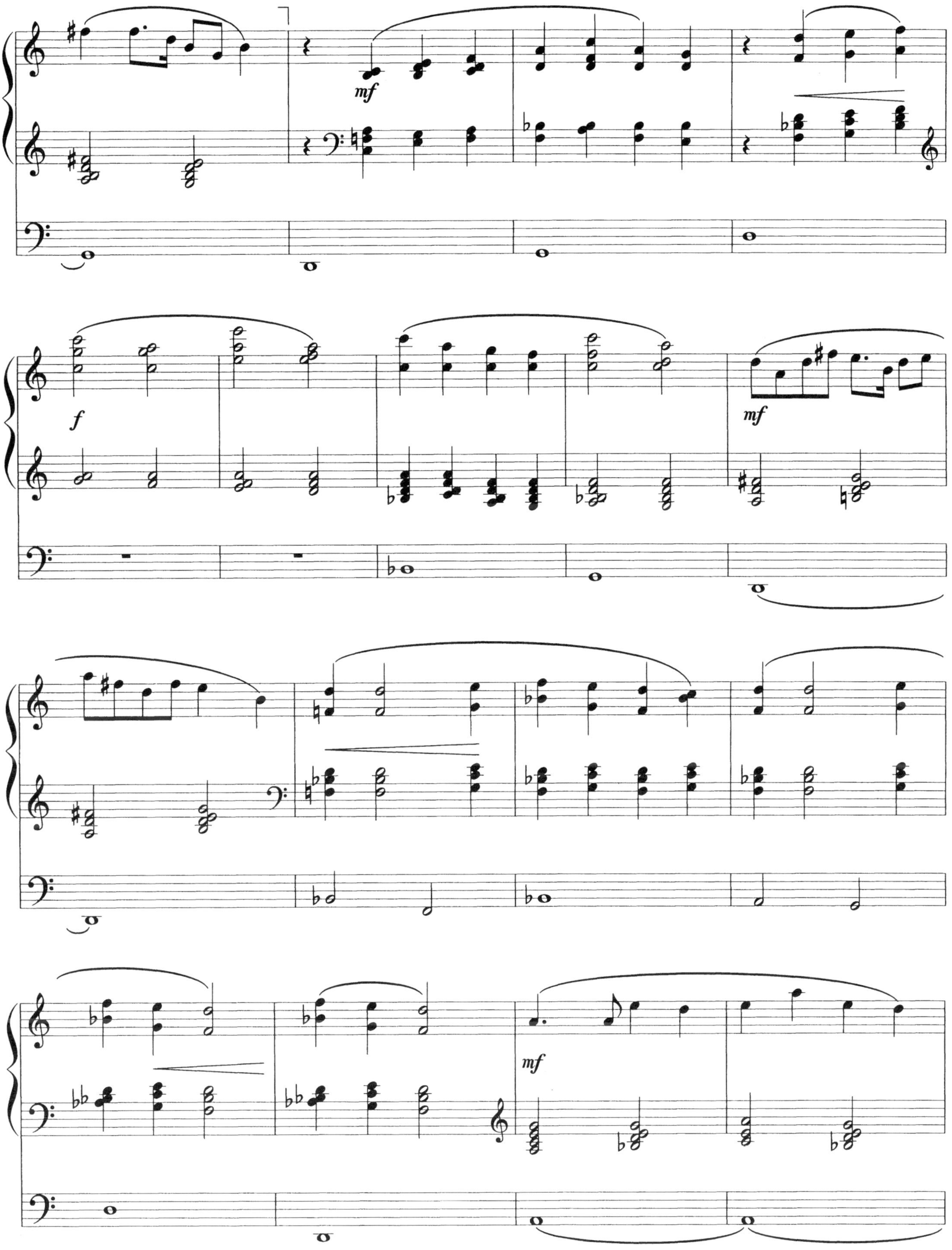
mf
f
mf
mf

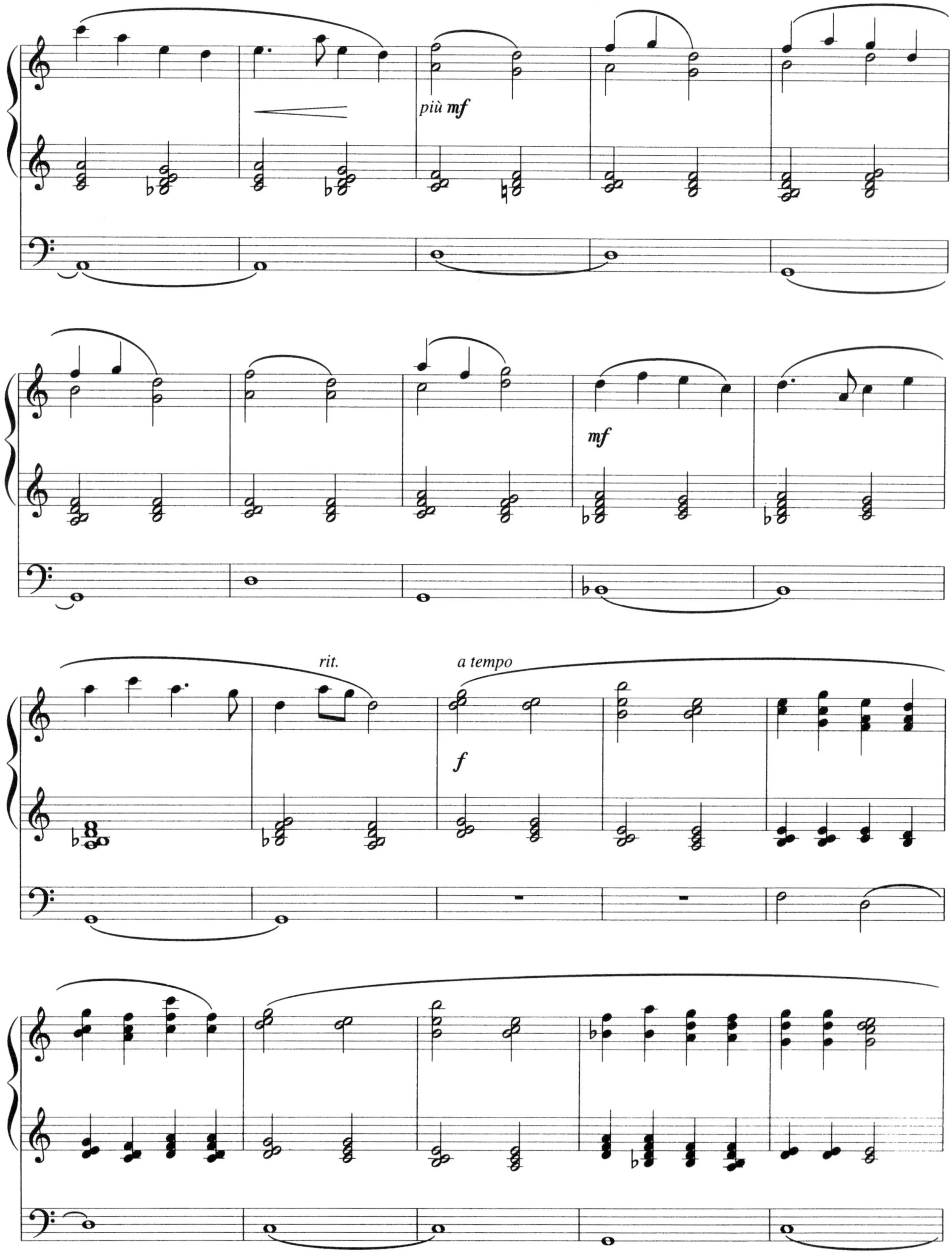
più mf
mf
rit.
a tempo
f

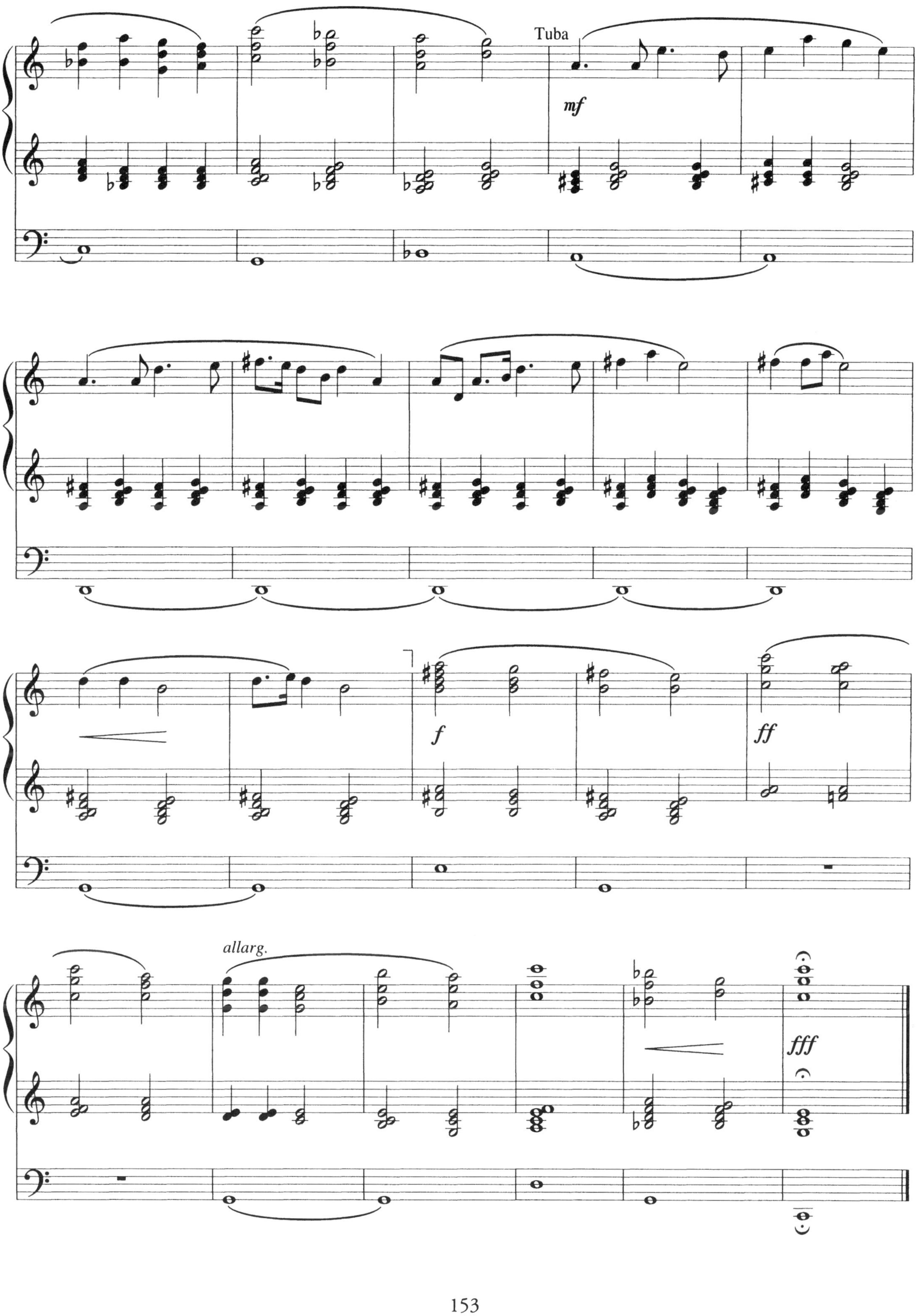

Tuba
mf
f
ff
allarg.
fff

to Frances and Winston

GRANDIOSO

Betty Roe

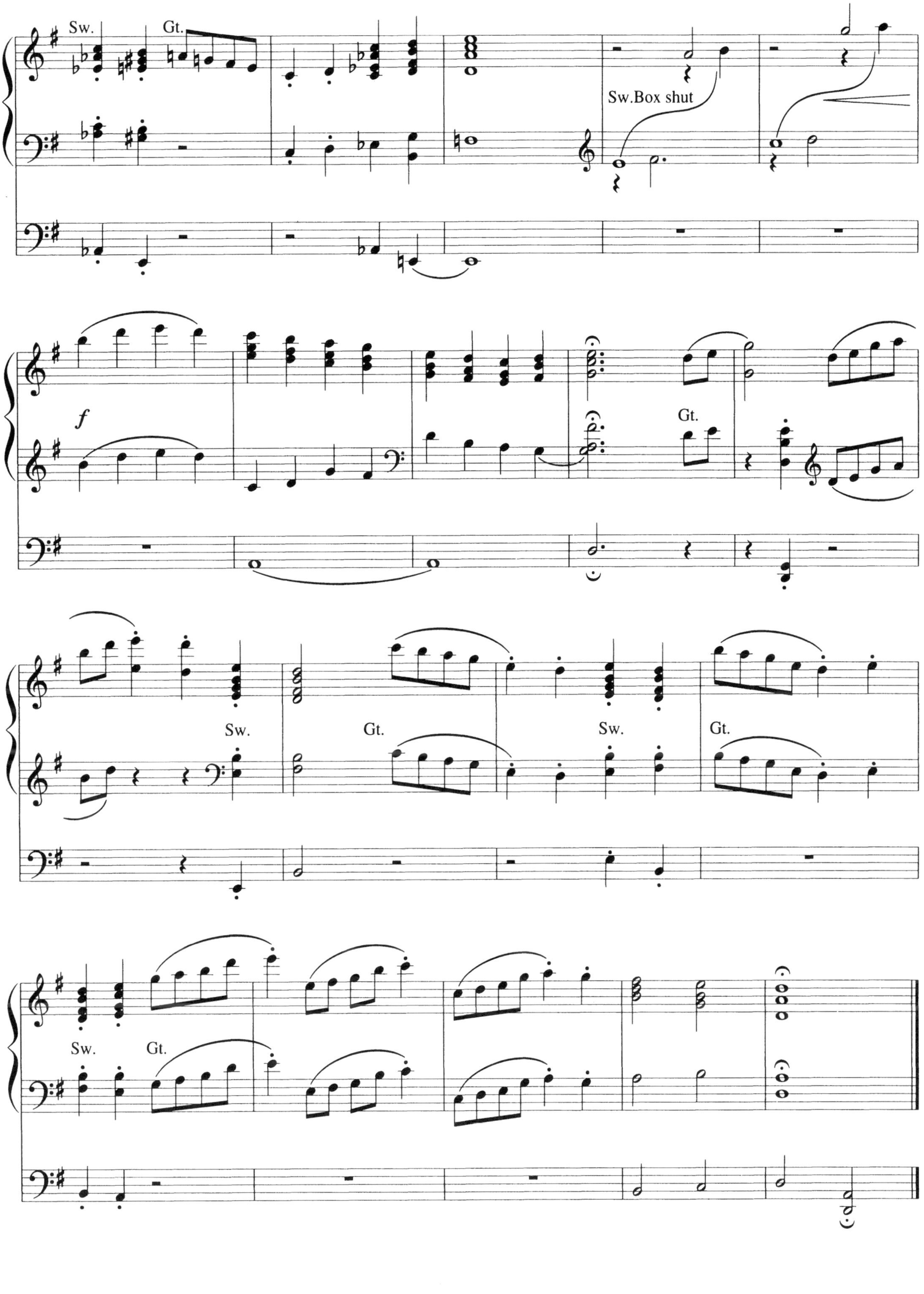
Sw.
Gt.
Sw.Box shut
f
Gt.
Sw.
Gt.
Sw.
Gt.
Sw.
Gt.

CARILLON FANFARE

for Mary

Paul Bryan

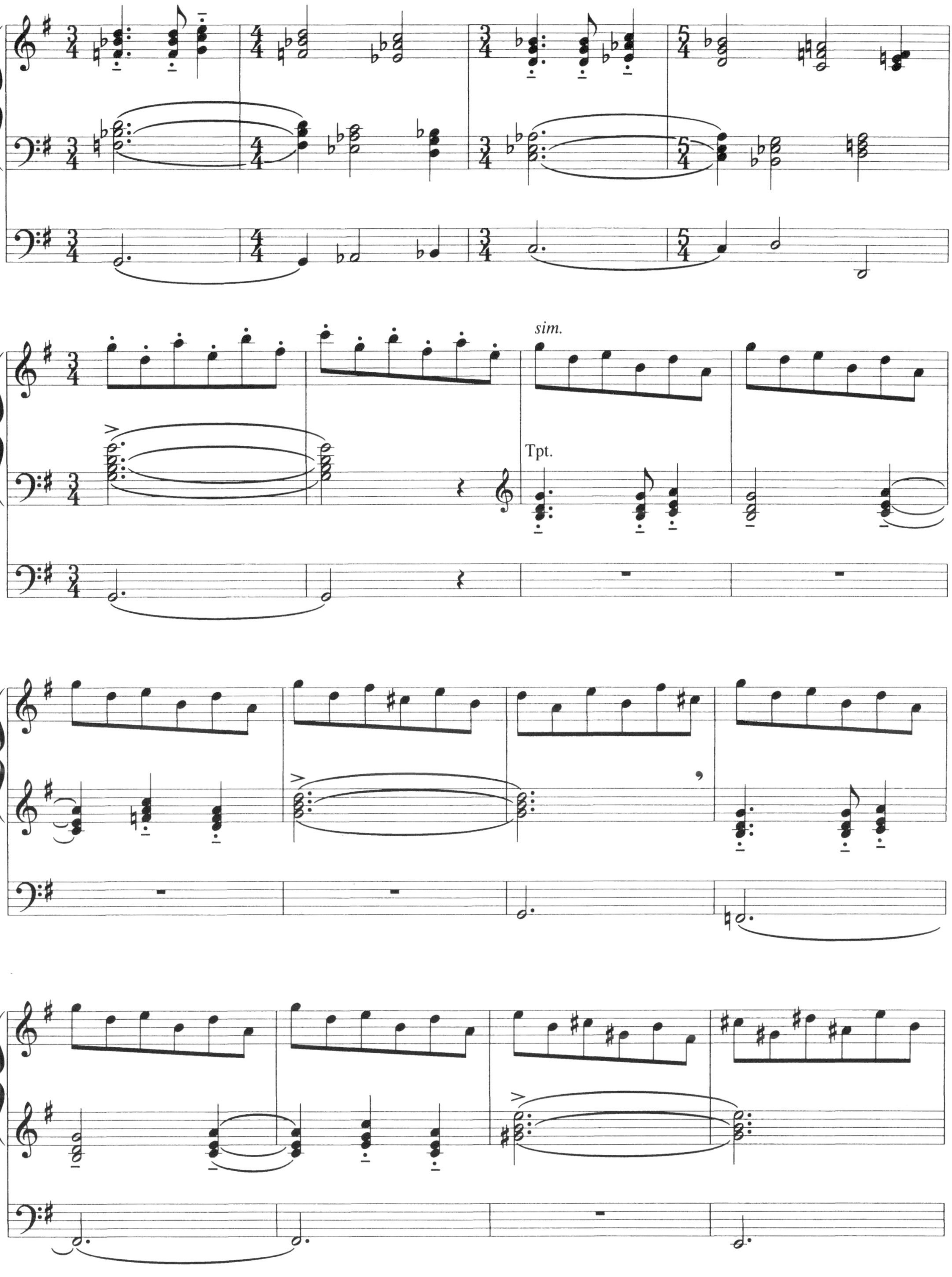
sim.
Tpt.

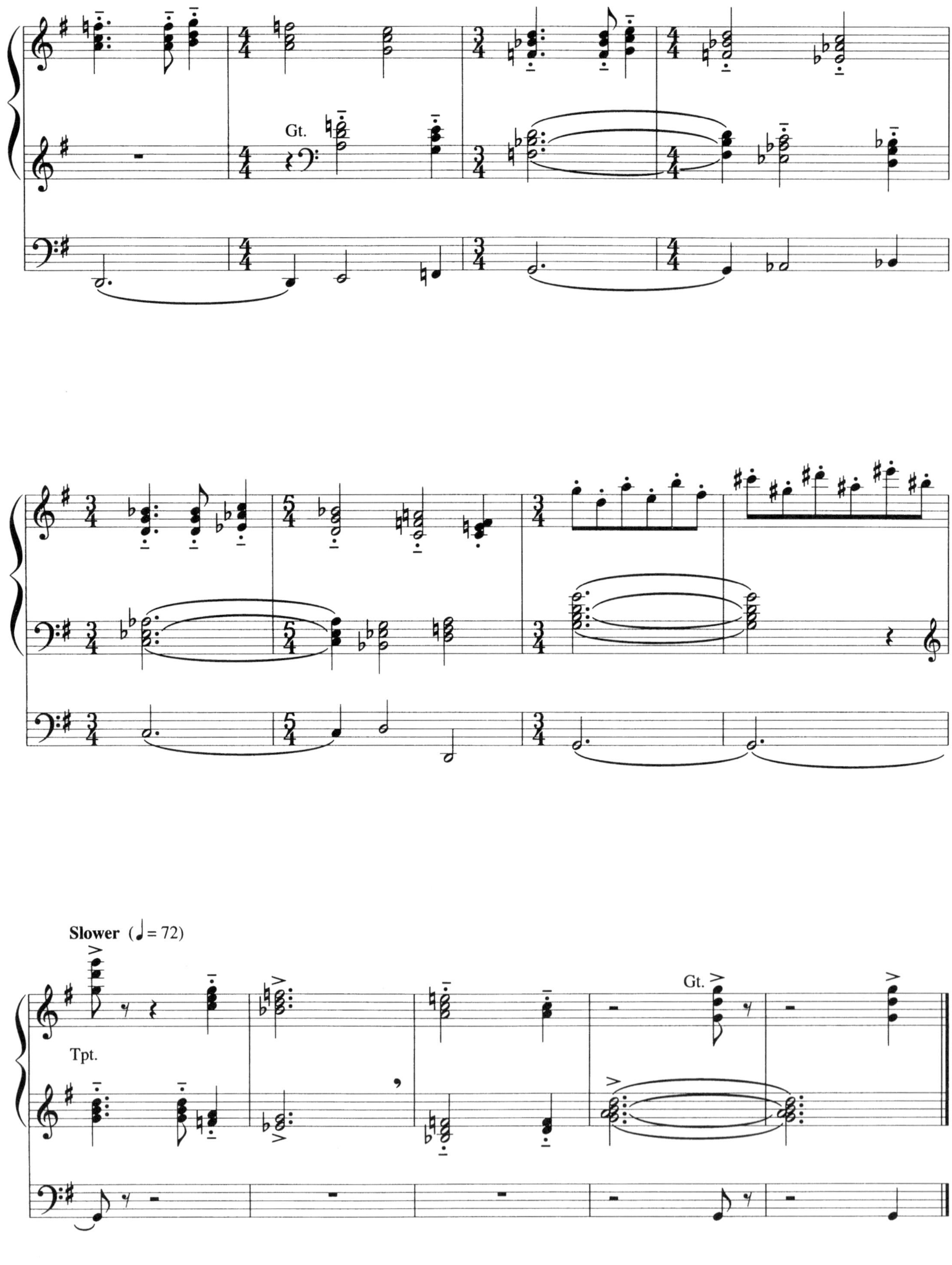
Gt.
Slower (♩ = 72)
Tpt.
Gt.

for Julia and Paul

LES DOUX YEUX

Richard Lloyd

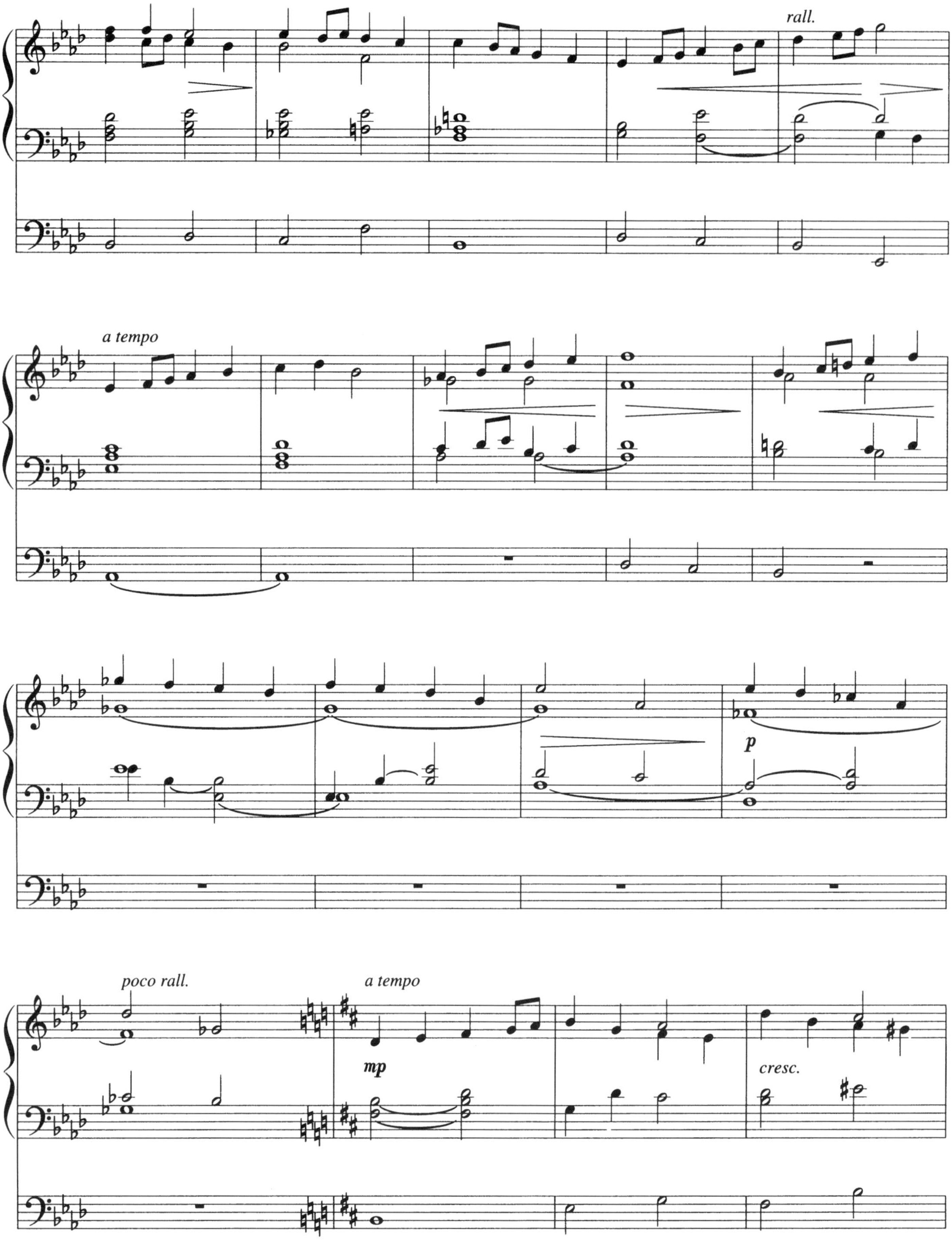
rall.
a tempo
p
poco rall.
a tempo
mp
cresc.

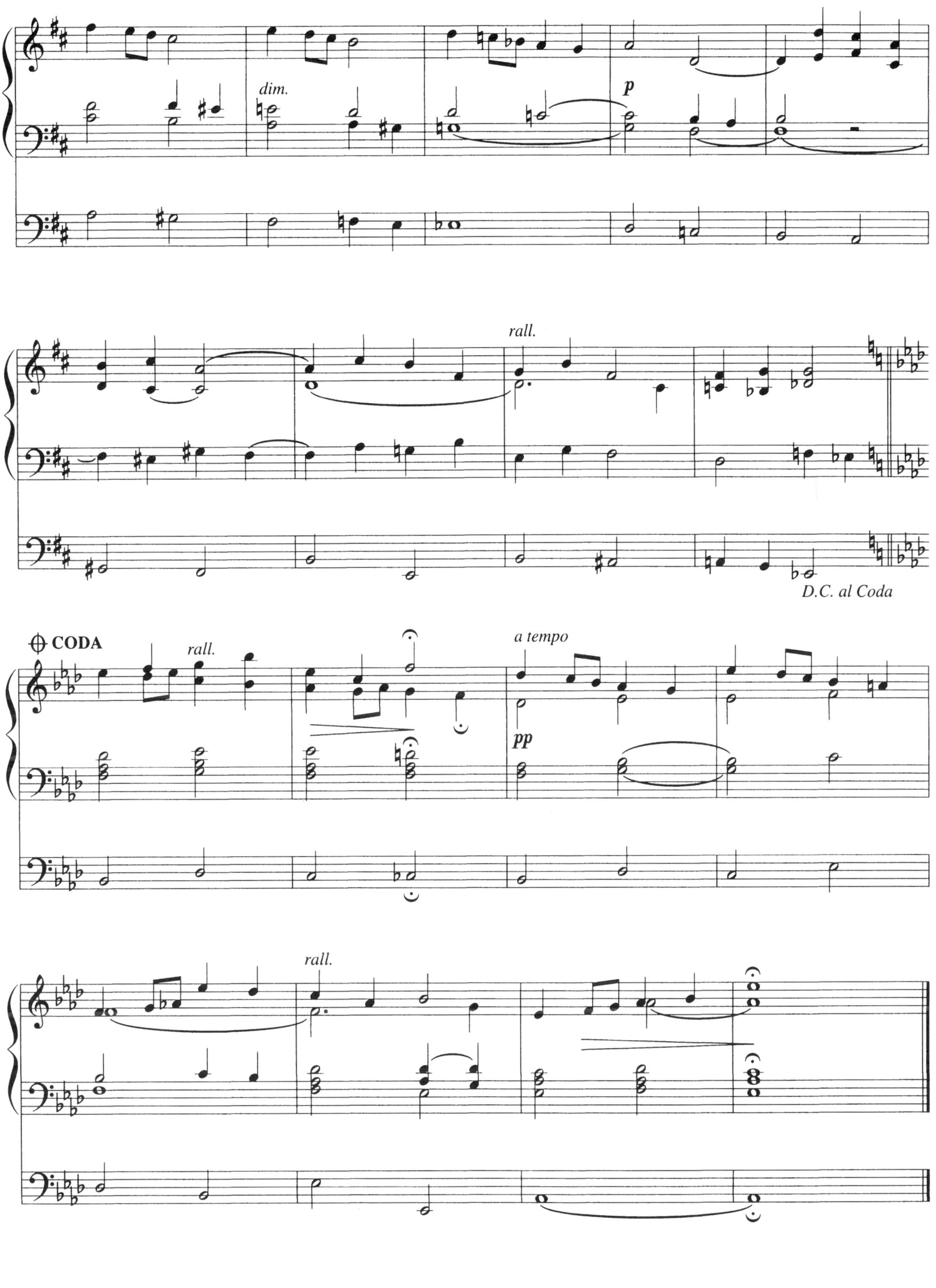
dim.
p
rall.
D.C. al Coda
CODA
rall.
a tempo
pp
rall.

FESTIVE RECESSIONAL

Owain Edwards

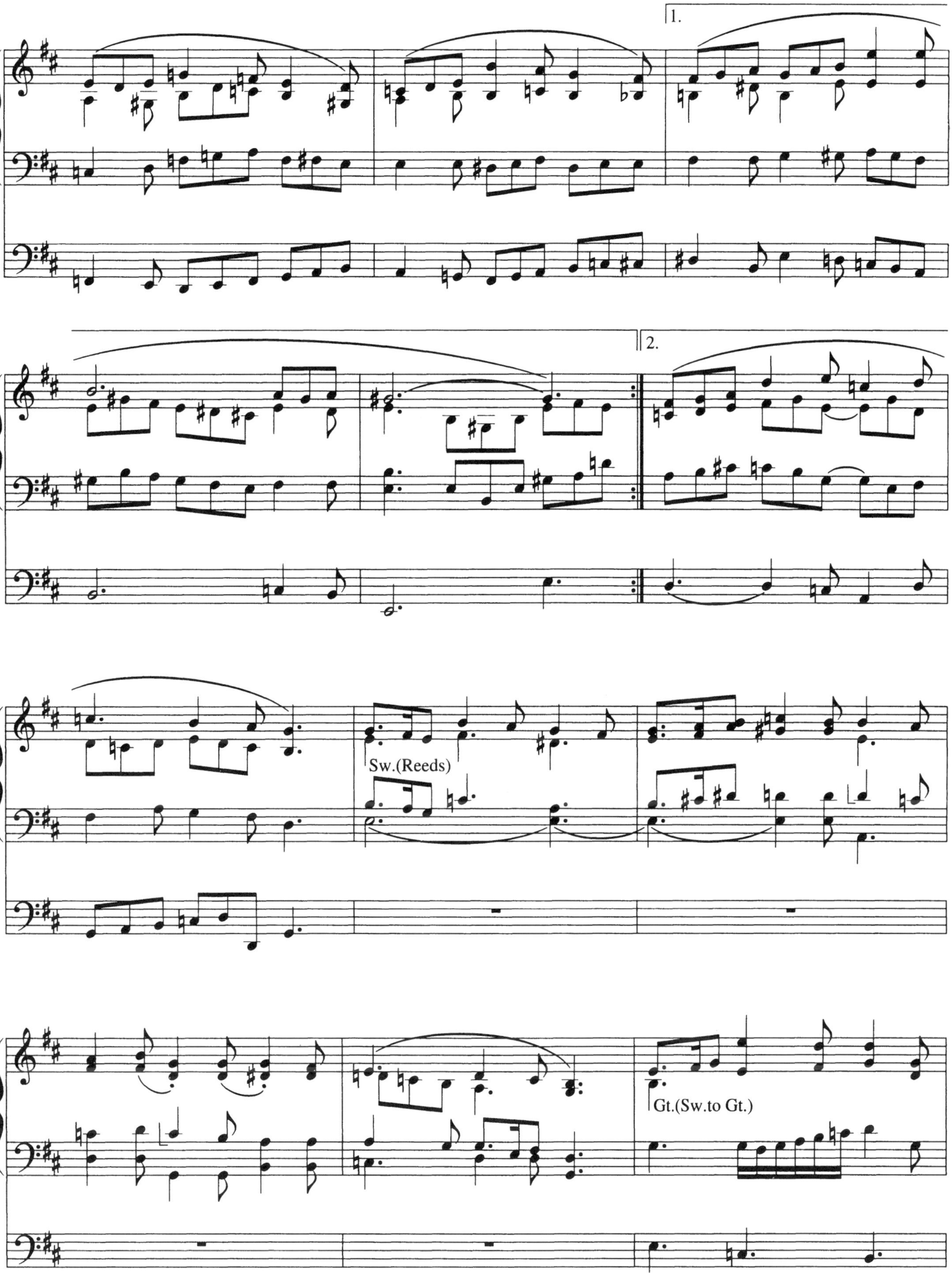
1.
2.
Sw.(Reeds)
Gt.(Sw.to Gt.)

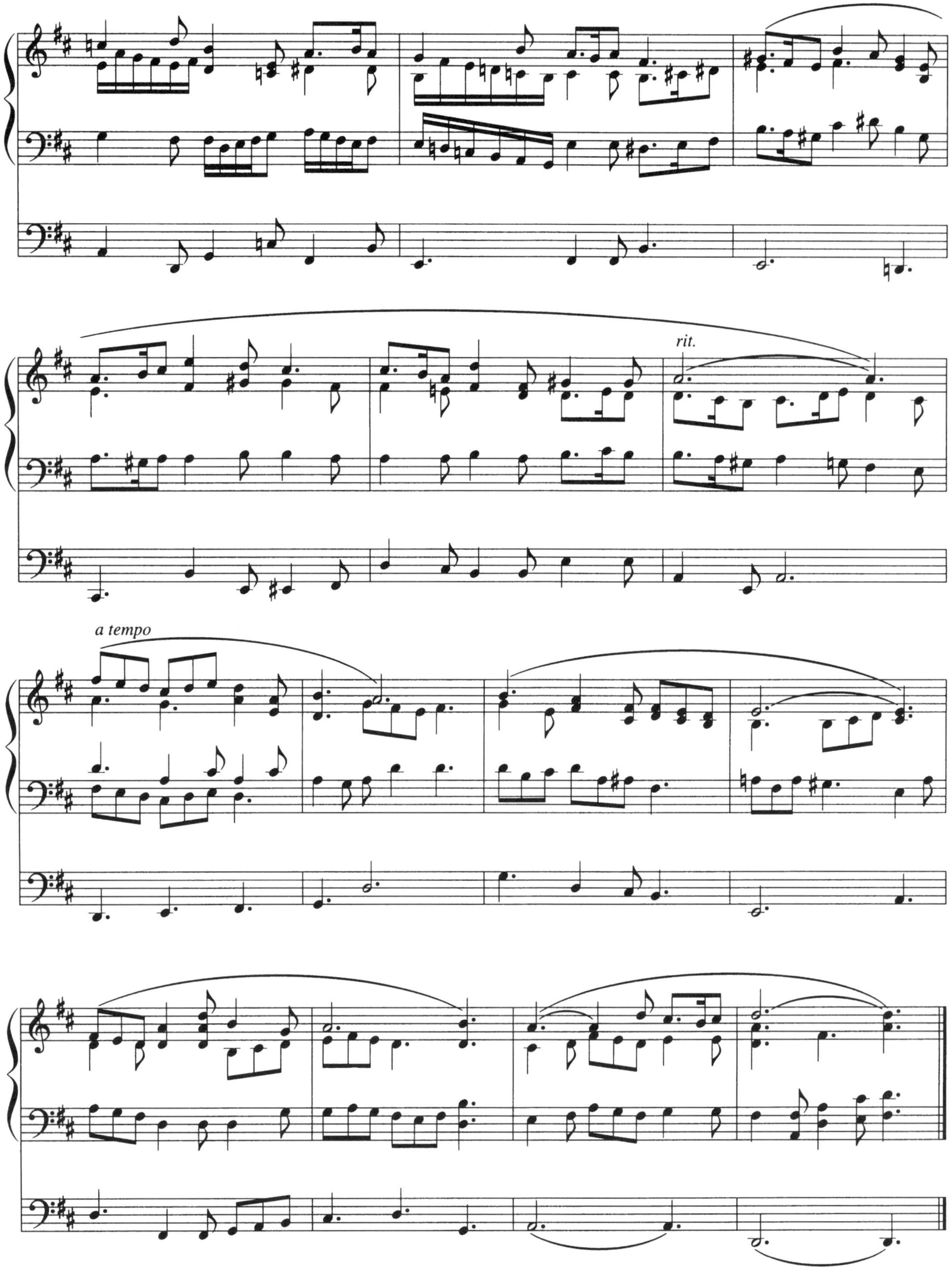
rit.
a tempo

ADVENT

Richard Knight

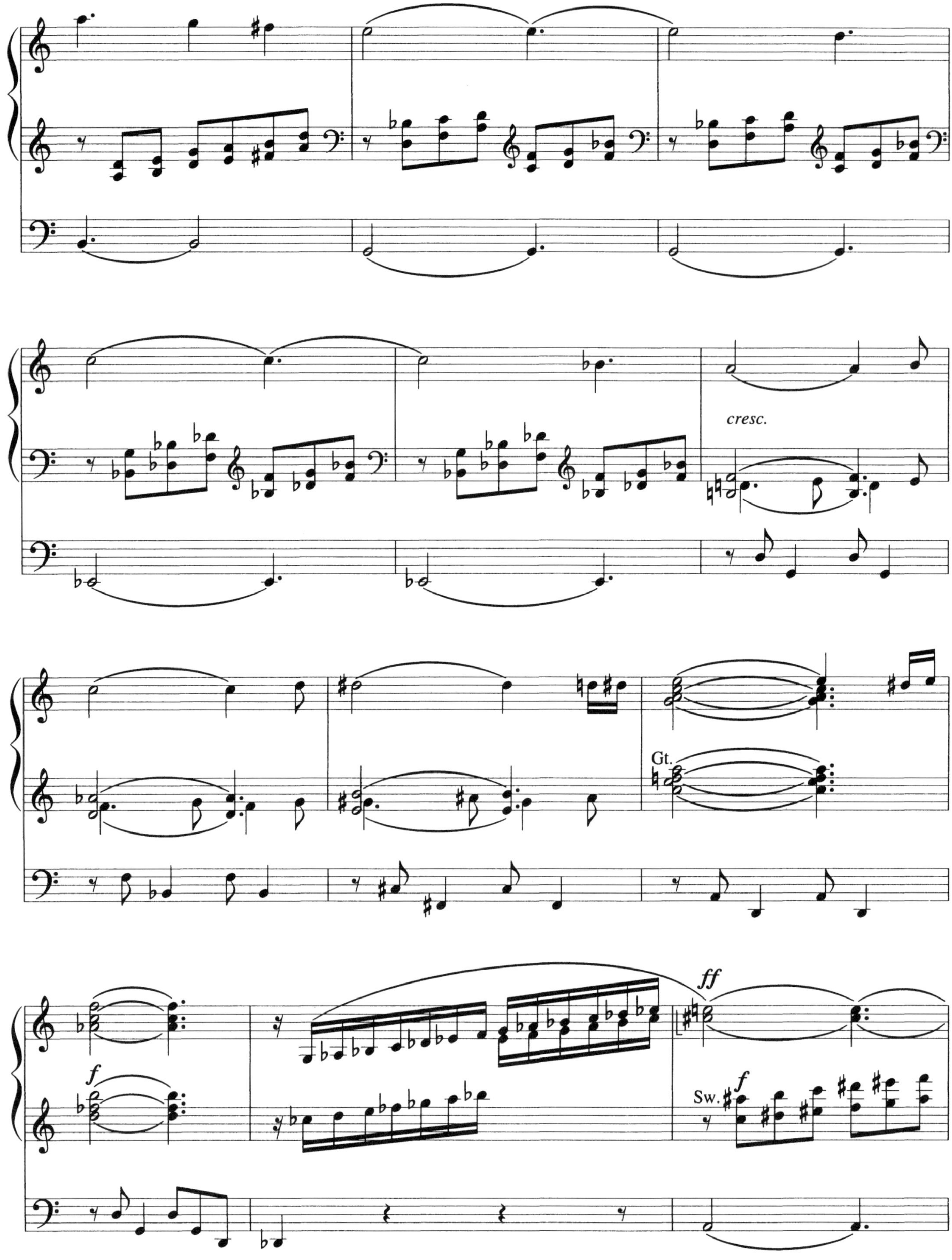
cresc.
Gt.
f
ff
Sw.
f

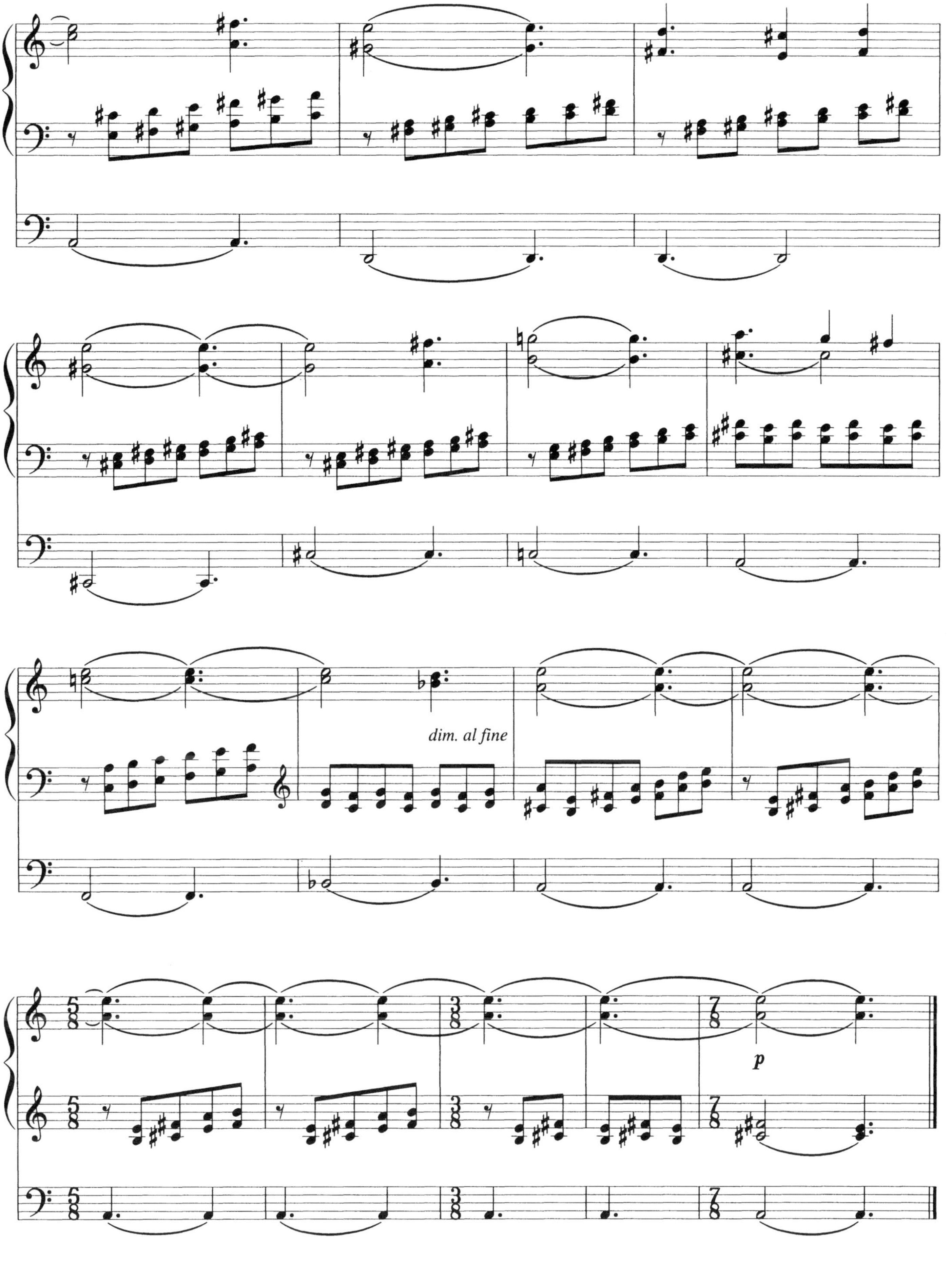
dim. al fine
p

INTRADA

Alan Viner

Reduce
ff
a tempo
rall.
dim.
mp
Sw.p
– Gt. to Ped.
rit.
(Reduce)
pp
dim.
niente
pp

CIACCONA

Robert Fielding

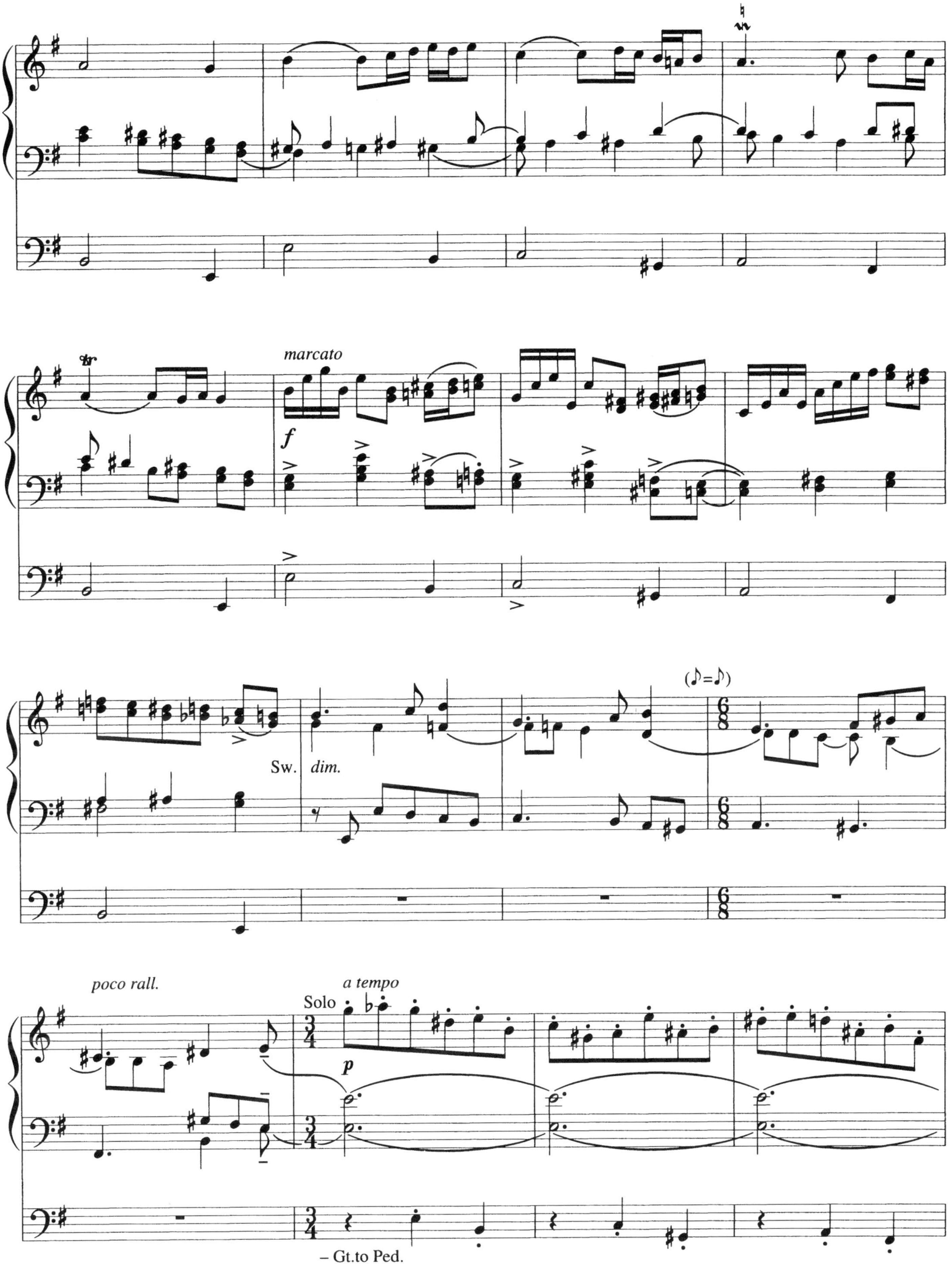
marcato
f
Sw.
dim.
poco rall.
Solo
a tempo
p
– Gt.to Ped.

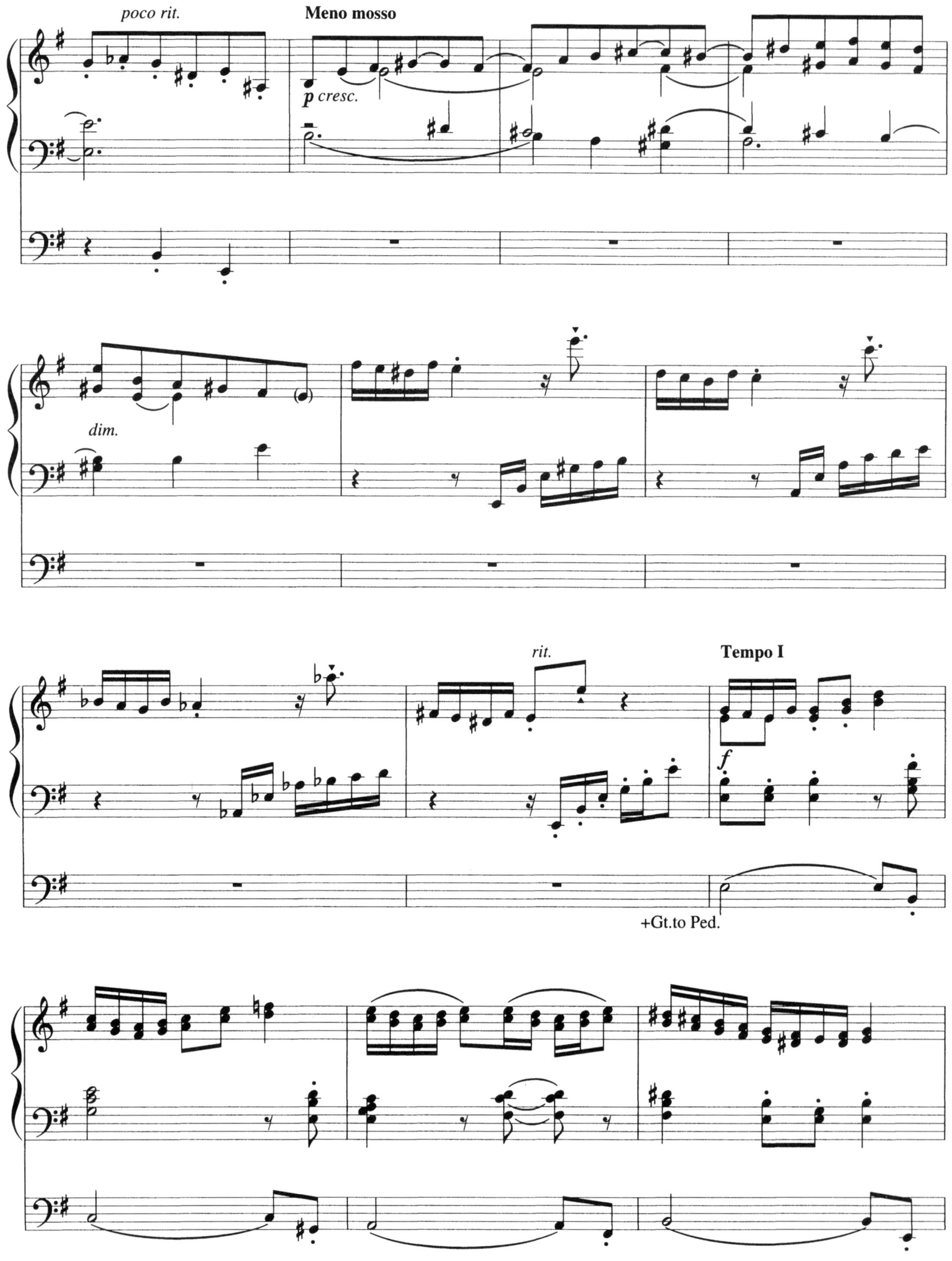
poco rit.
Meno mosso
p cresc.
dim.
rit.
Tempo I
f
+Gt.to Ped.

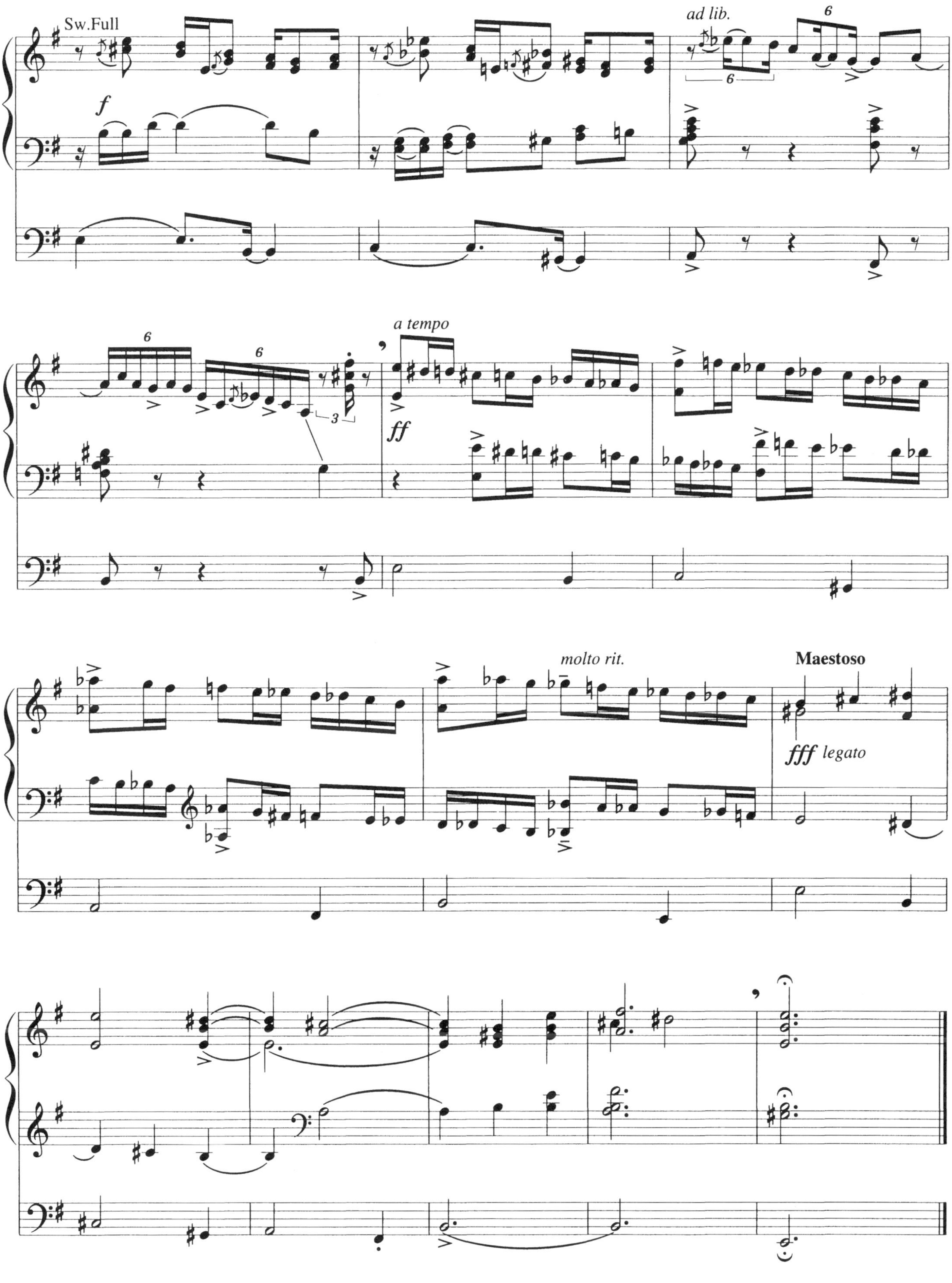
Sw.Full
f
ad lib.
a tempo
ff
molto rit.
Maestoso
fff legato

for Mavis Murphy
RED-HOT CHOIR
Quentin Thomas

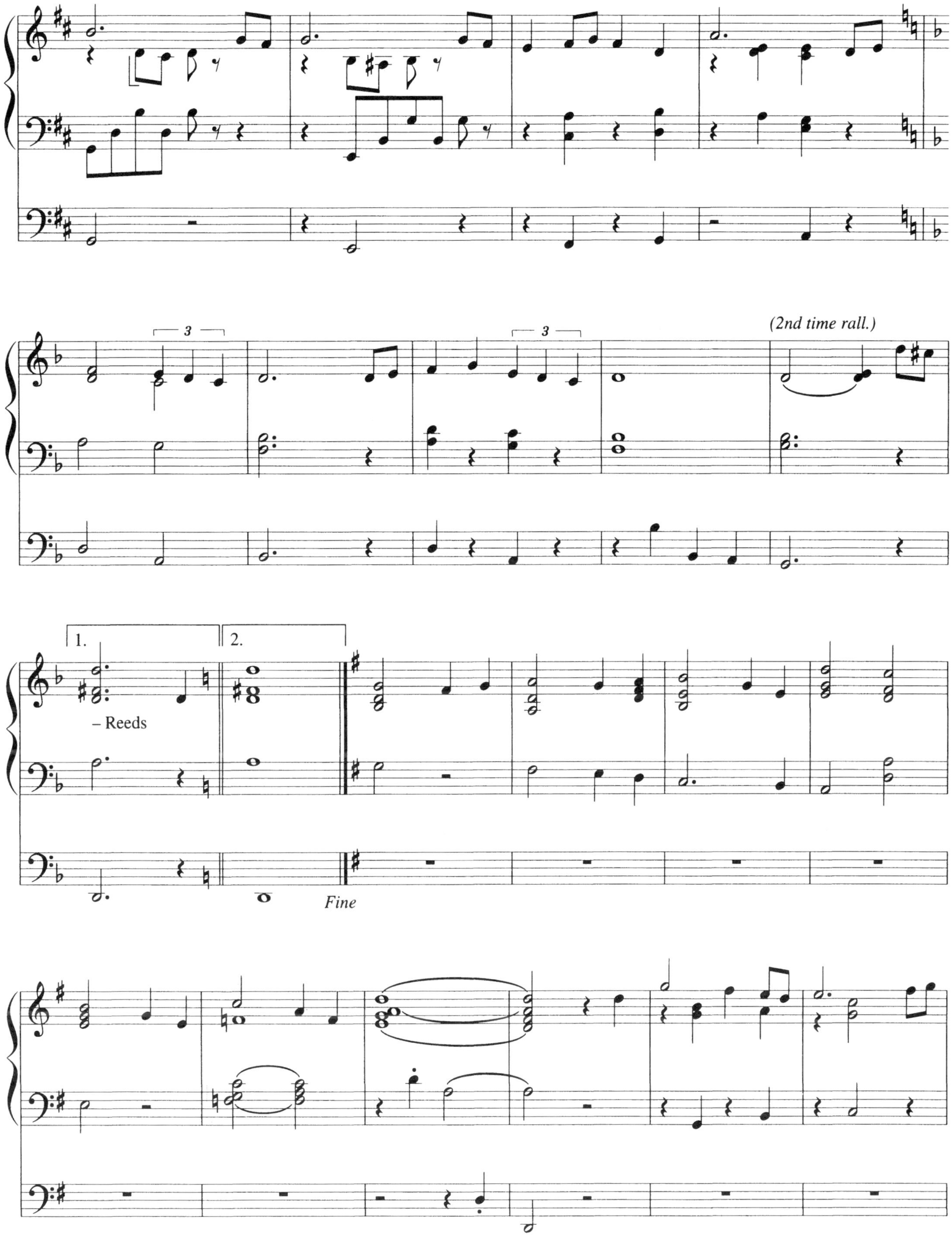
(2nd time rall.)
1.
2.
– Reeds
Fine

D.S. al Fine

TOCCATA

Stanley Vann

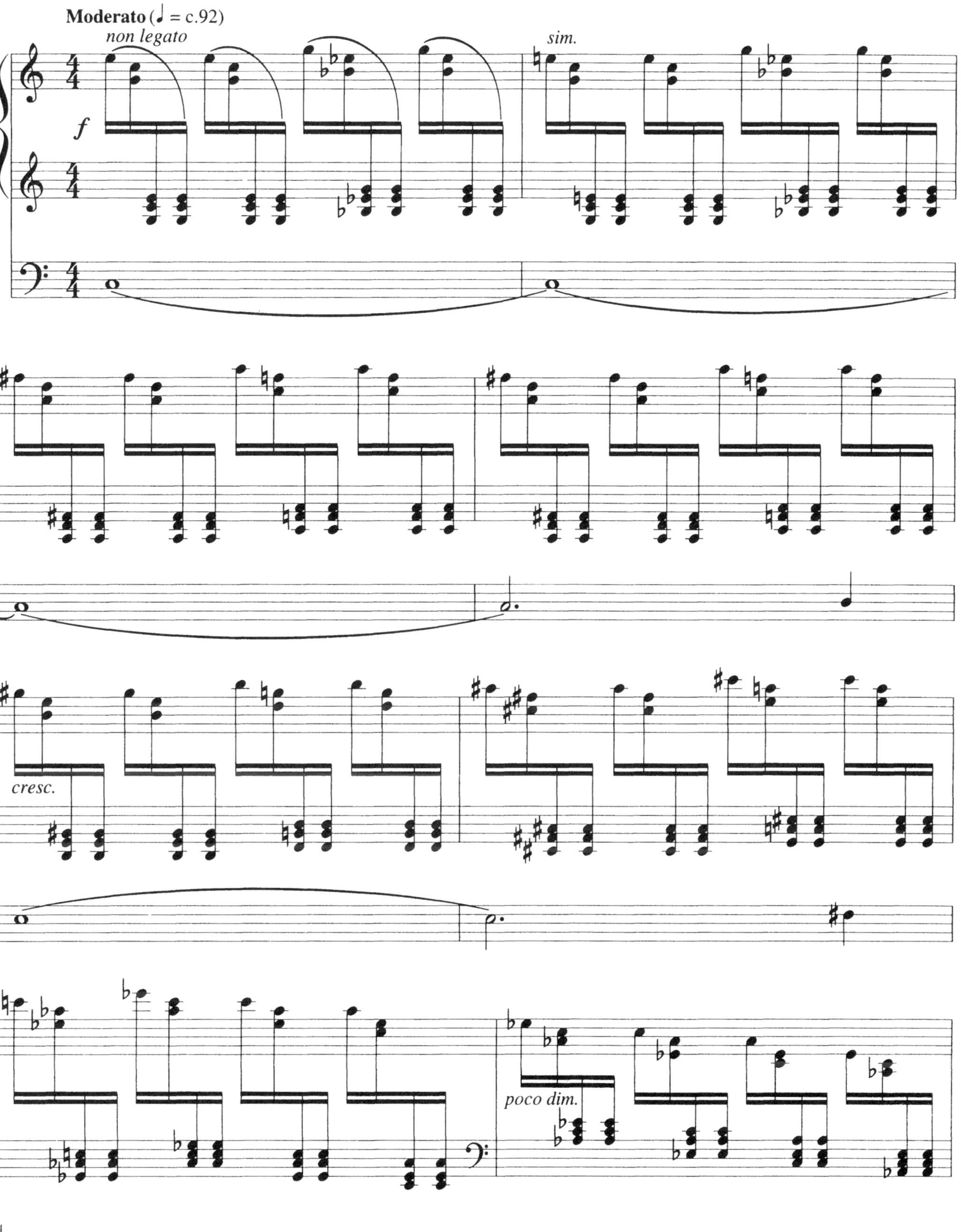

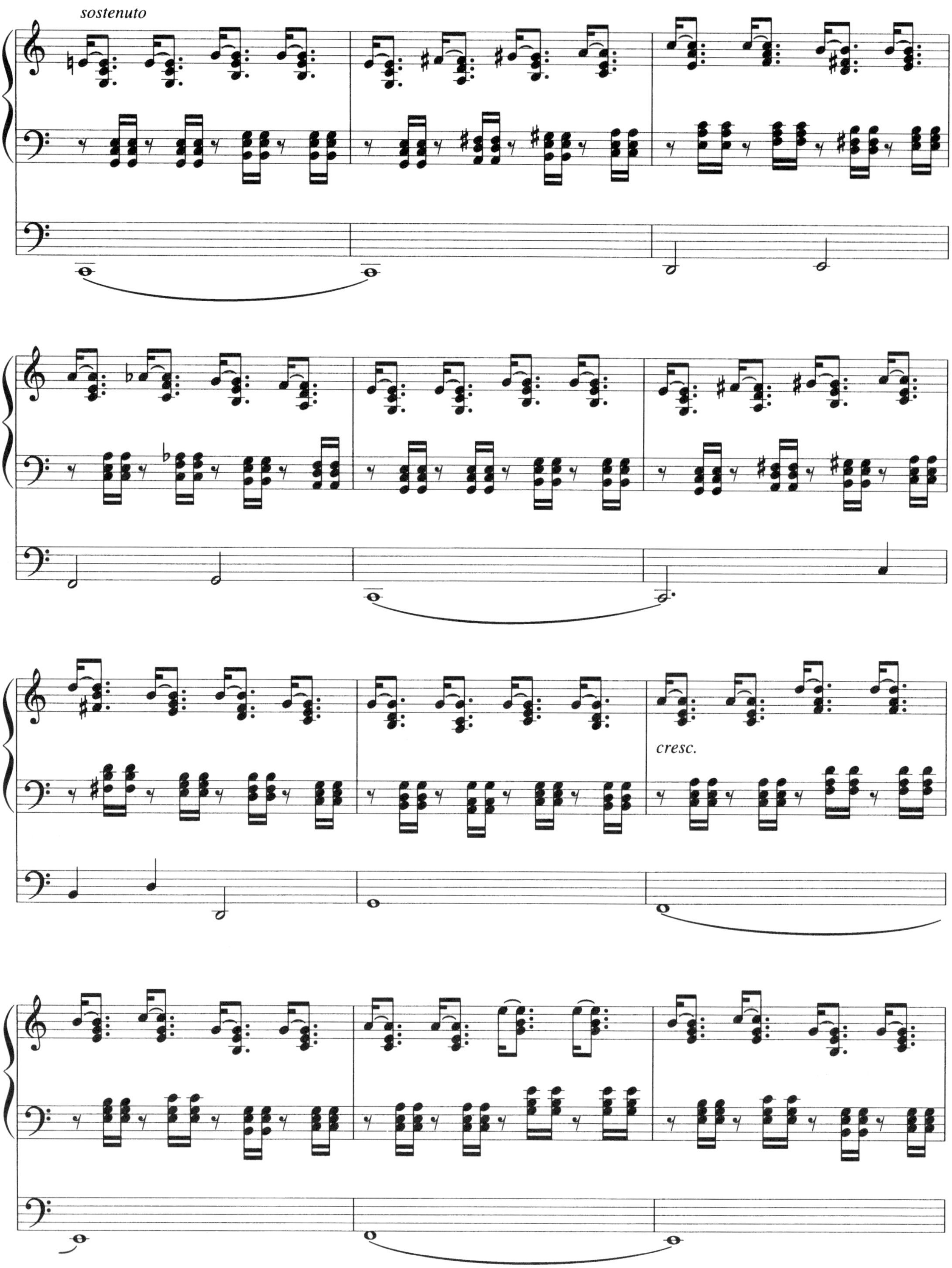
sostenuto
cresc.

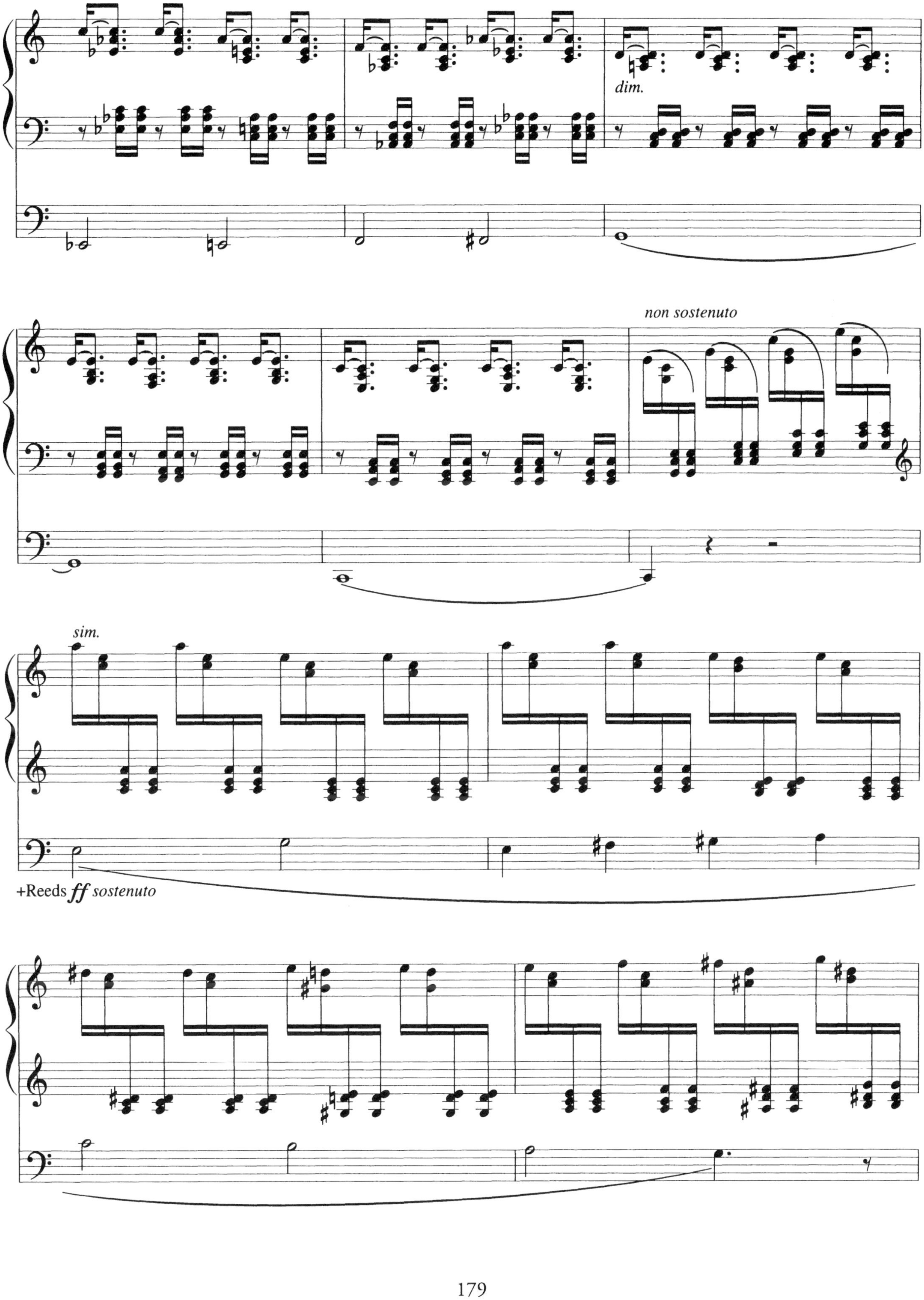
dim.
non sostenuto
sim.
+Reeds ff sostenuto

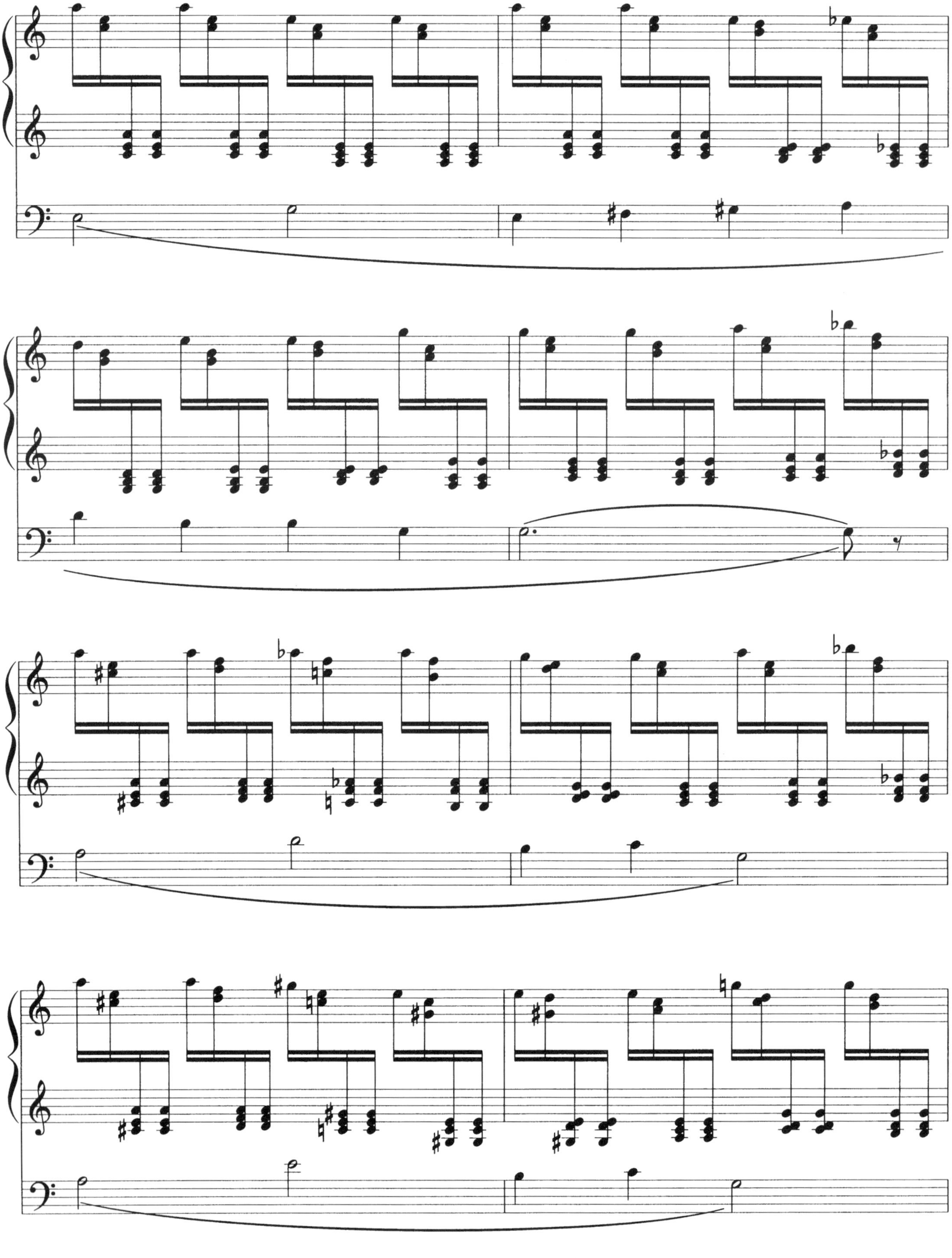

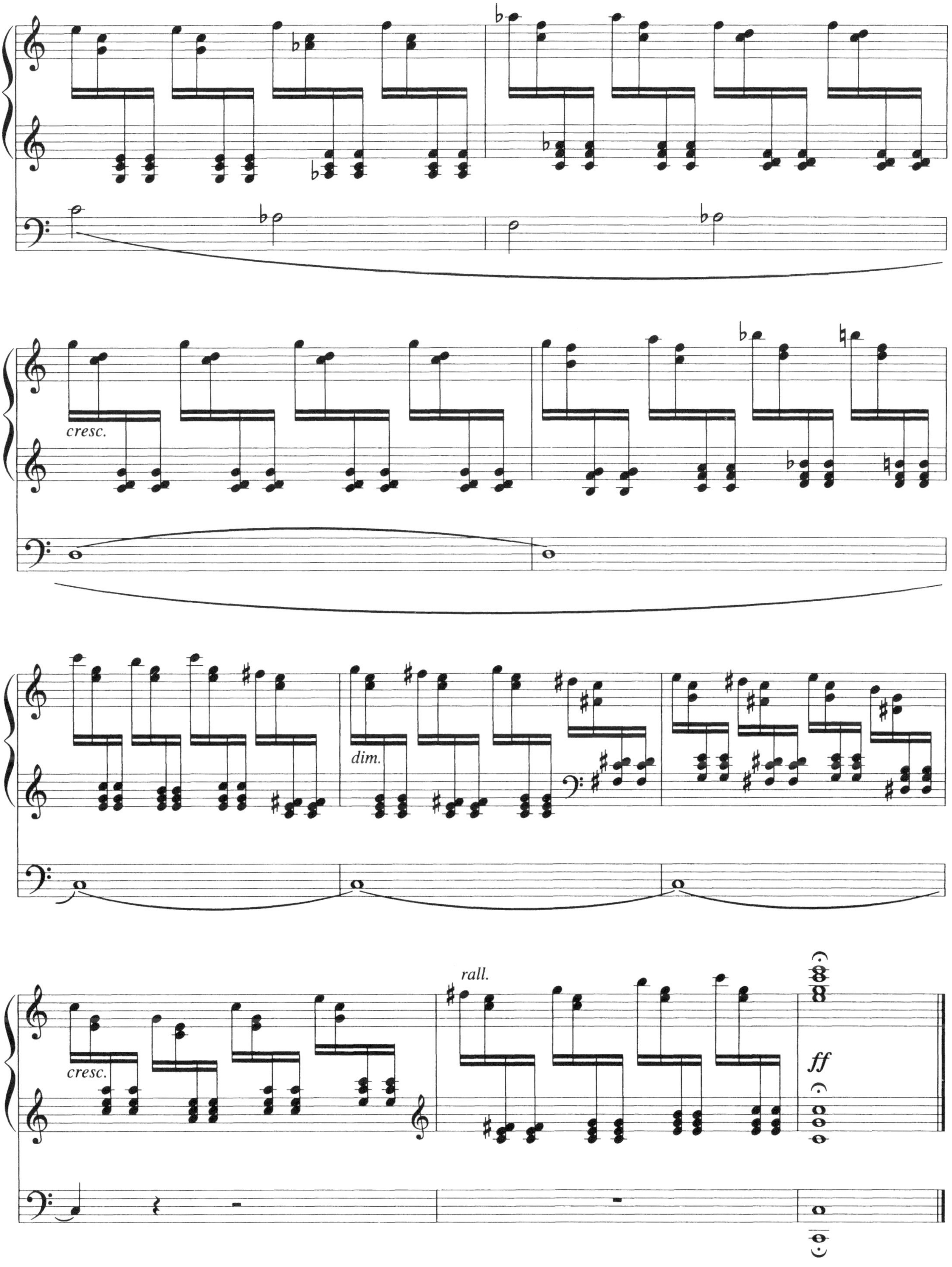
cresc.
dim.
cresc.
rall.
ff

PRELUDE

Norman Warren

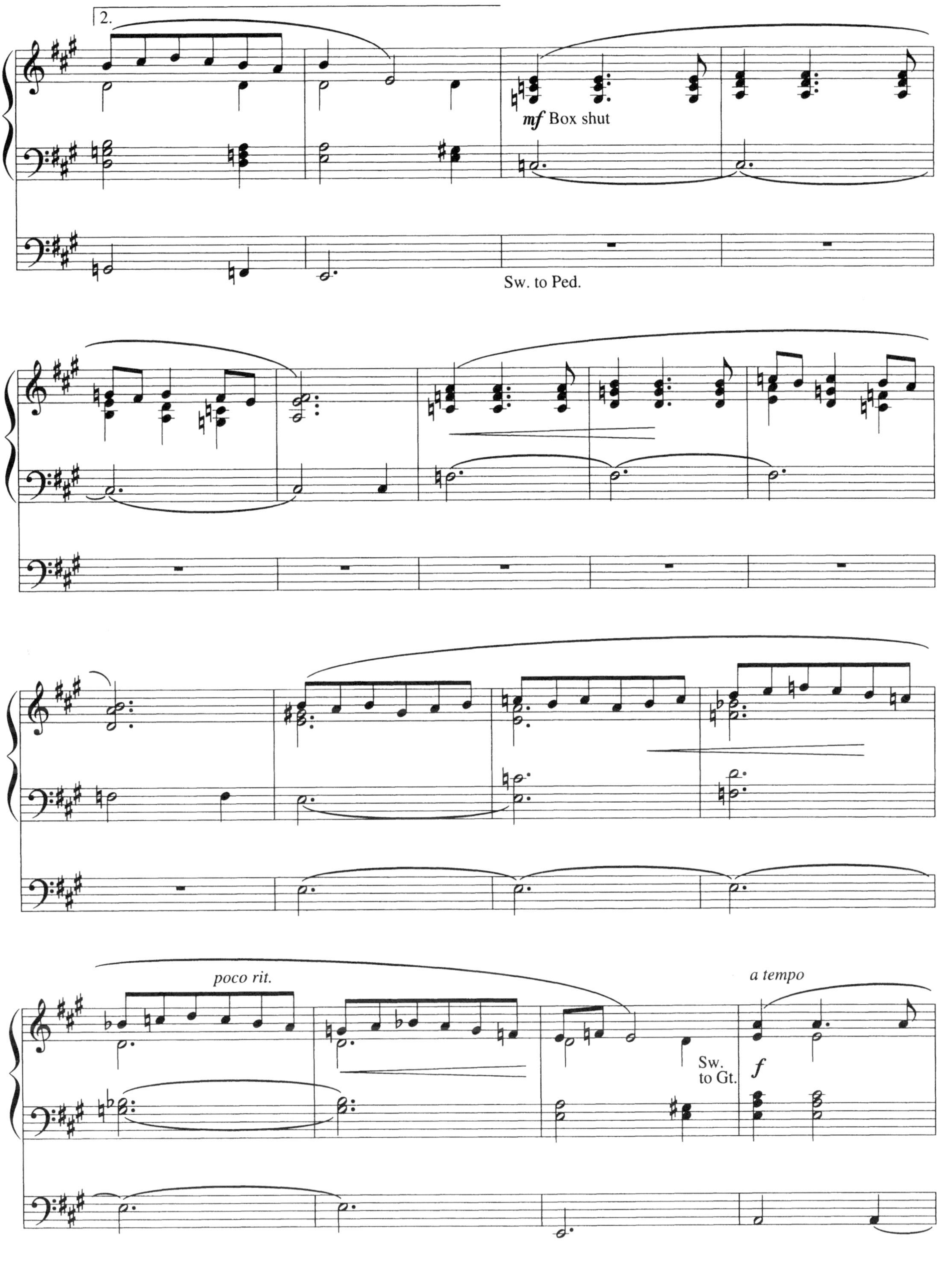
2.
mf Box shut
Sw. to Ped.
poco rit.
a tempo
Sw.
to Gt.
f

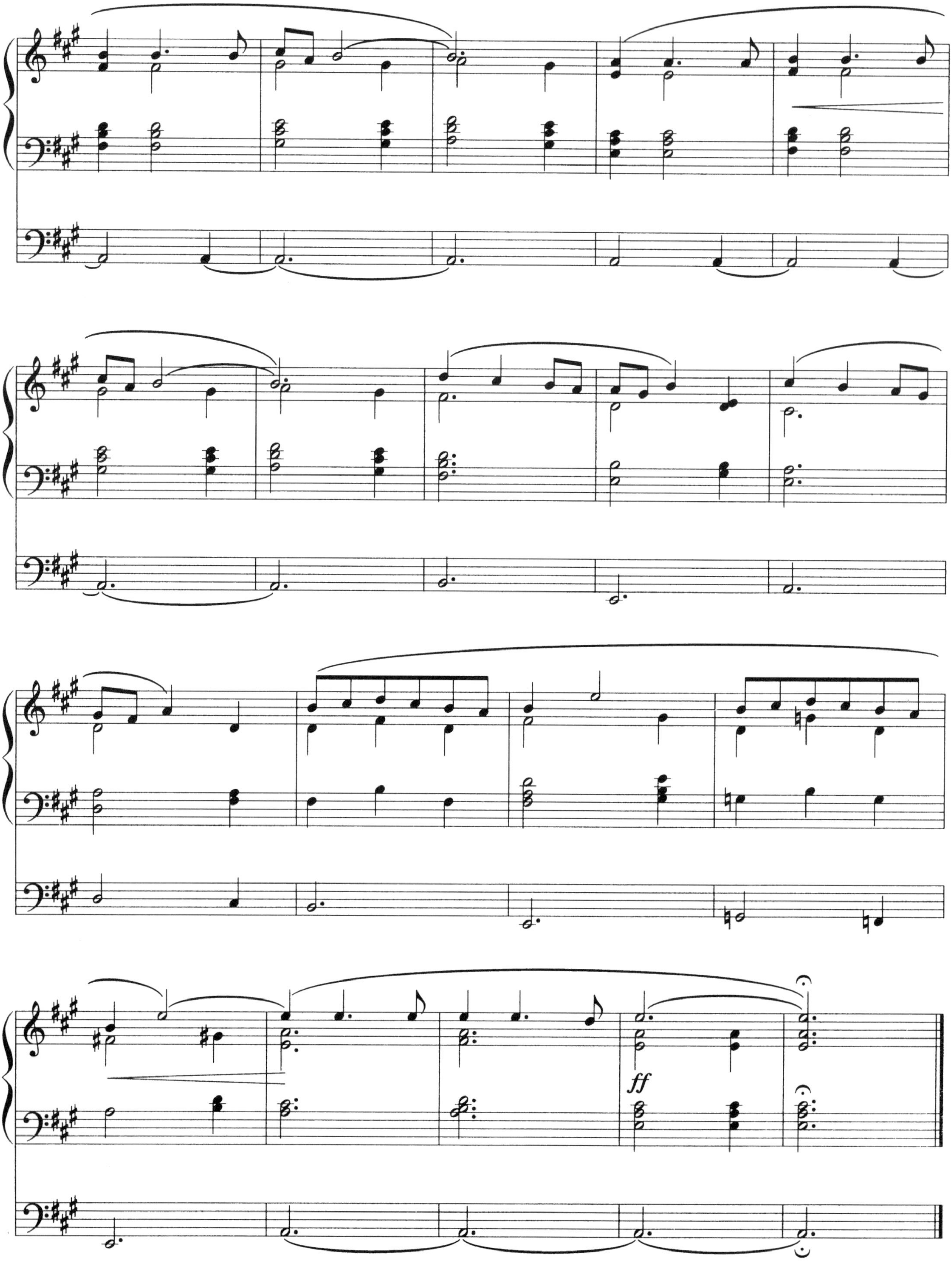
ff

REFLECTIVE PROCESSIONAL

Colin Mawby

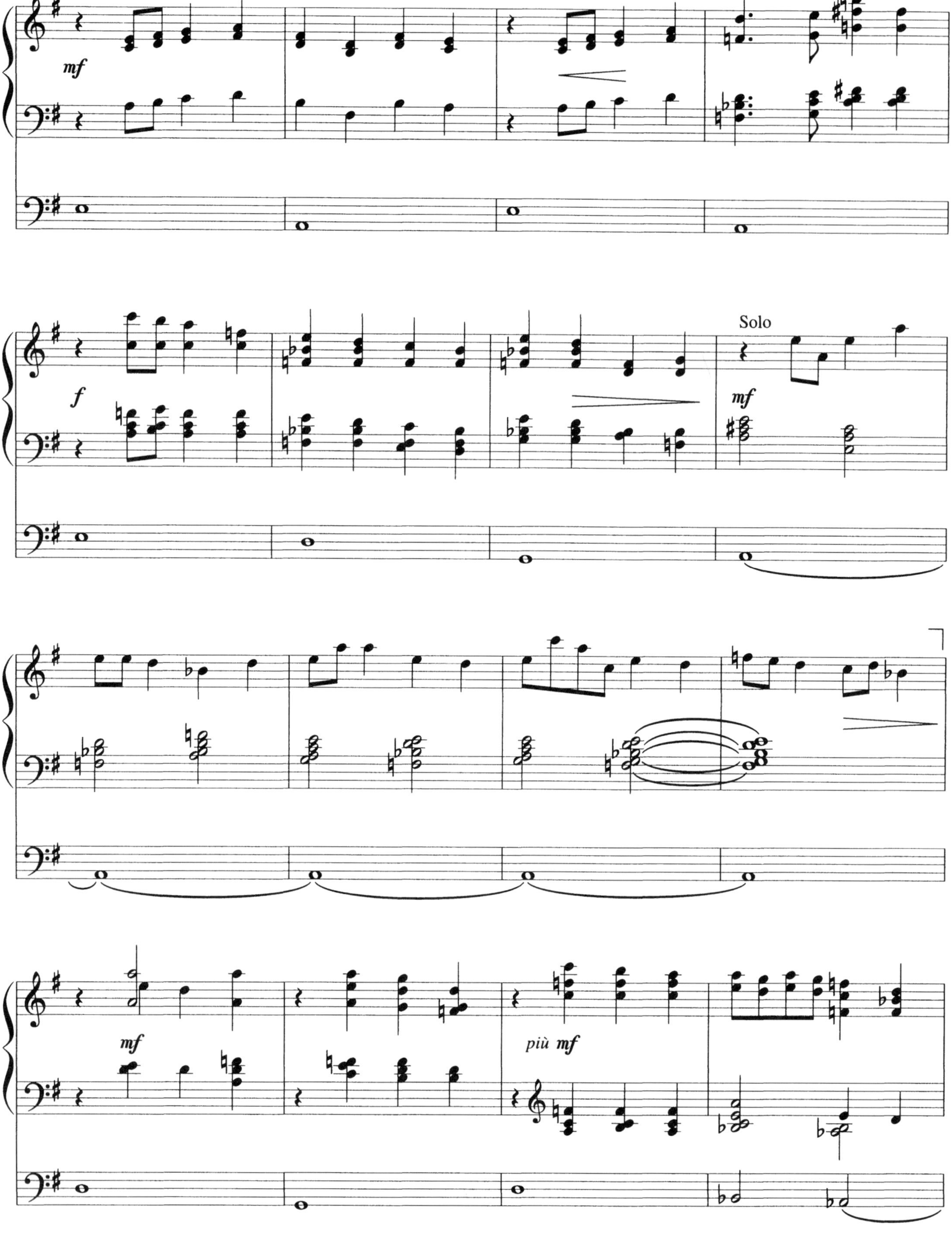
mf
f
Solo
mf
mf
più mf

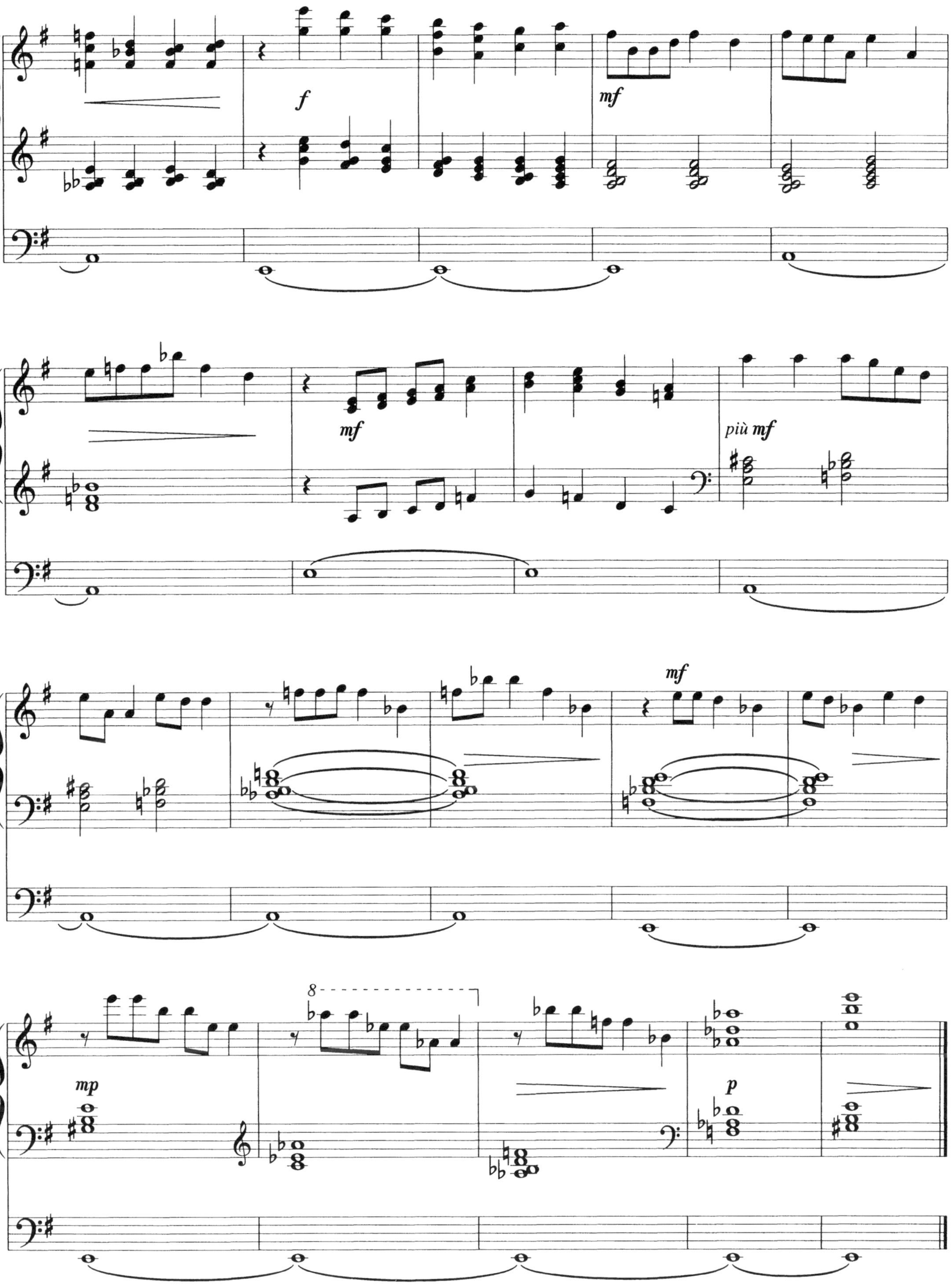
f
mf
mf
più mf
mf
mp
8
p

for Julia and Paul

SORTIE

Richard Lloyd

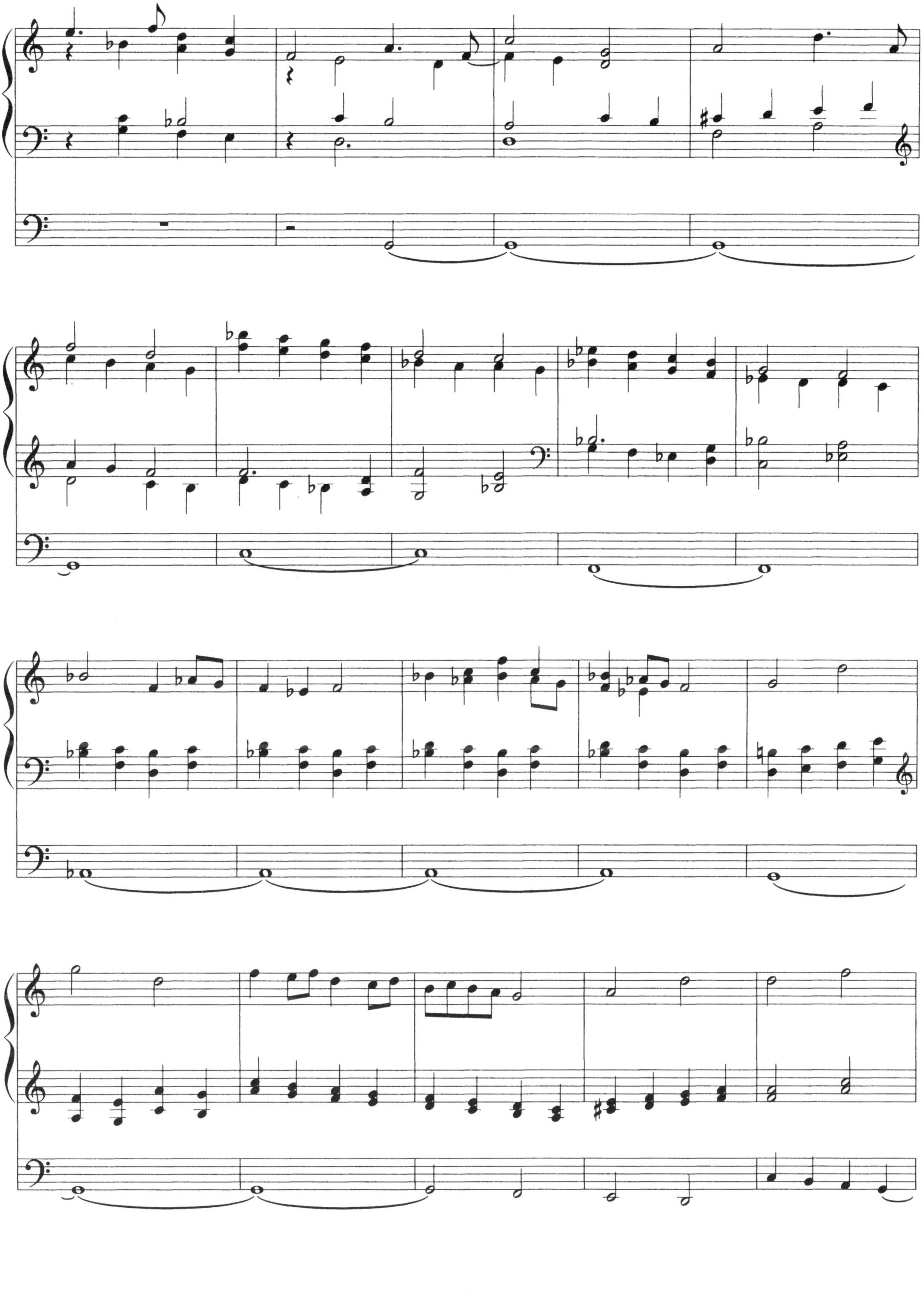

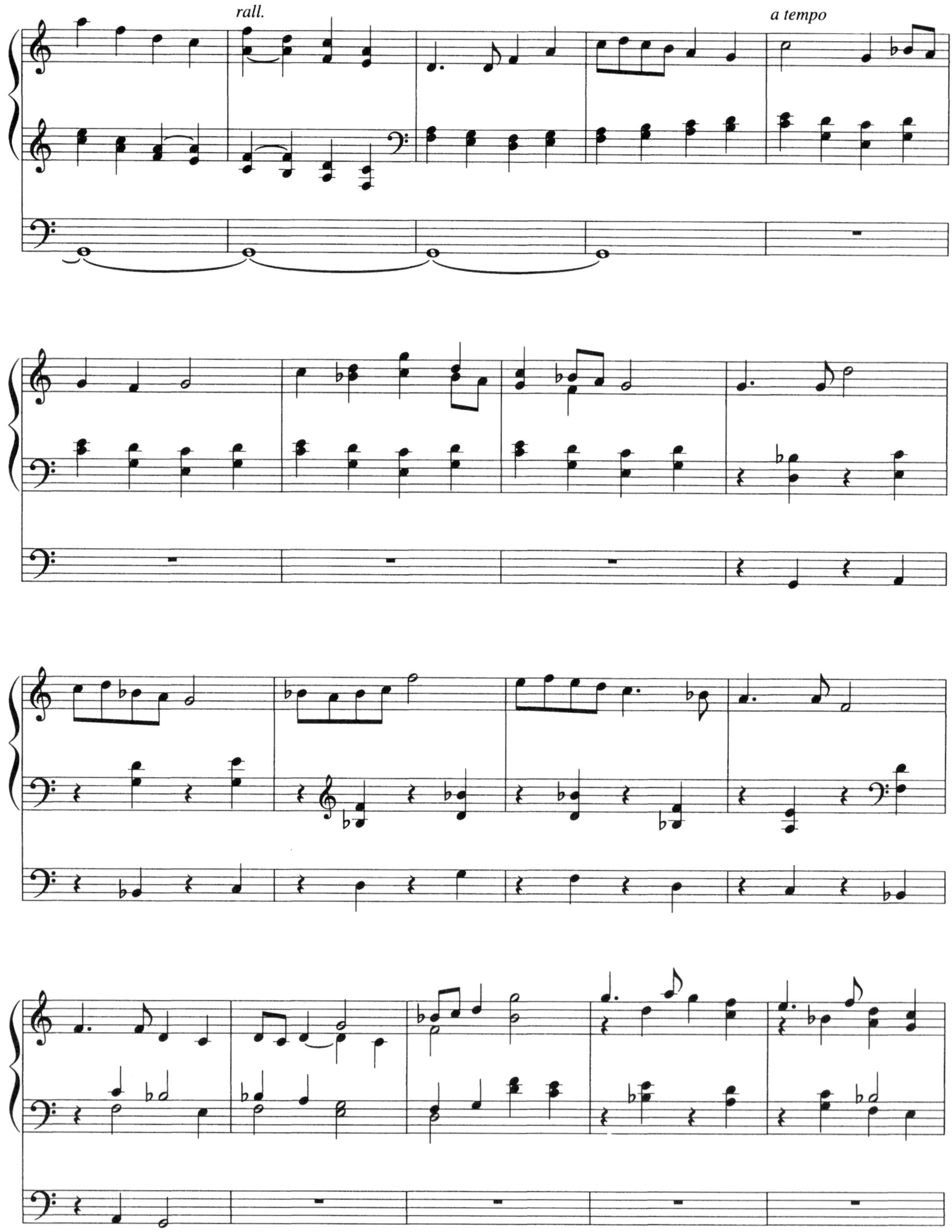
rall.
a tempo

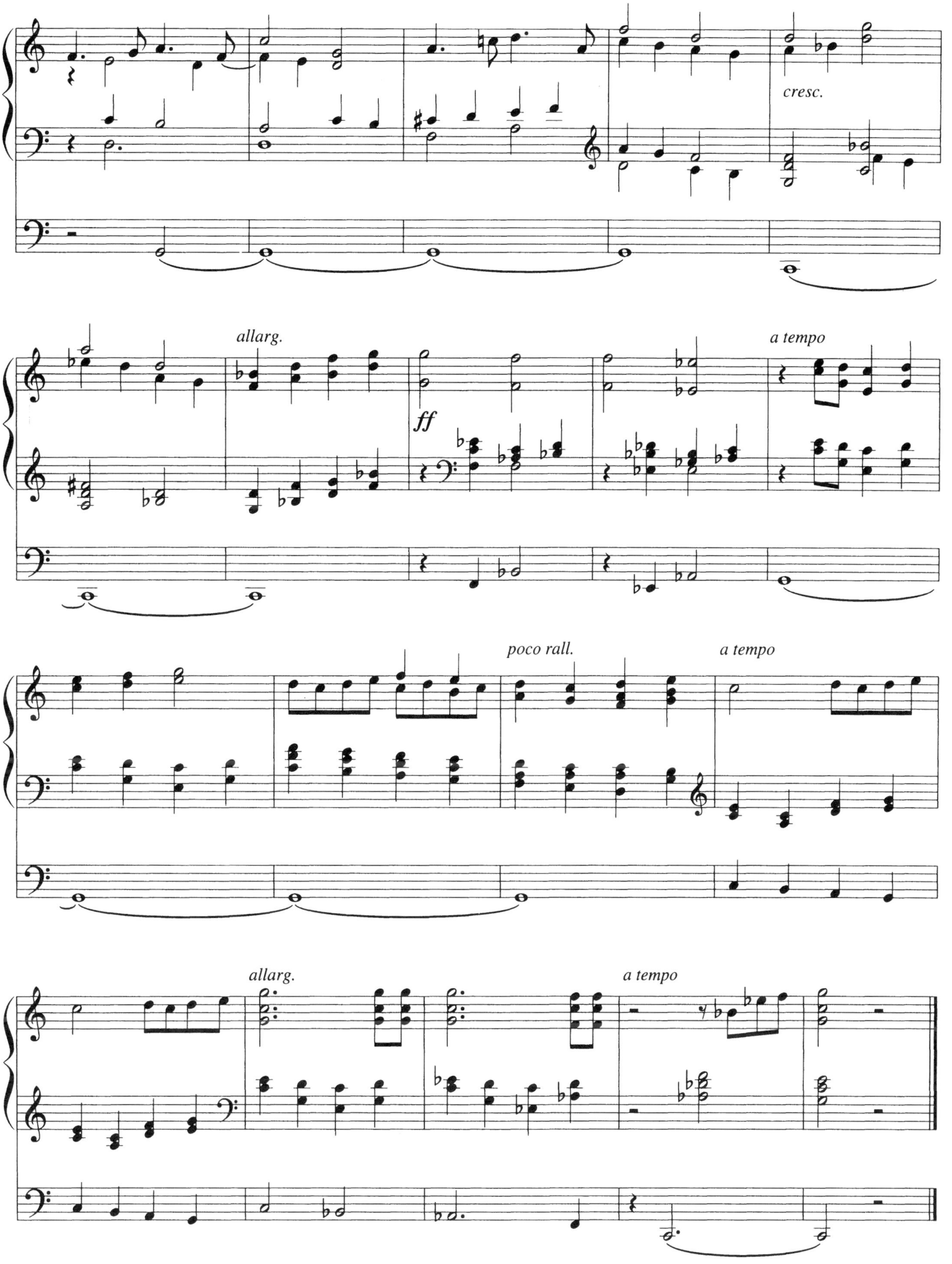
cresc.
allarg.
ff
a tempo
poco rall.
a tempo
allarg.
a tempo

FESTIVAL PROCESSIONAL

Andrew Gant

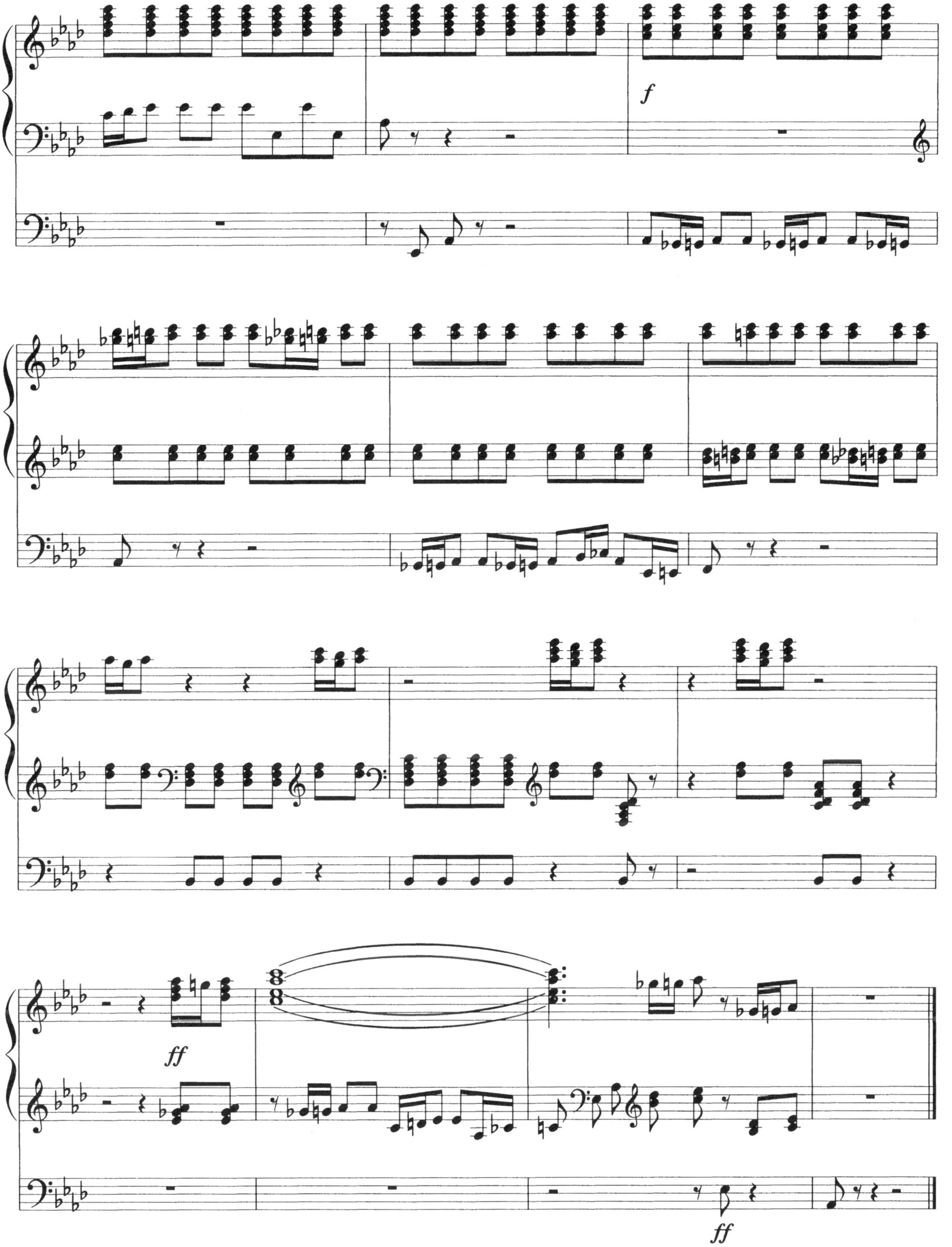
f
ff
ff

FLOURISH

Rosalie Bonighton

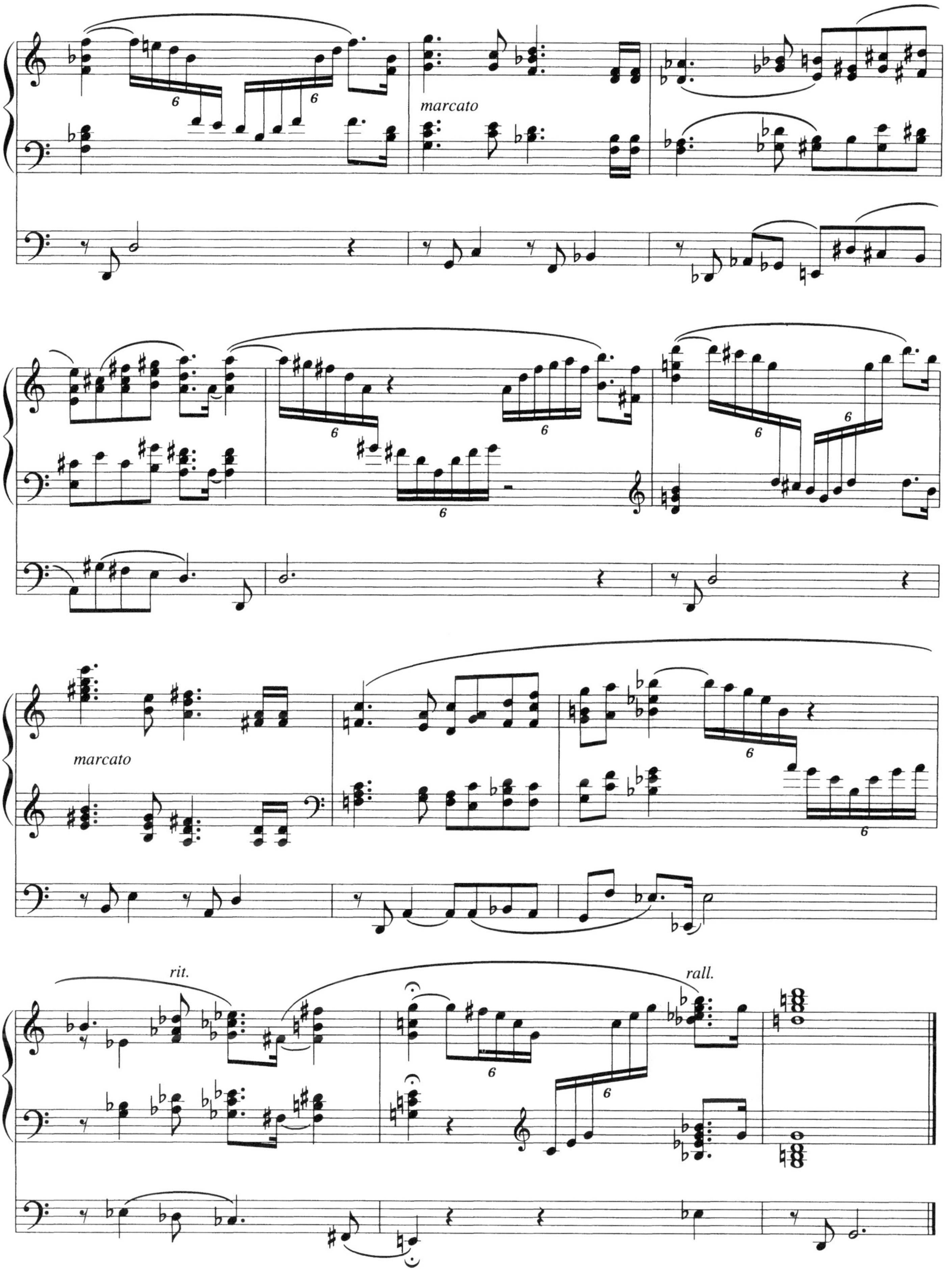
marcato
marcato
rit.
rall.

for W Richard Hixson

FANFARE

Stephen Kemp

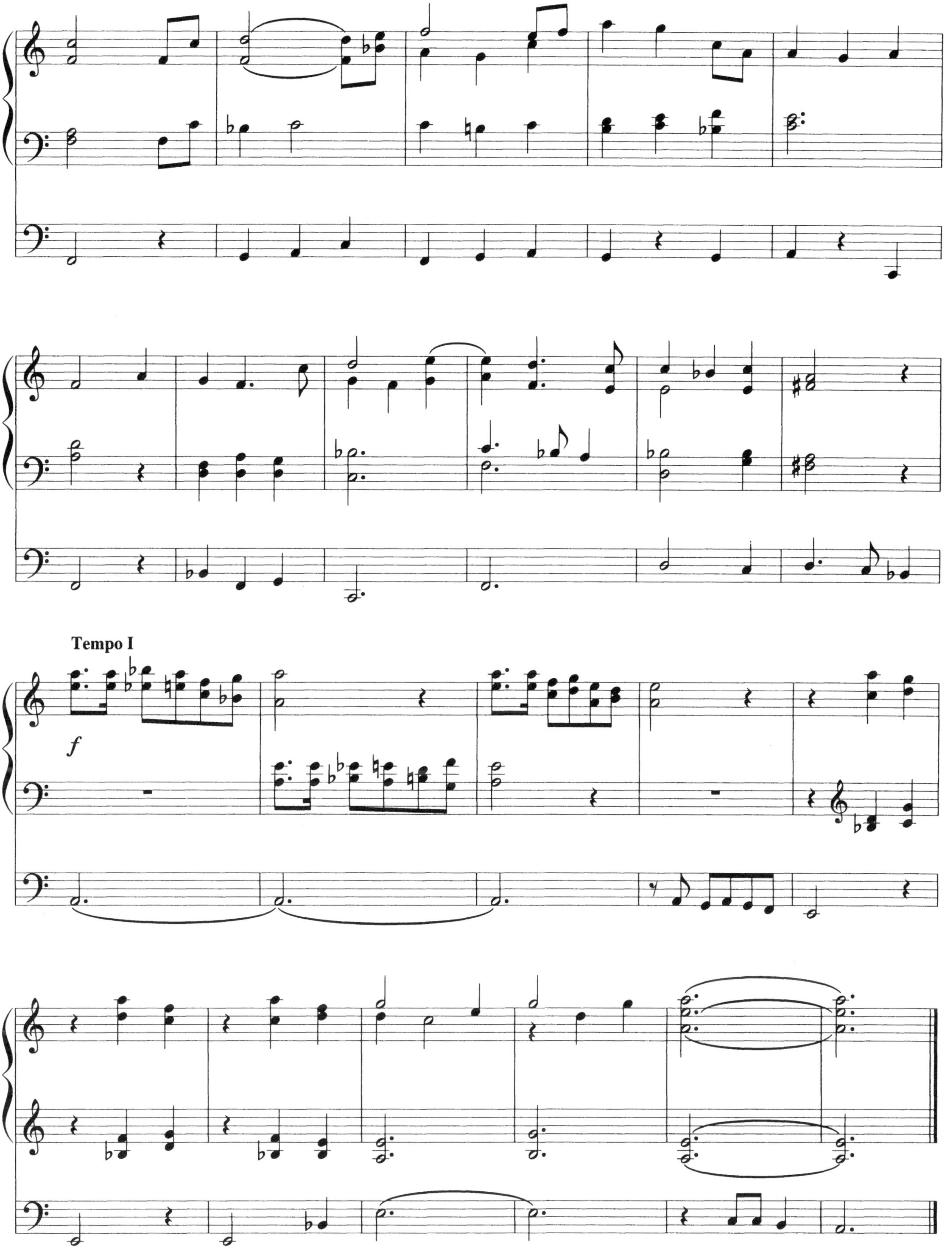
Tempo I
f

CHOIR'S WANDERING

Quentin Thomas

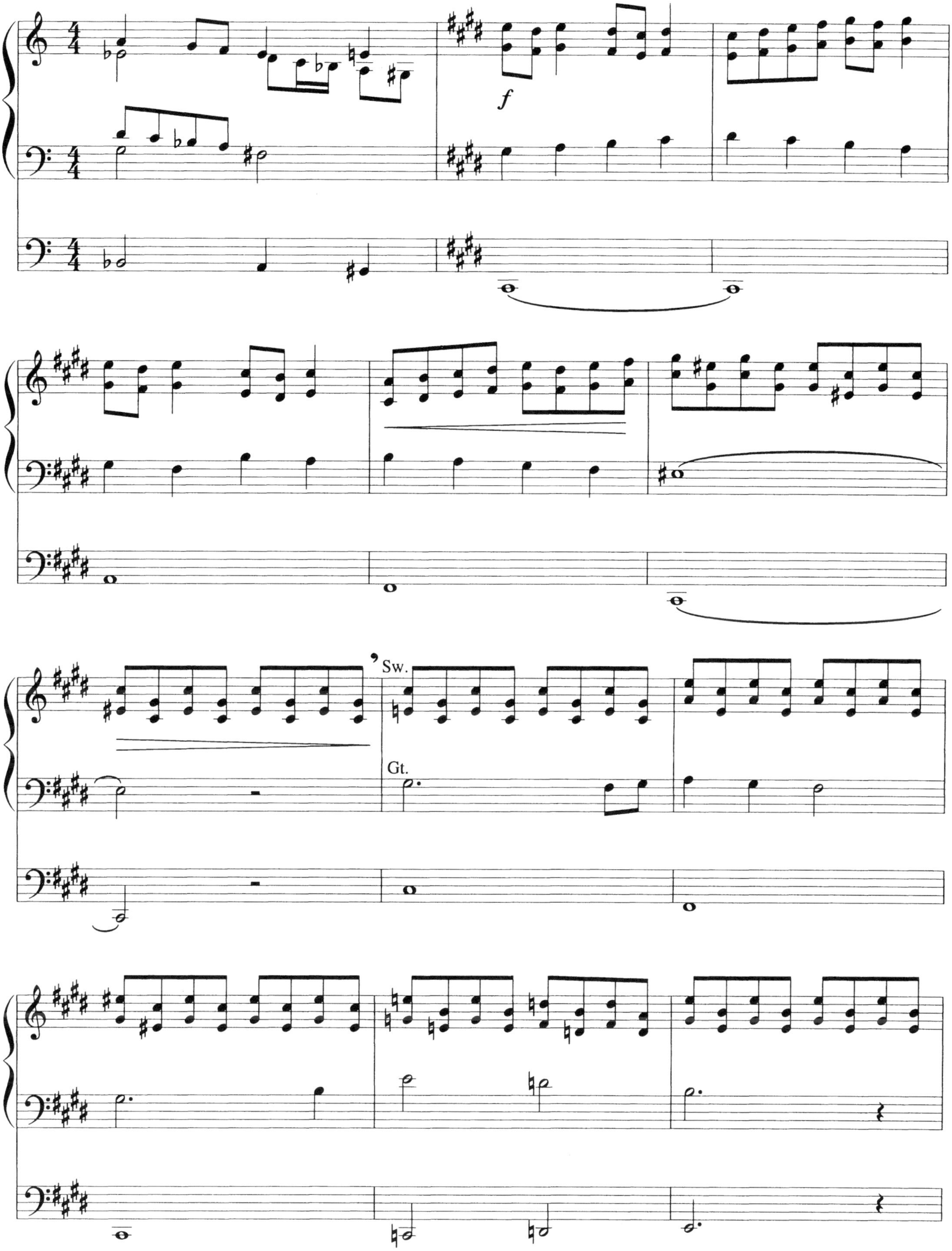
f
Sw.
Gt.

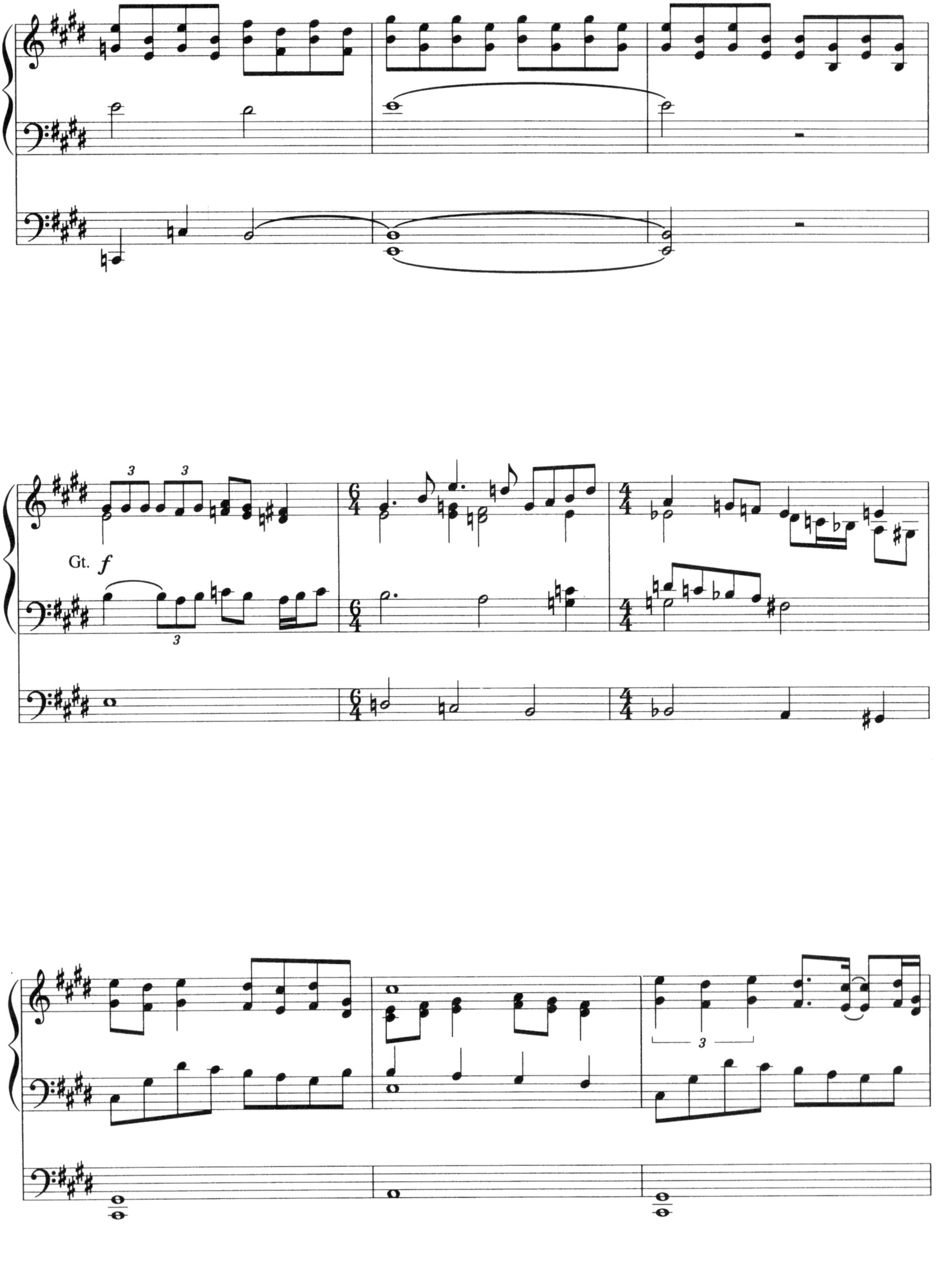
Gt. f

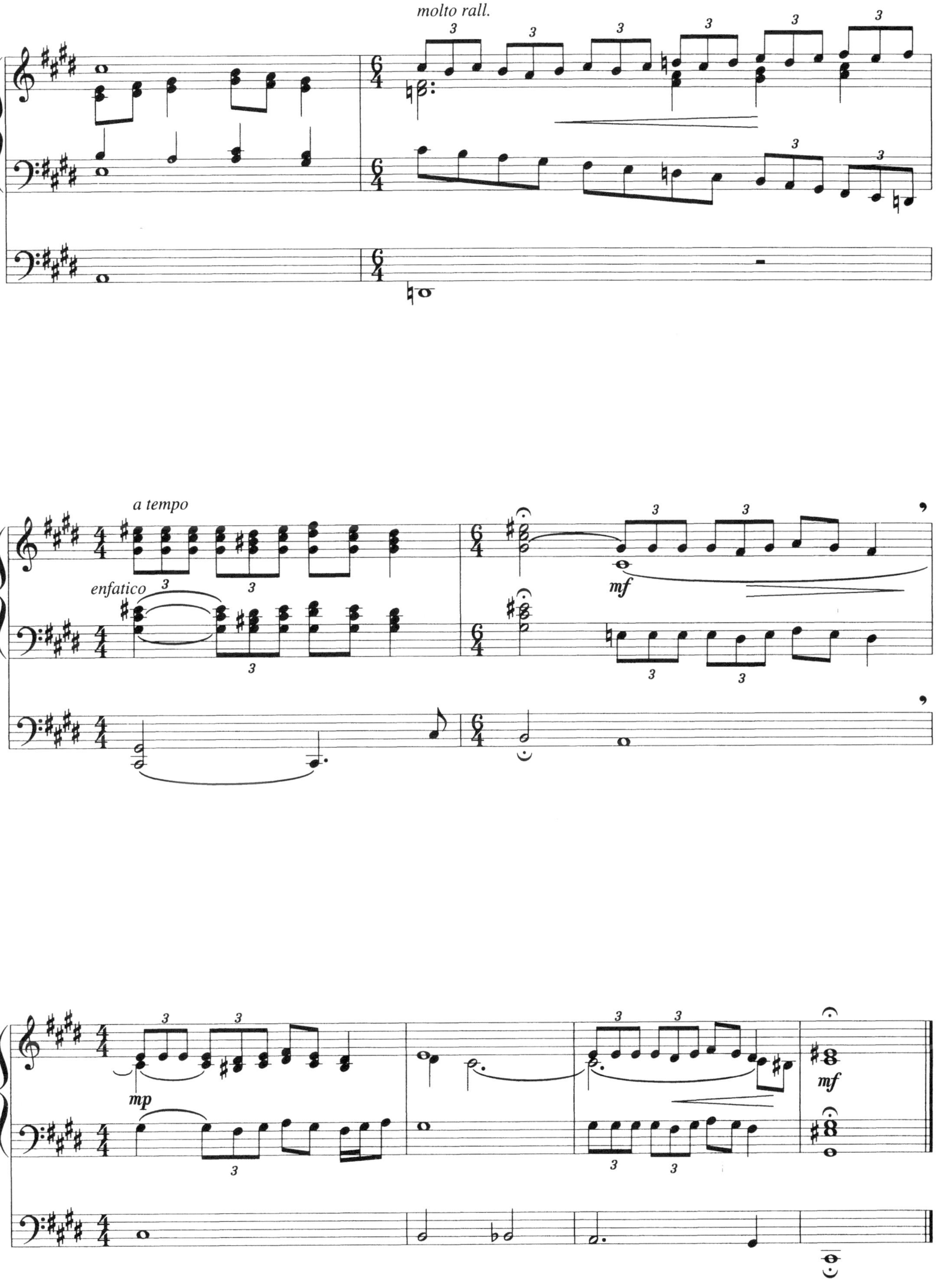
molto rall.
a tempo
enfatico
mf
mp
mf

REGALIA

Andrew Moore

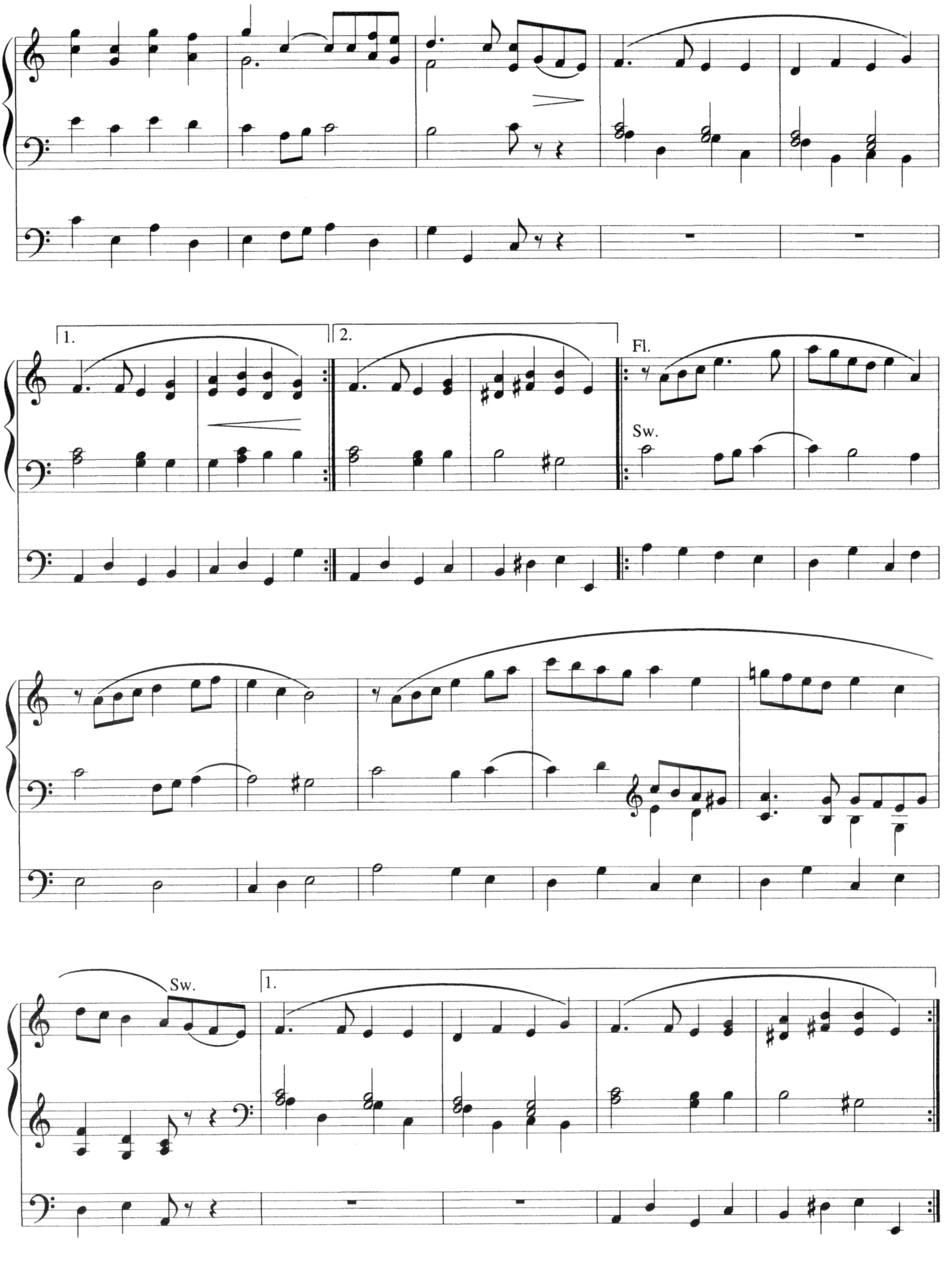
1.
2.
Fl.
Sw.
Sw.
1.

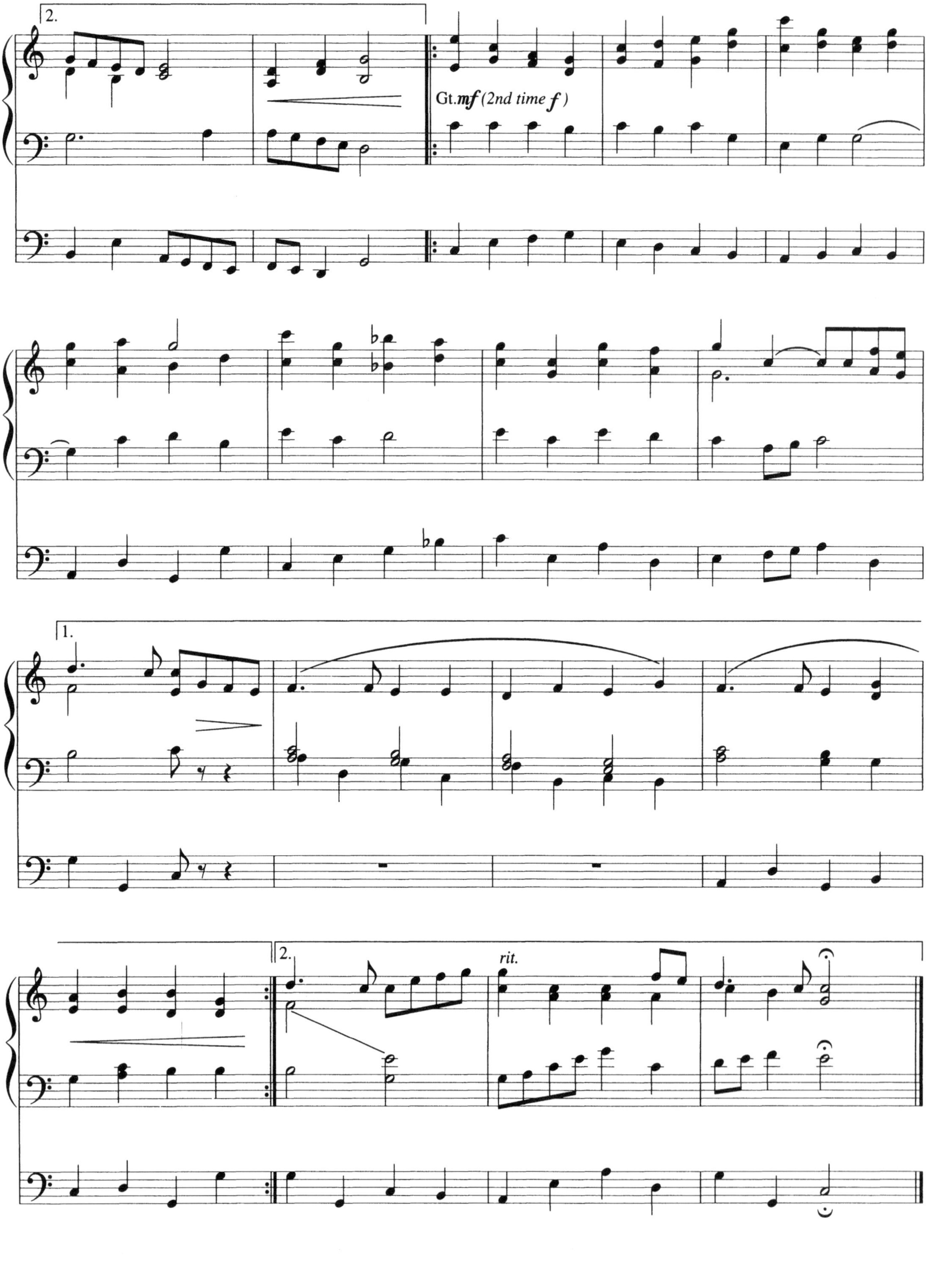
2.
Gt. mf (2nd time f)
1.
2.
rit.

SORTIE

Robert Fielding

I+II
ff
poco rit.
a tempo
2nd time to Coda
I
+I
senza rall.
II (bright stops)
mf

molto rit.
a tempo
mf
rit.
I+II
ff
D.C. al Coda
CODA
molto rall.
a tempo
rit.

ITE MISSA EST

Philip Moore

Un poco allegro (♩. = c.60)

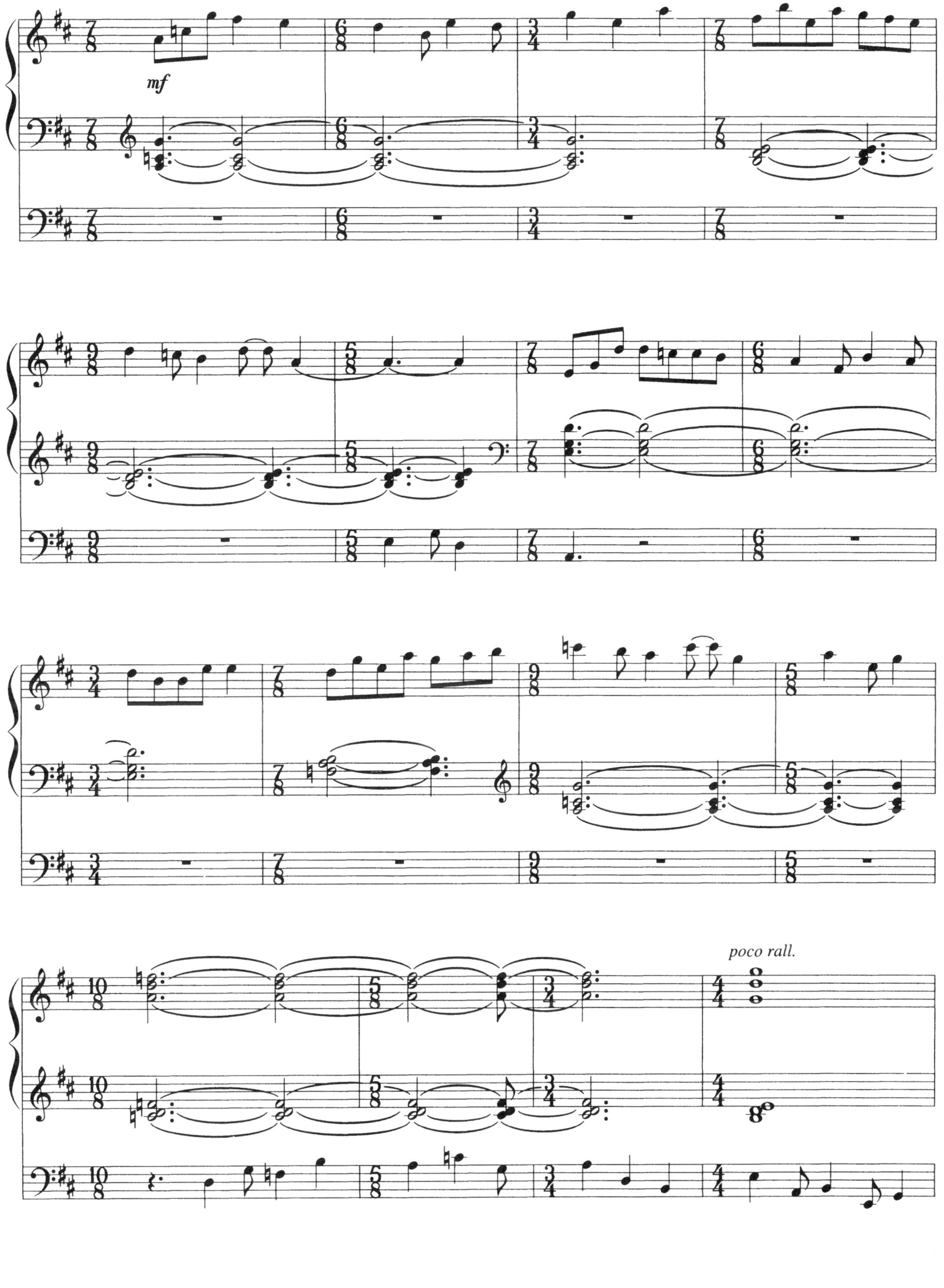
mf
poco rall.

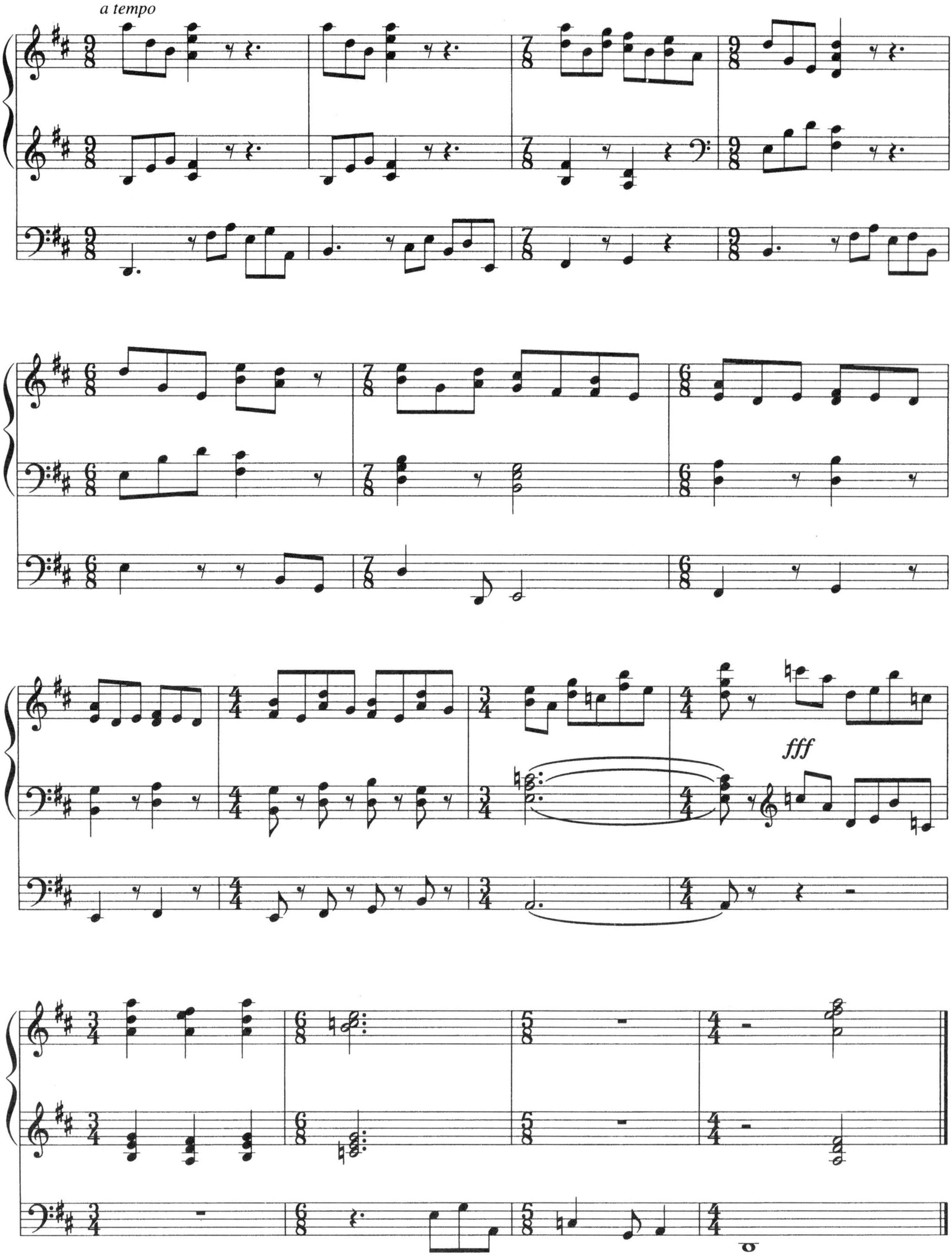
a tempo
fff

PASTORALE

Richard Shephard

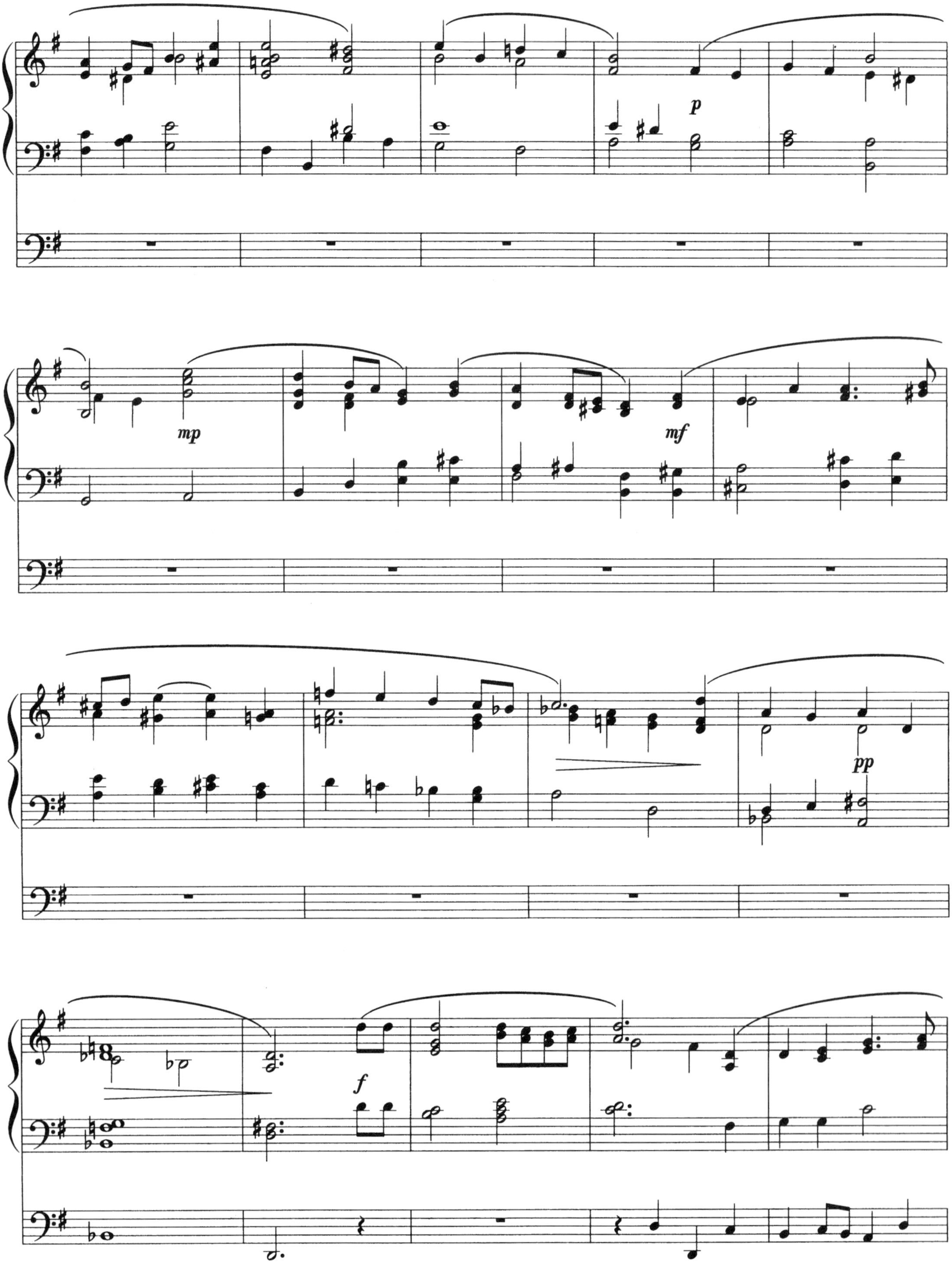
p
mp
mf
pp
f

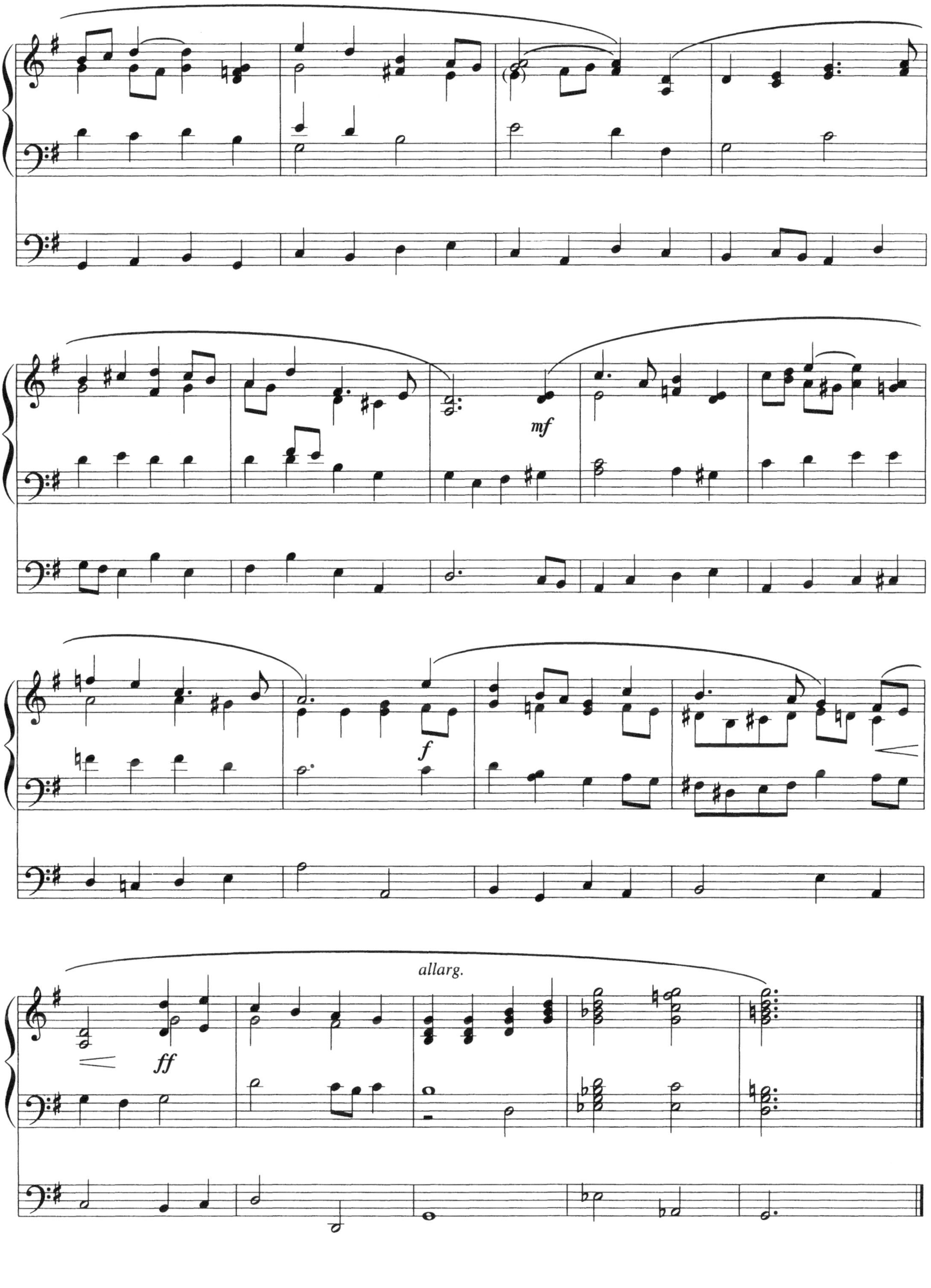
mf
f
allarg.
ff

PAEAN

Richard Pantcheff

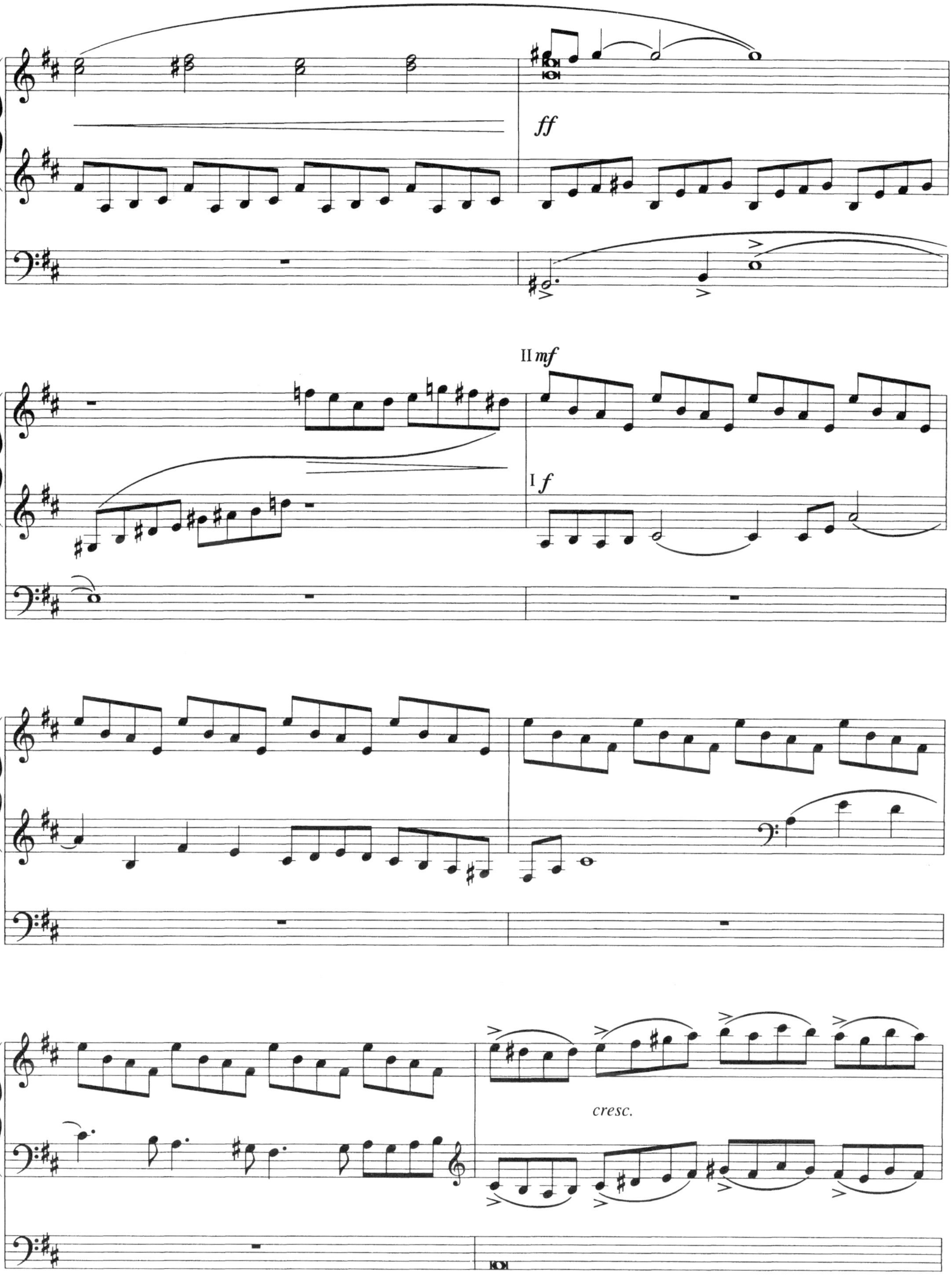
ff
II mf
I f
cresc.

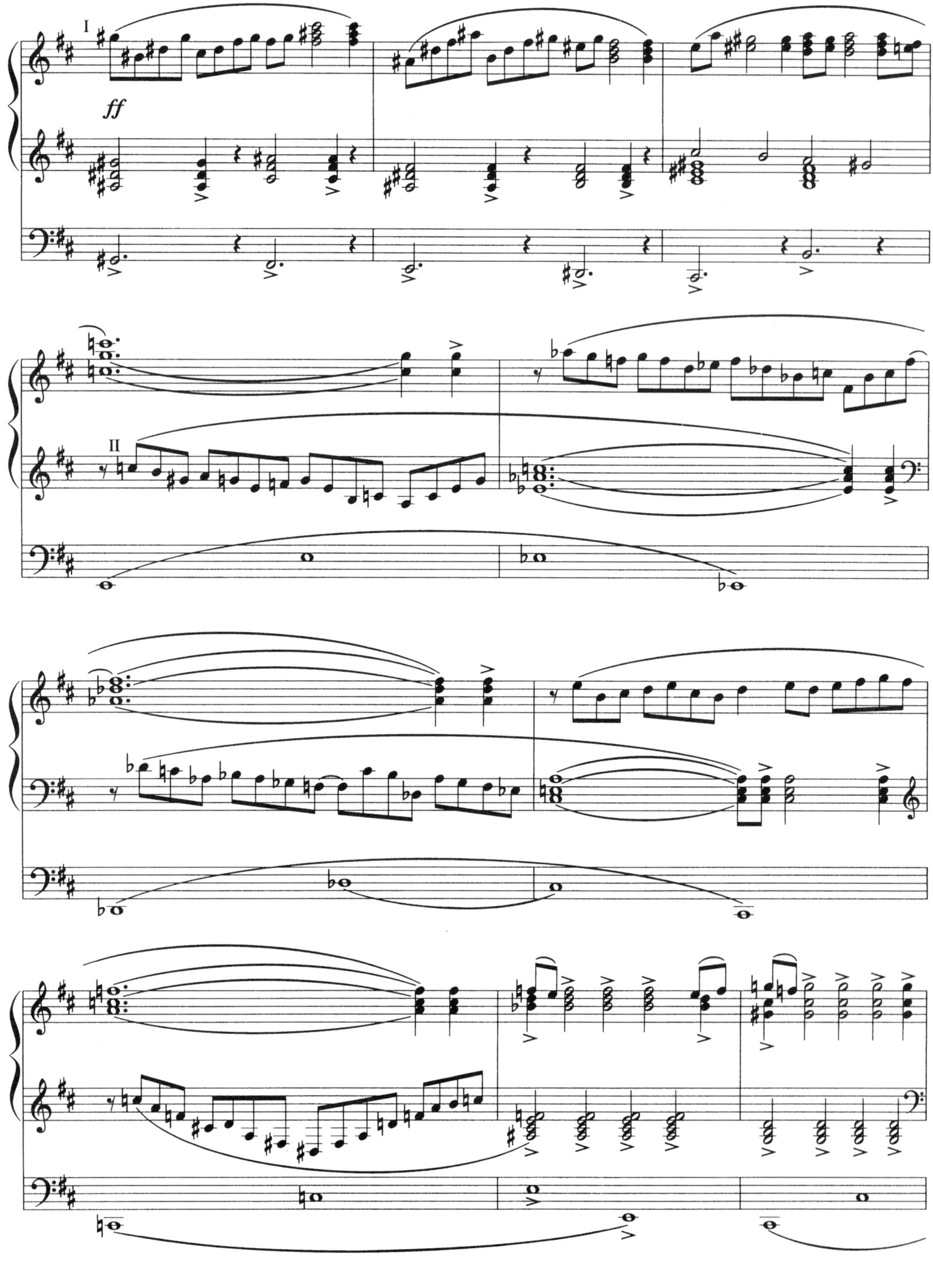
I
ff
II

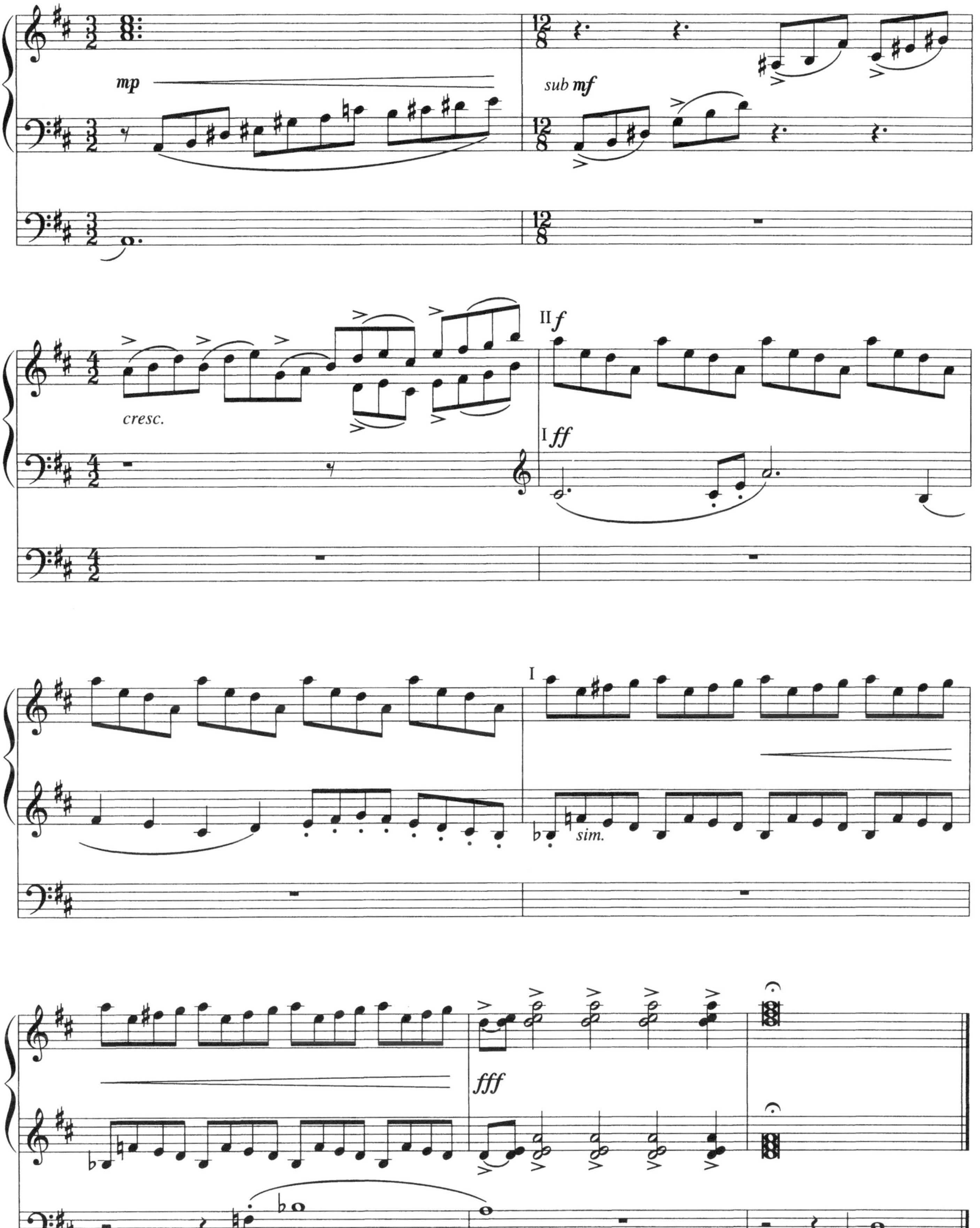
mp
sub mf
cresc.
II f
I ff
I
sim.
fff

PROLOGUE TO A CEREMONY

June Nixon

rit.

a tempo

Add

Add

3

[D.C.*]

allarg.

* optional Da Capo if required

for Martin and Lisa

THE BRIDE'S PROCESSION

Andrew Fletcher

Maestoso

poco a poco cresc.
1. (optional repeat più f)
2. Solo Reed
(or Full Gt.+Sw.)
ff
Gt.
rall.
fff

VENITE

Norman Warren

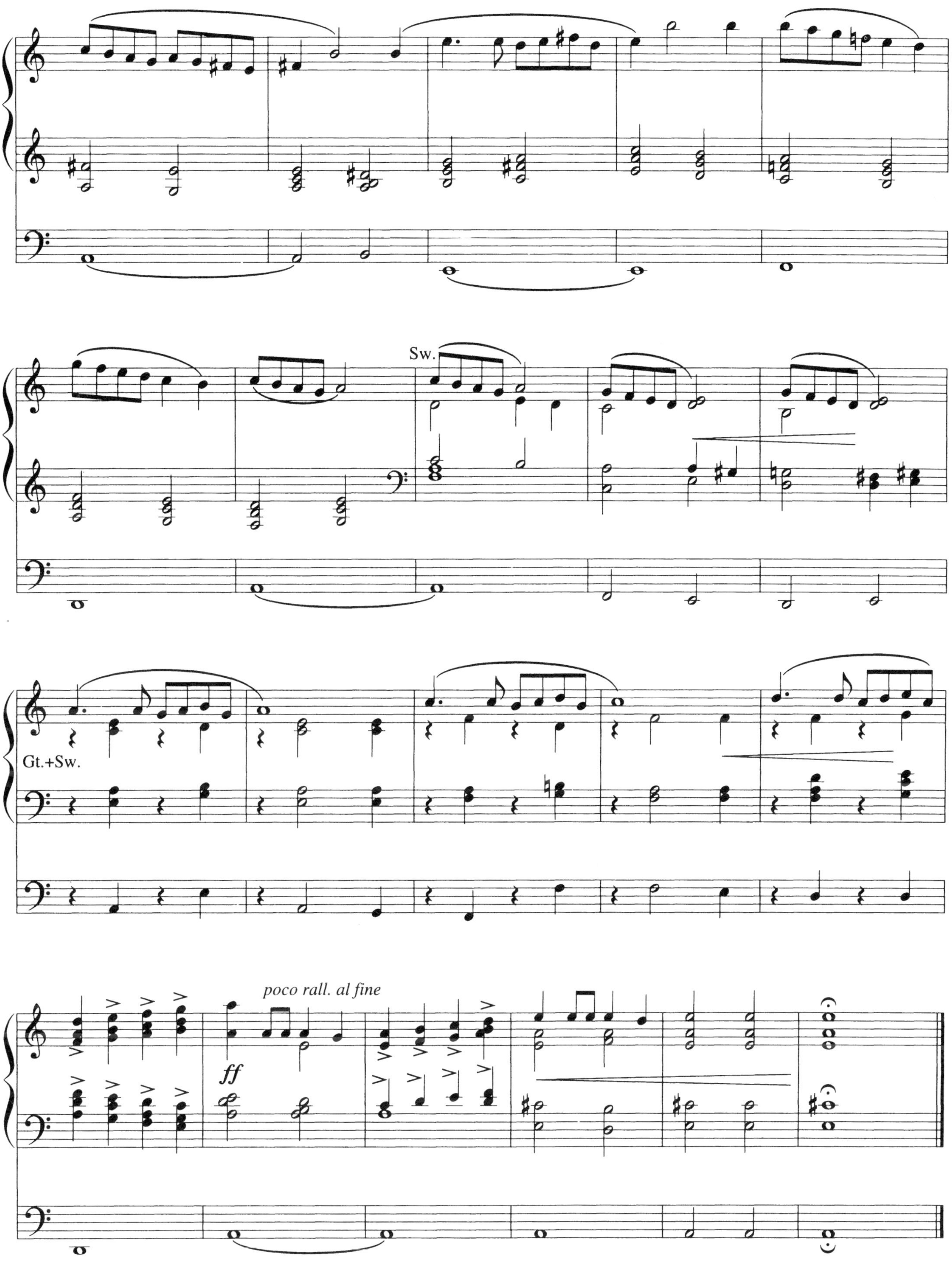

116 114 222 211

TOCCATINO

Andrew Moore

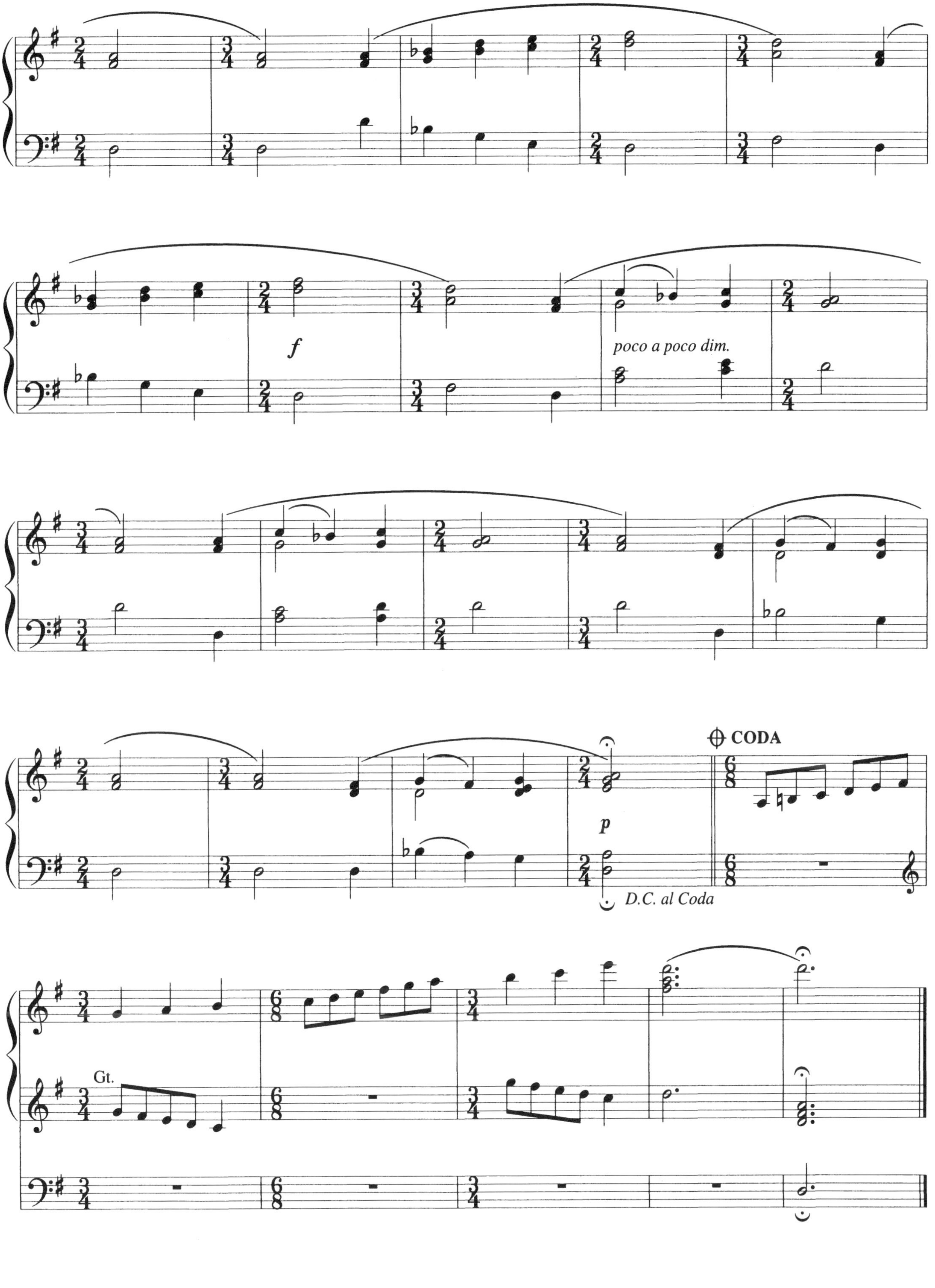
f
poco a poco dim.
CODA
p
D.C. al Coda
Gt.

TRUMPET TUNE

Stephen Kemp

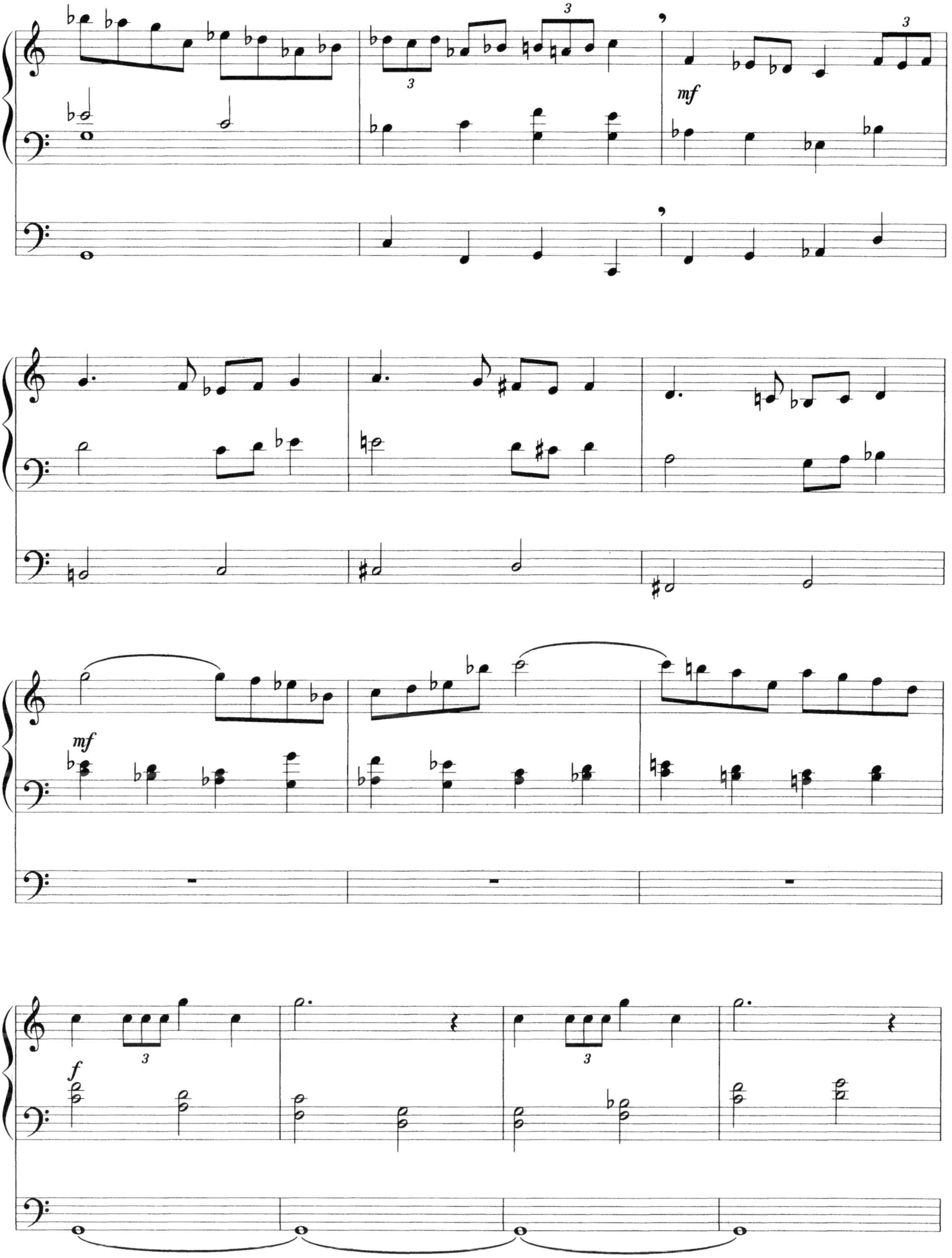
mf
mf
f

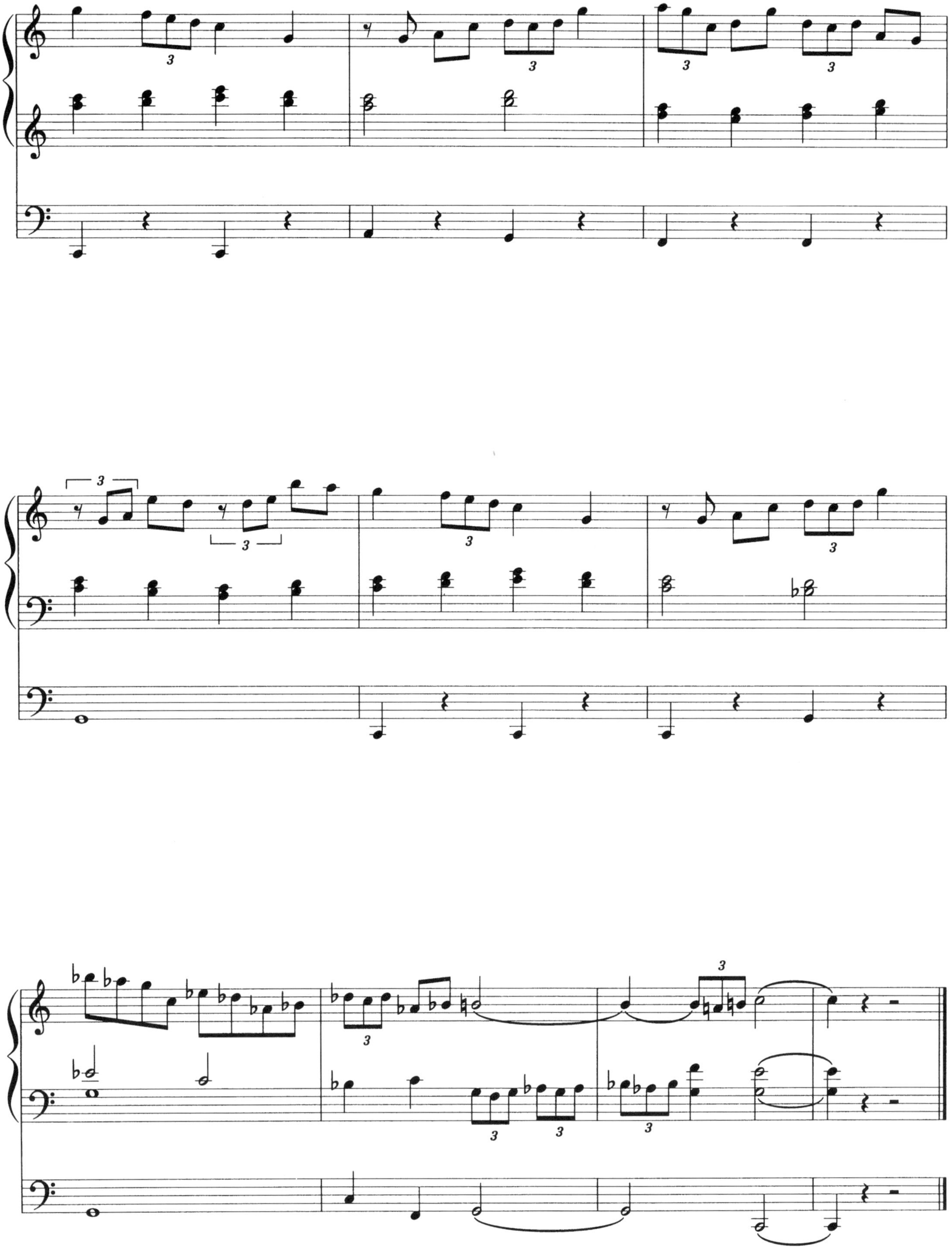

for Andrew Fletcher

FESTIVE STUDY

Quentin Thomas

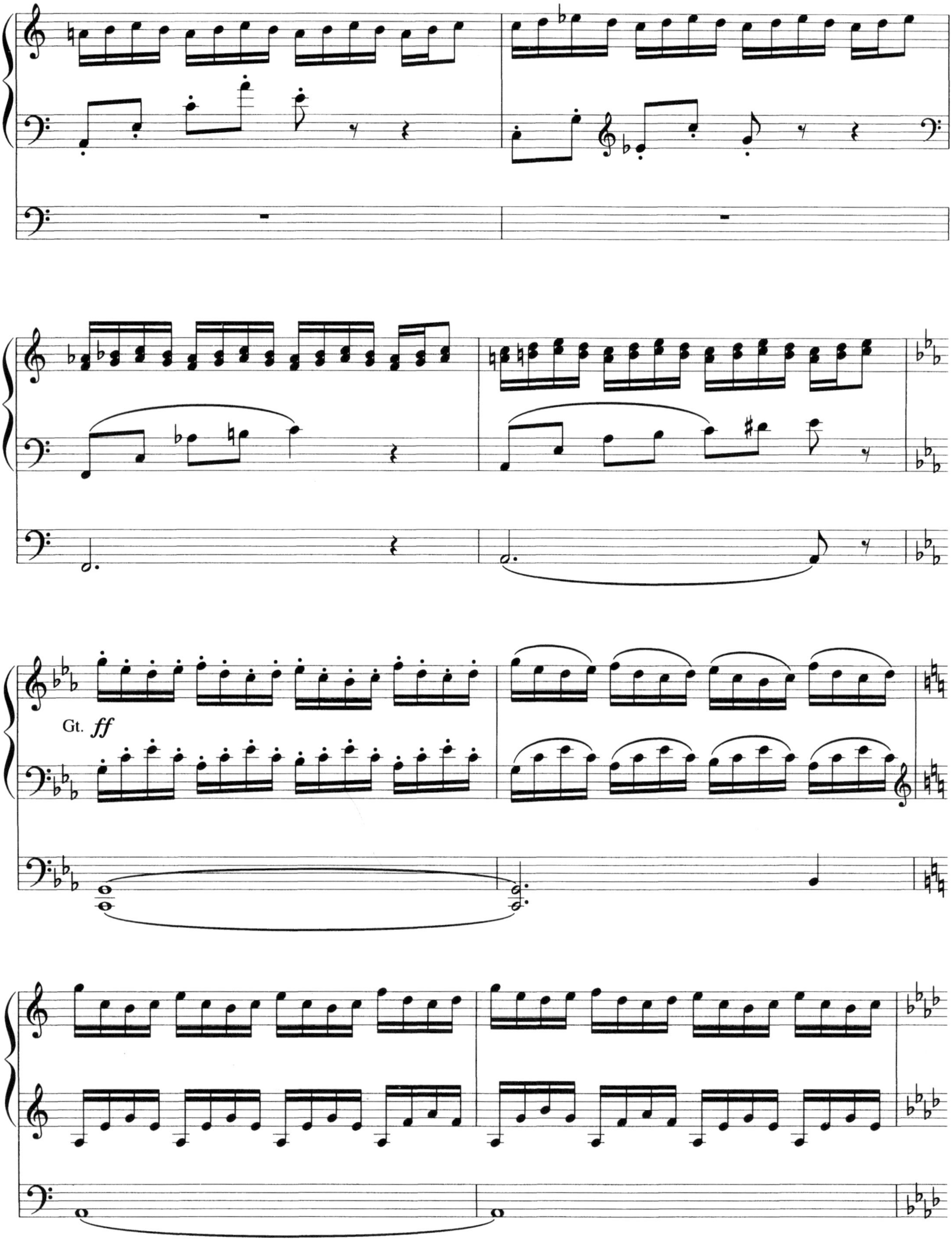
Gt. ff

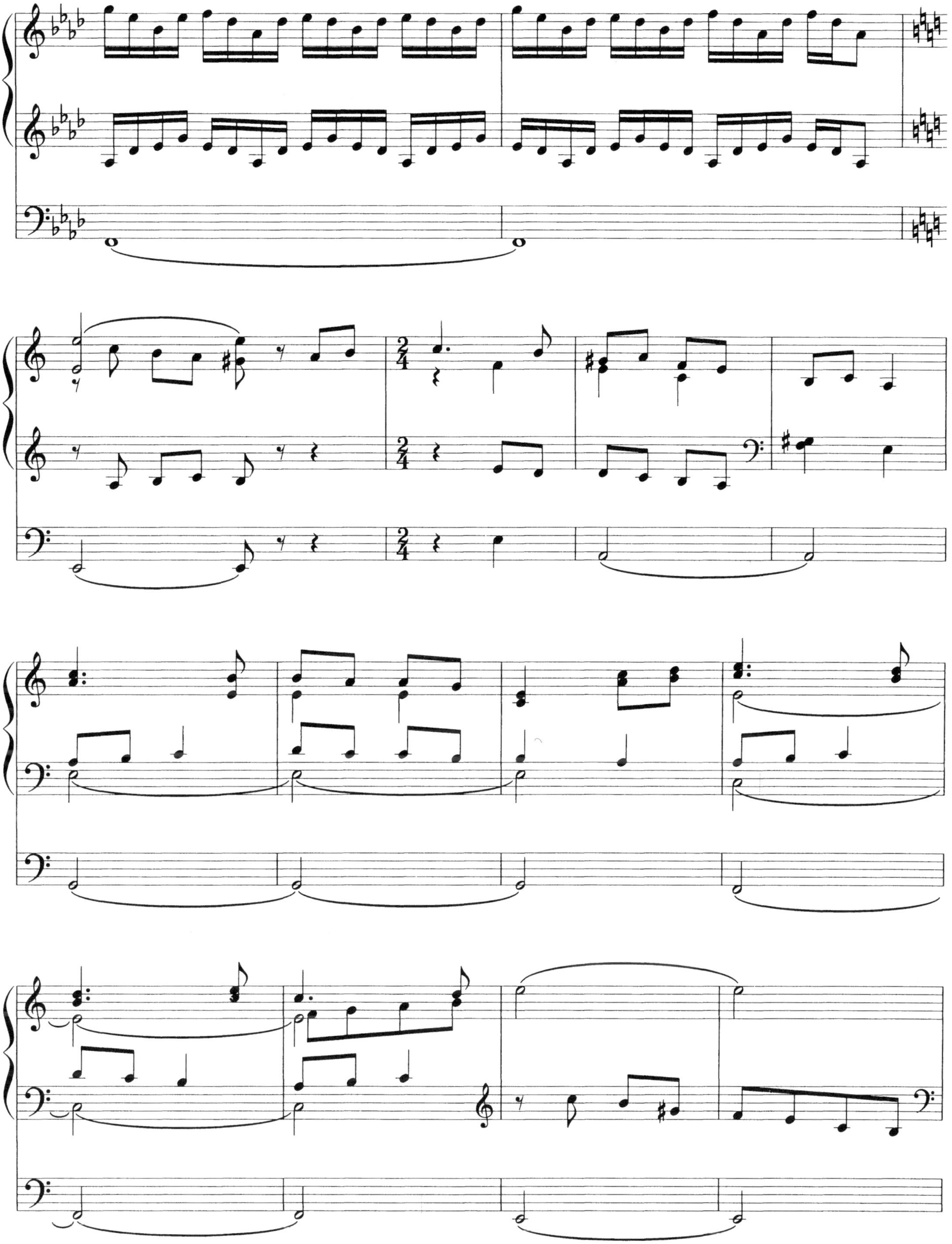

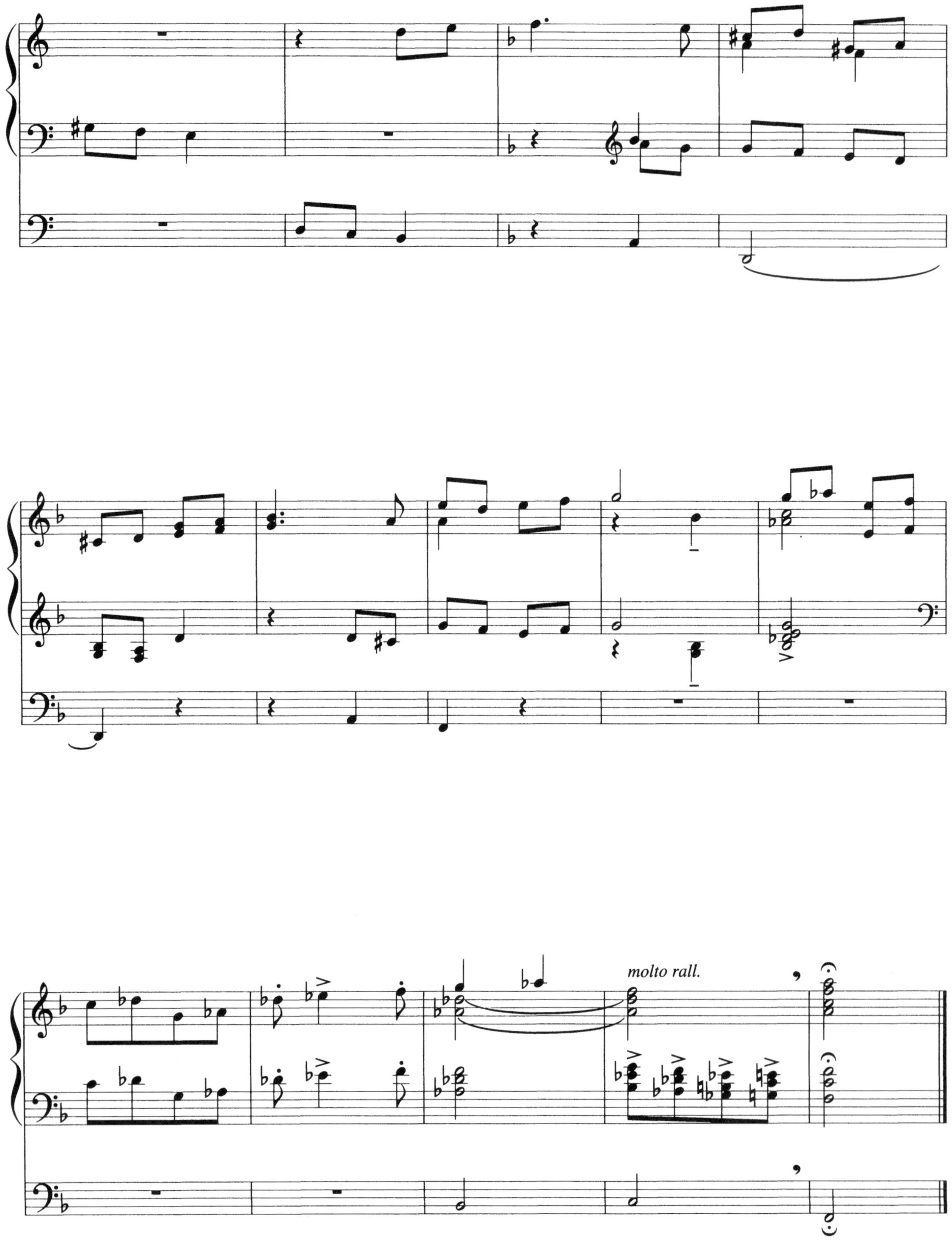
molto rall.

to Summer

ANDANTE

Betty Roe

234

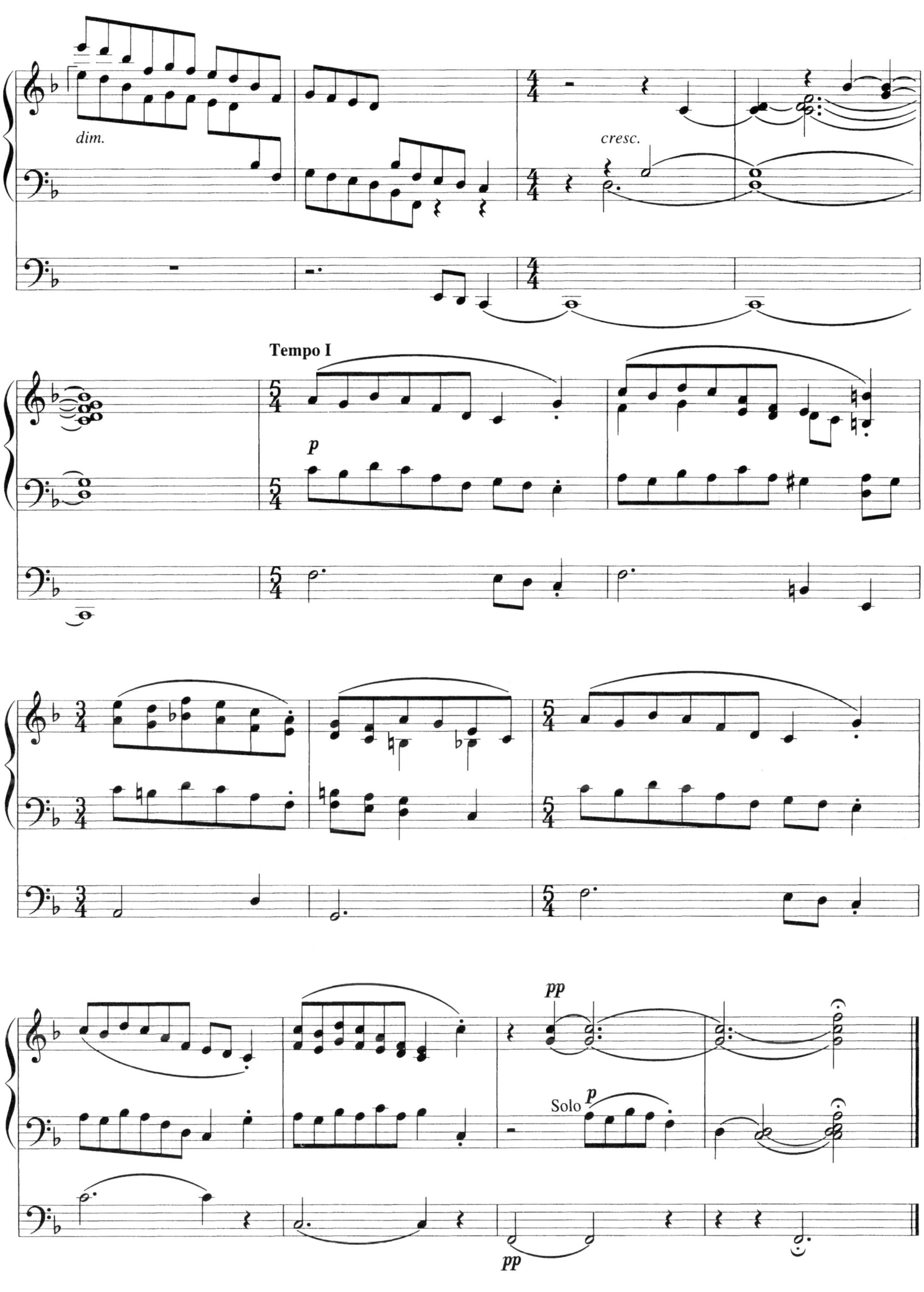
dim.
cresc.
Tempo I
p
pp
Solo
p
pp

GAUDETE

John Marsh

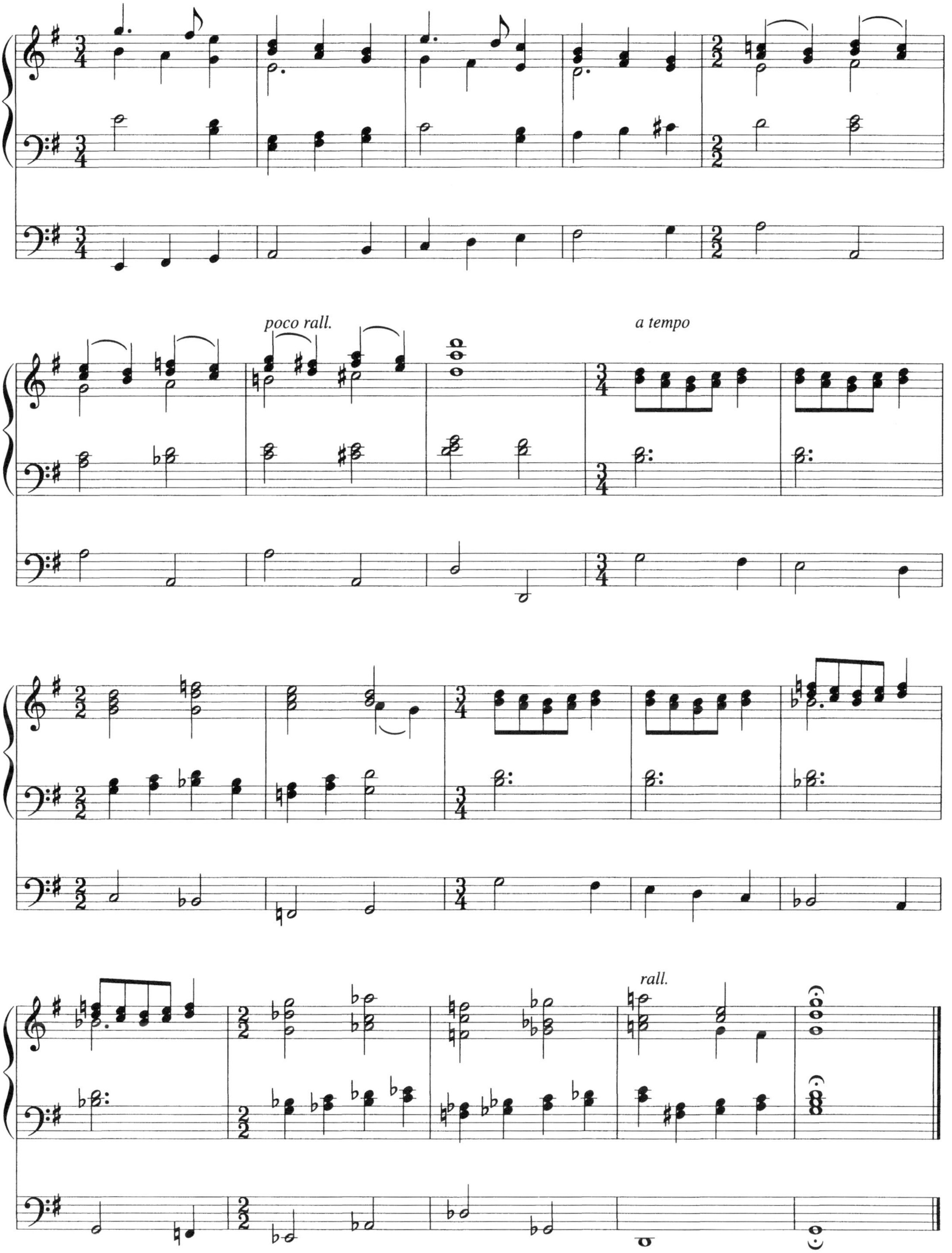
poco rall.
a tempo
rall.

for Sarah and Ian on their Wedding Day

TRIUMPHANT MARCH

Christopher Tambling

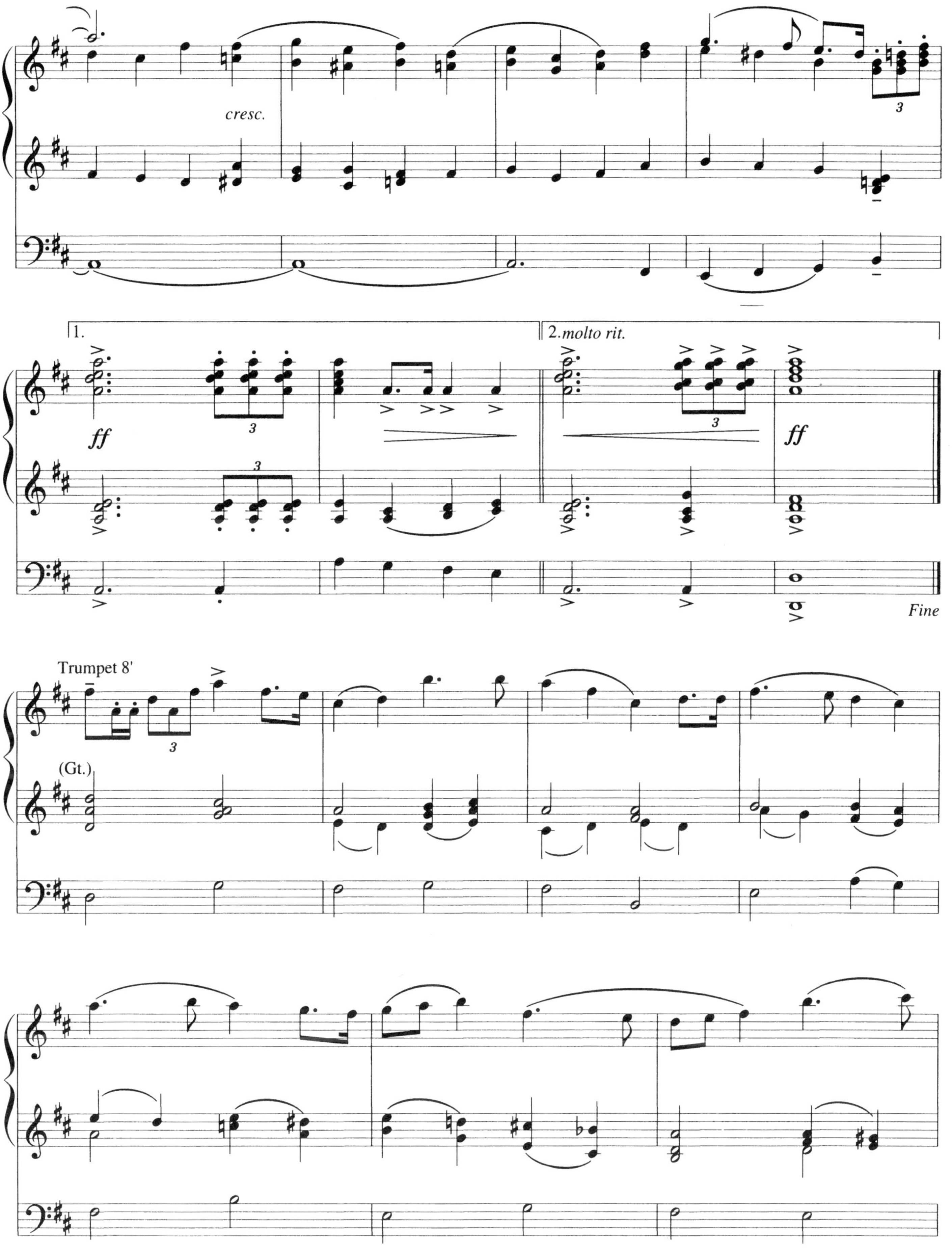

cresc.
1.
ff
2. molto rit.
ff
Fine
Trumpet 8'
(Gt.)

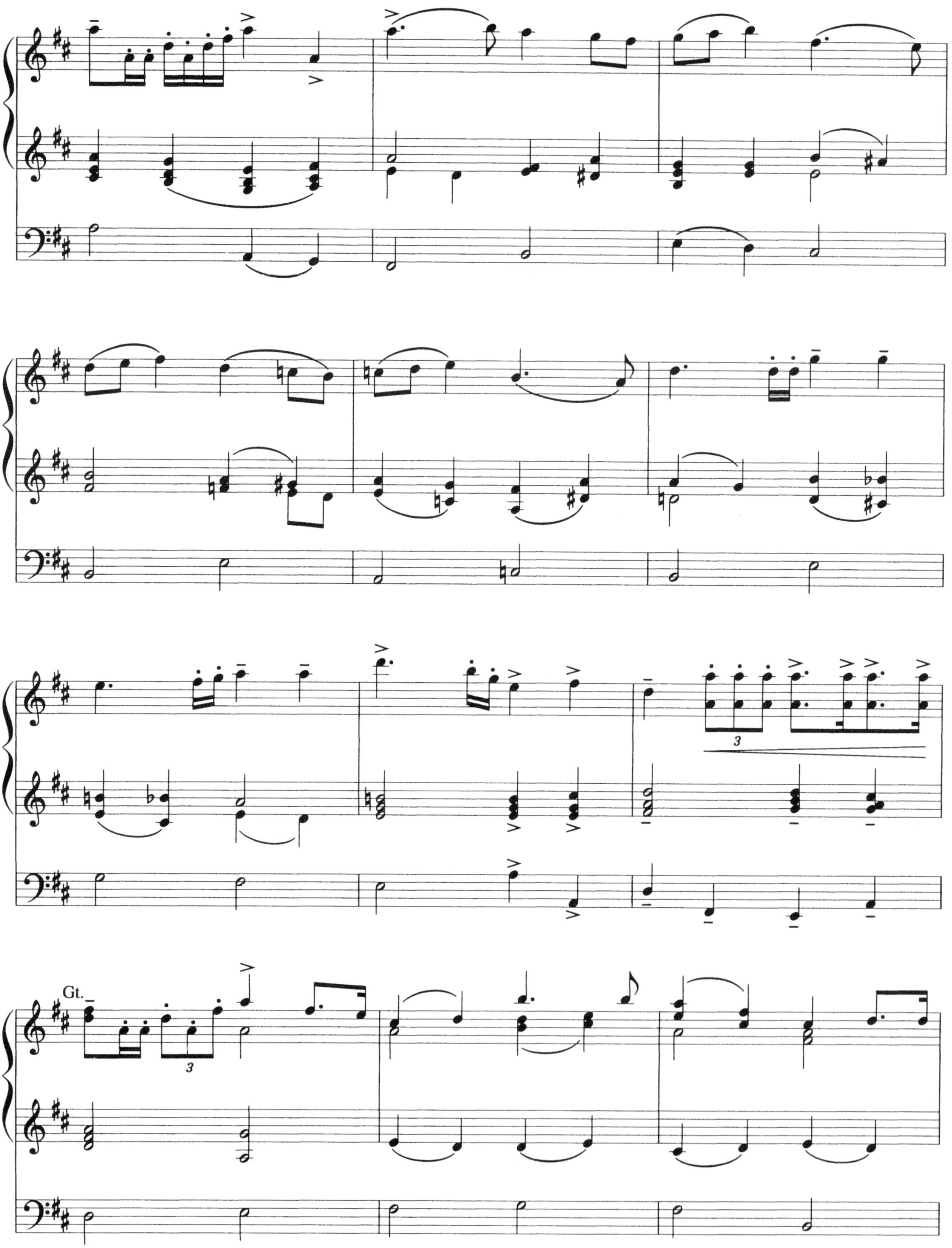
Gt.

D.C. al Fine

241

FINALE

Stanley Vann

poco rall.
dim.
a tempo, ma un poco meno mosso
mf
poco a poco cresc.
poco rall.

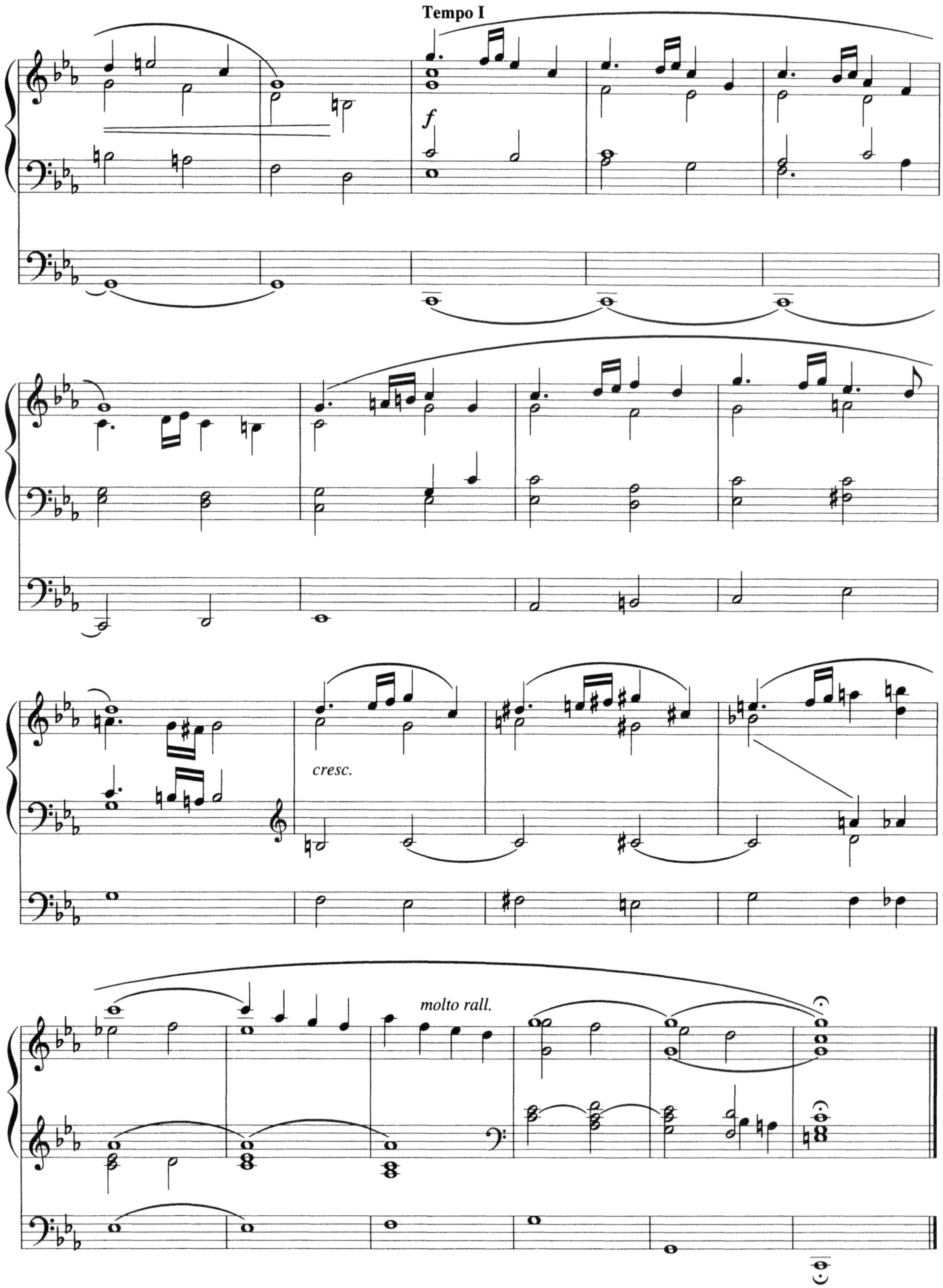
Tempo I
f
cresc.
molto rall.

POSTLUDE

Andrew Gant

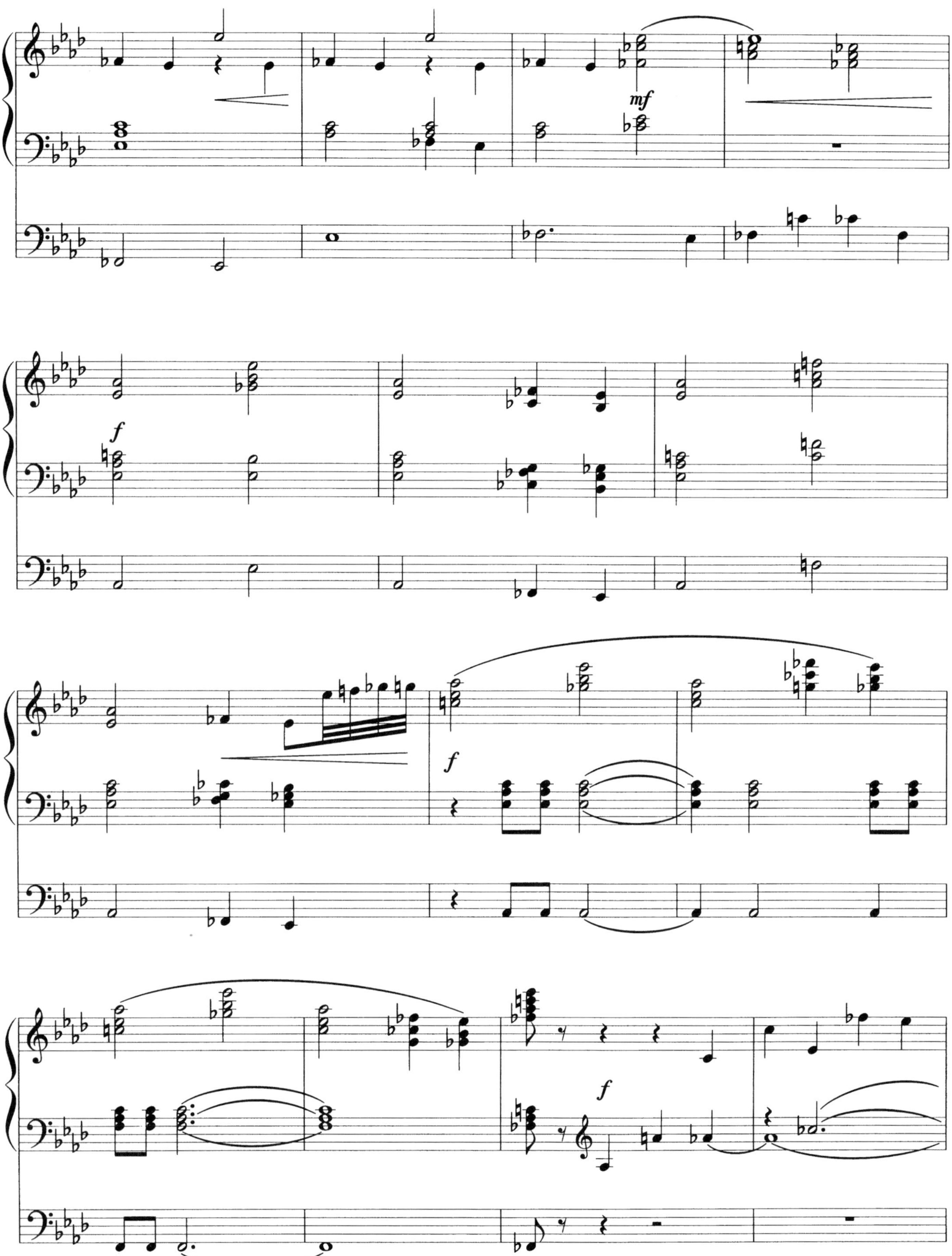
mf
f
f
f

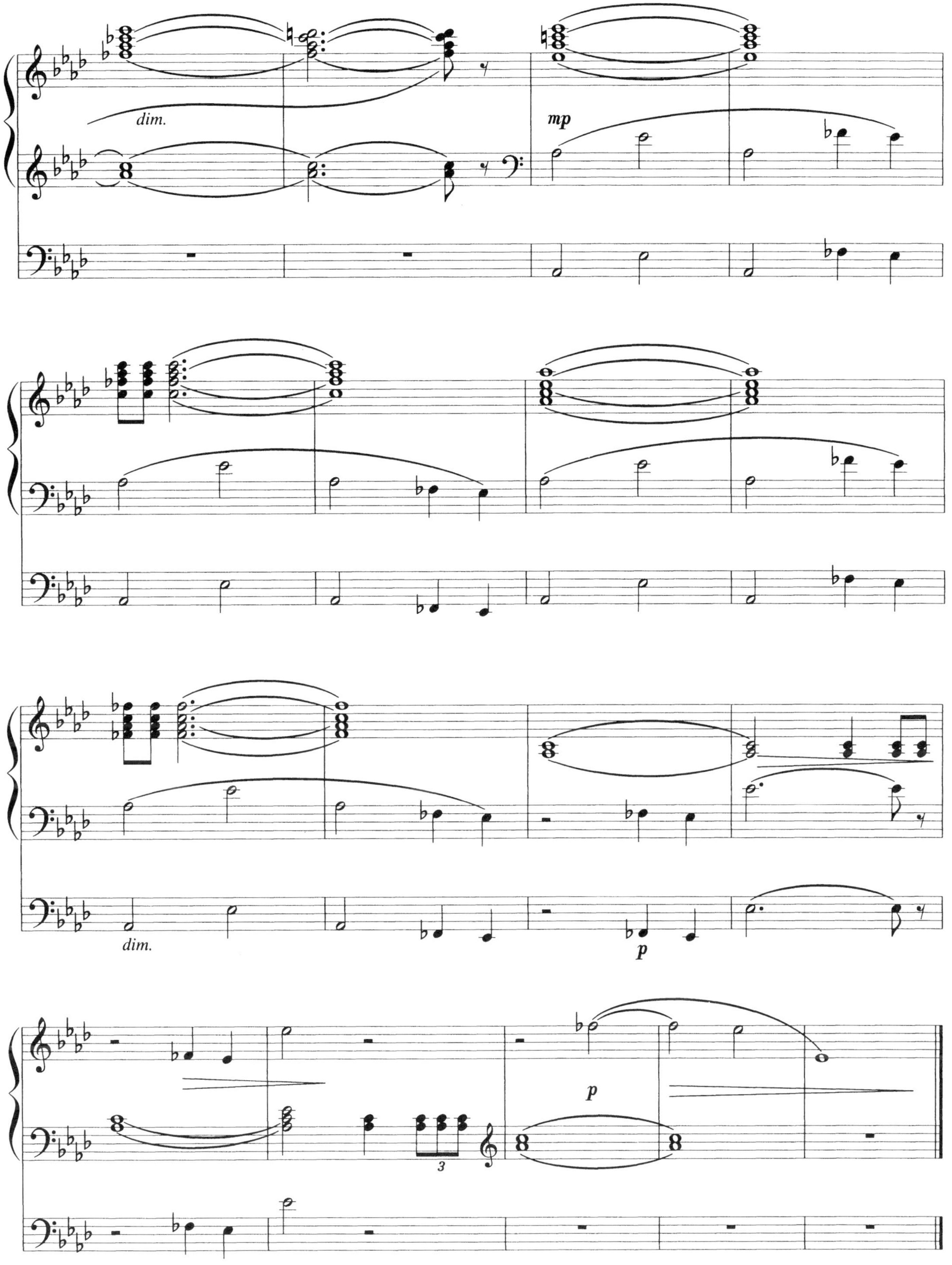
dim.
mp
dim.
p
3
p

LIGHT-HEARTED RECESSIONAL

Rosalie Bonighton

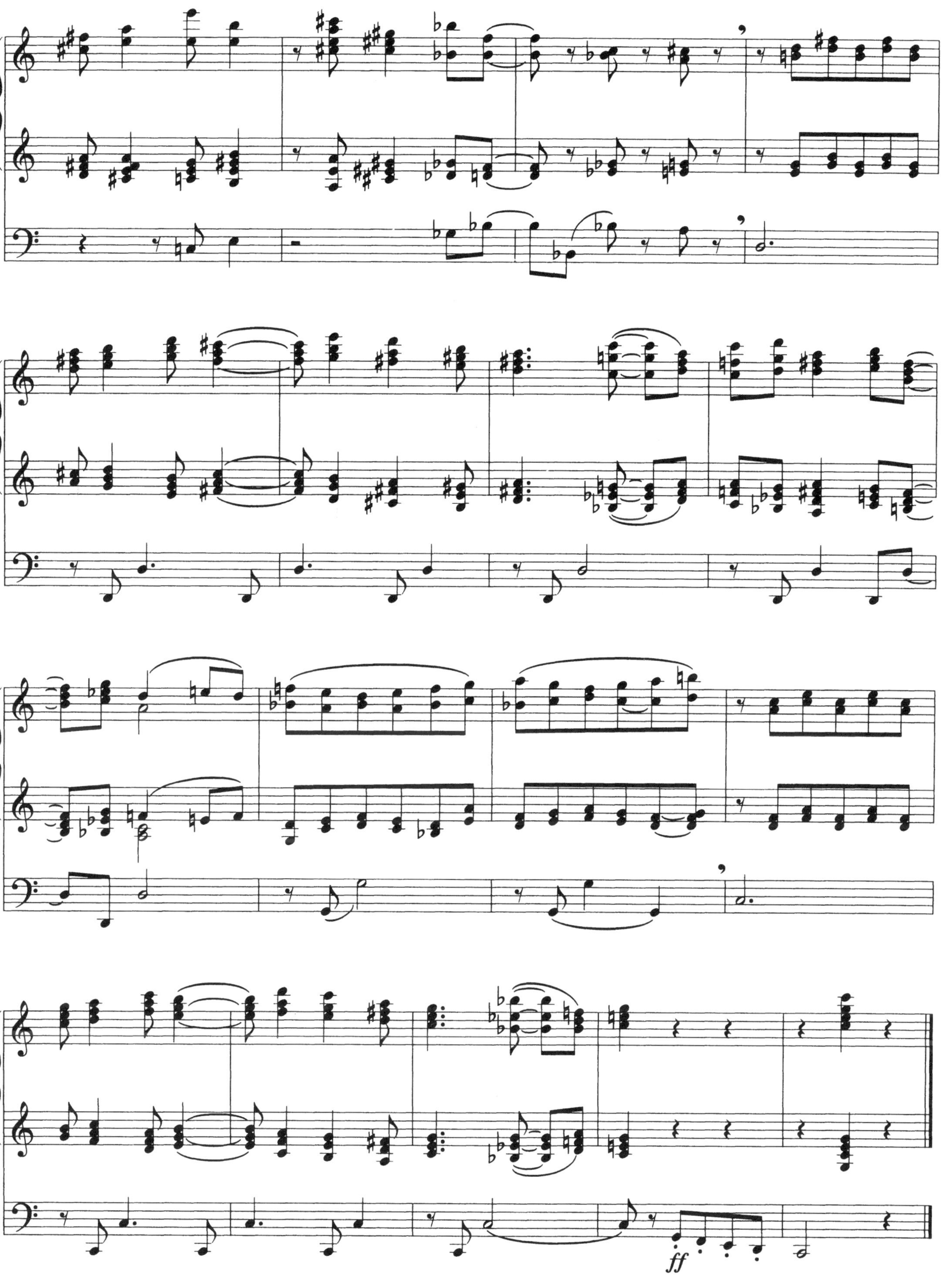
ff

for Trevor

CHORALE PROCESSION

Paul Bryan

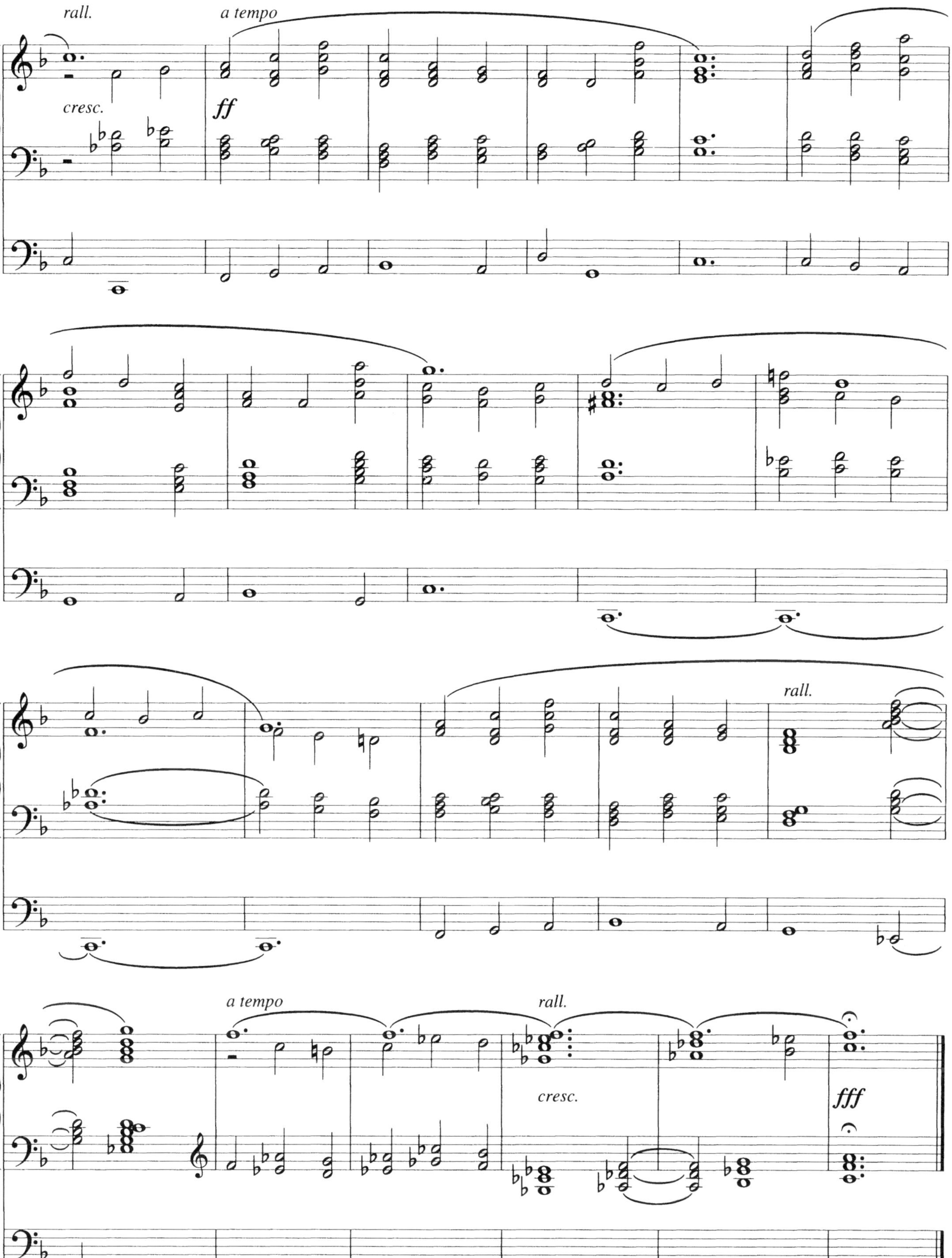
rall.
a tempo
cresc.
ff
rall.
a tempo
rall.
cresc.
fff

EPILOGUE

June Nixon

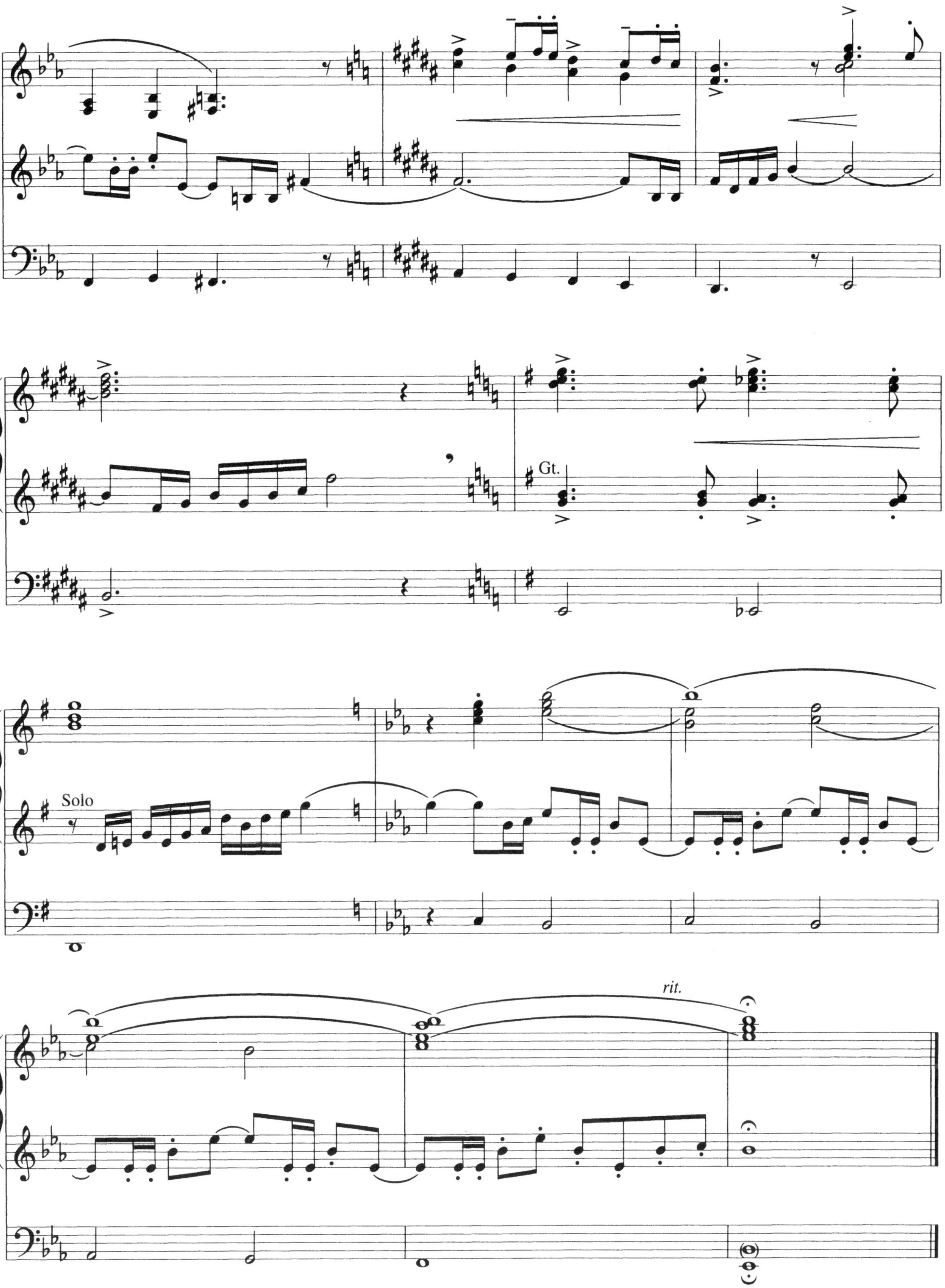
Gt.
Solo
rit.

PAGEANT

Richard Knight

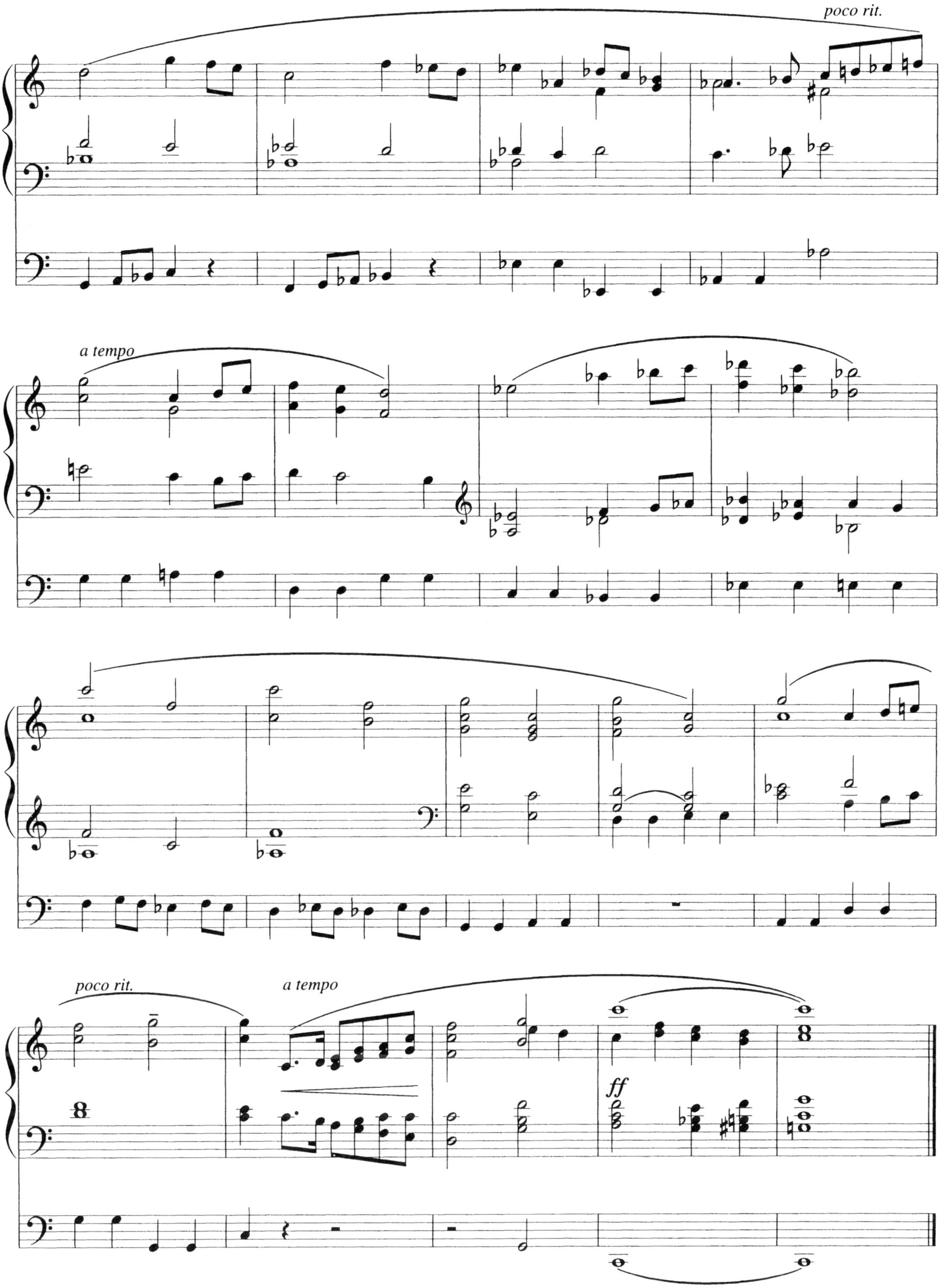
poco rit.
a tempo
poco rit.
a tempo
ff

NOBILMENTE

Quentin Thomas

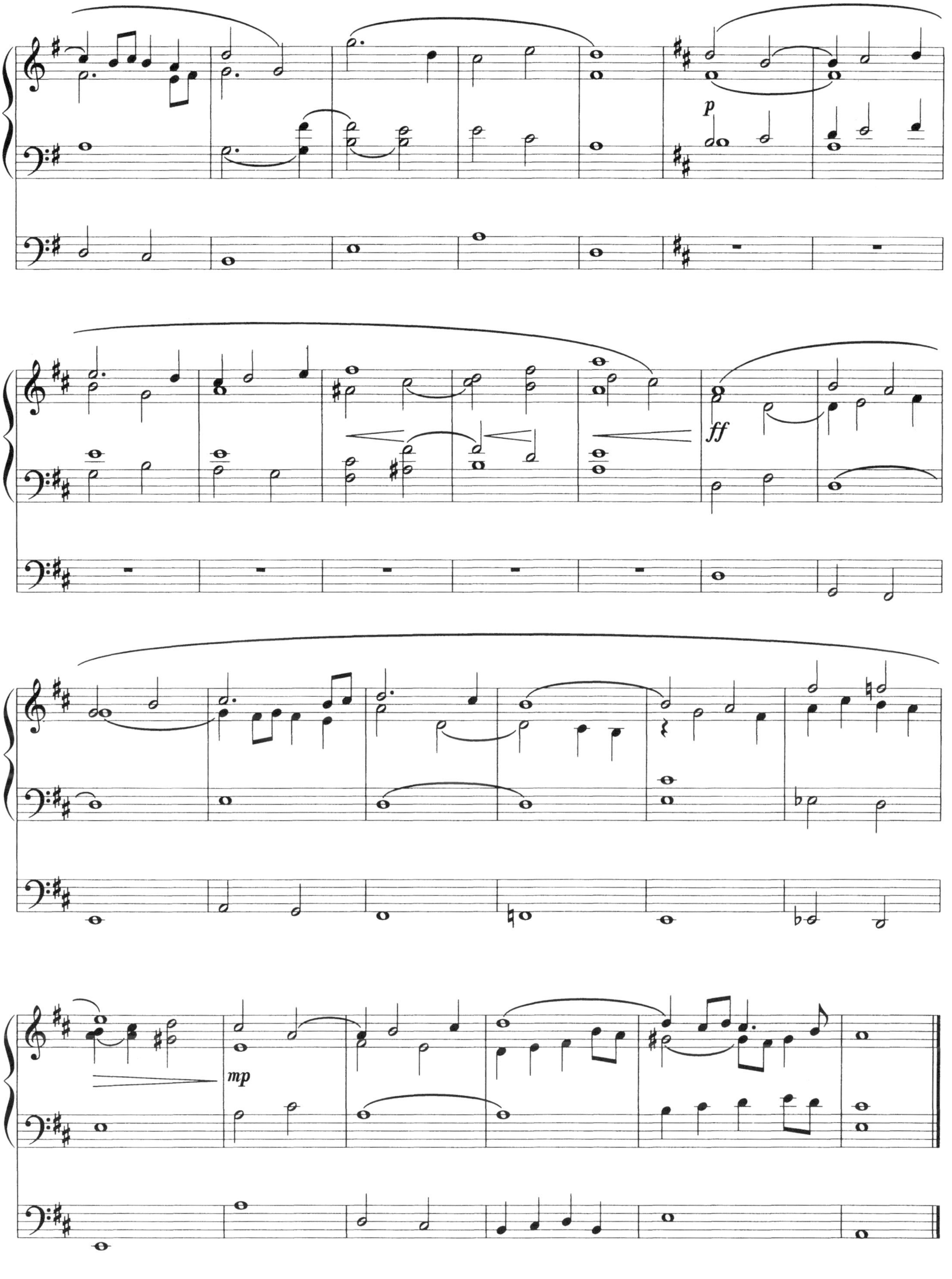
p
ff
mp

for Eleri and Richard, 23 May 1964; Rhiannon and Paul, 30 July 1994

WEDDING MARCH (Like Mother, Like Daughter)

Owain Edwards

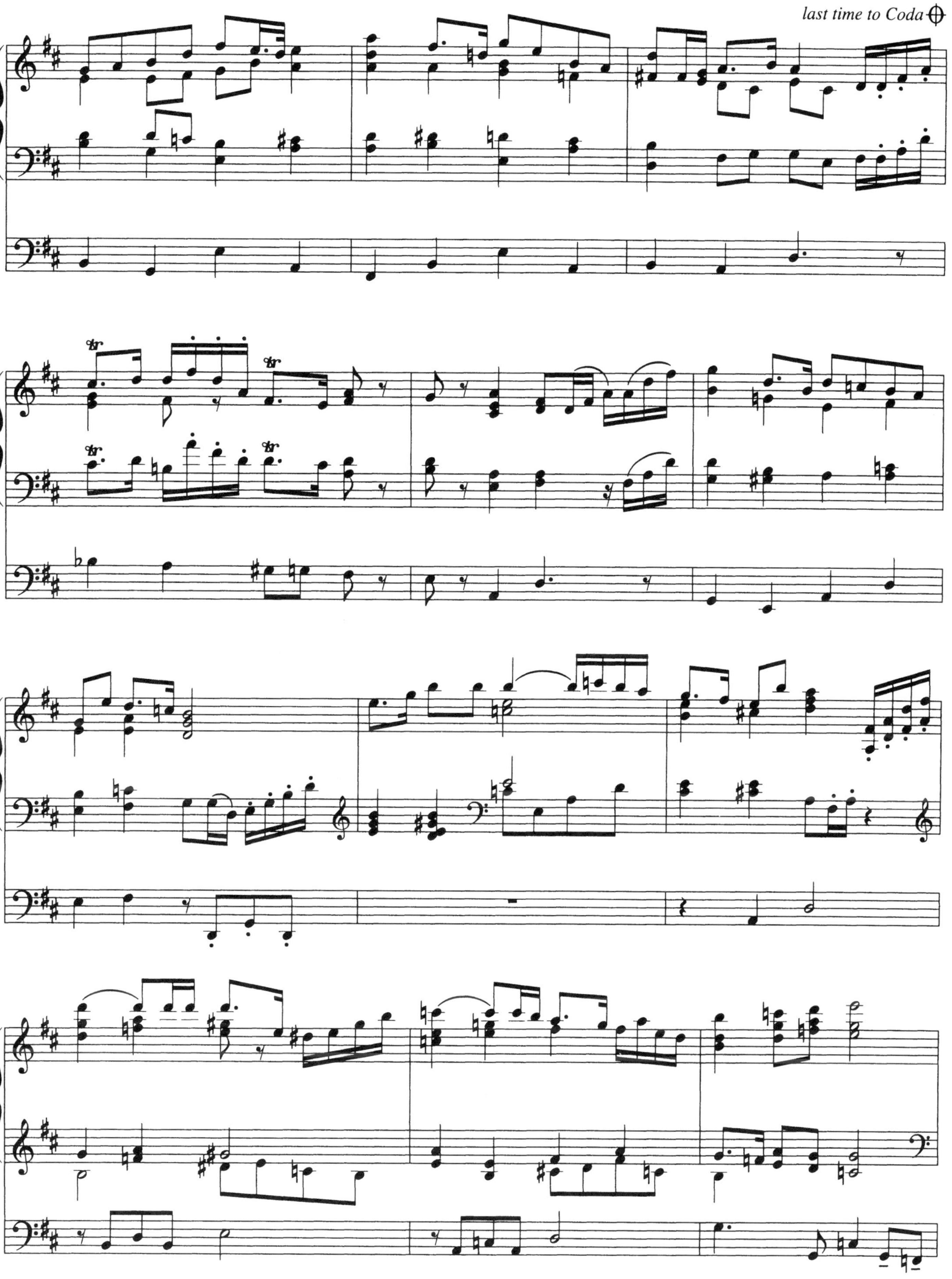
last time to Coda

D.S. al Coda

✛ CODA

JOYFUL PROCESSIONAL

Colin Mawby

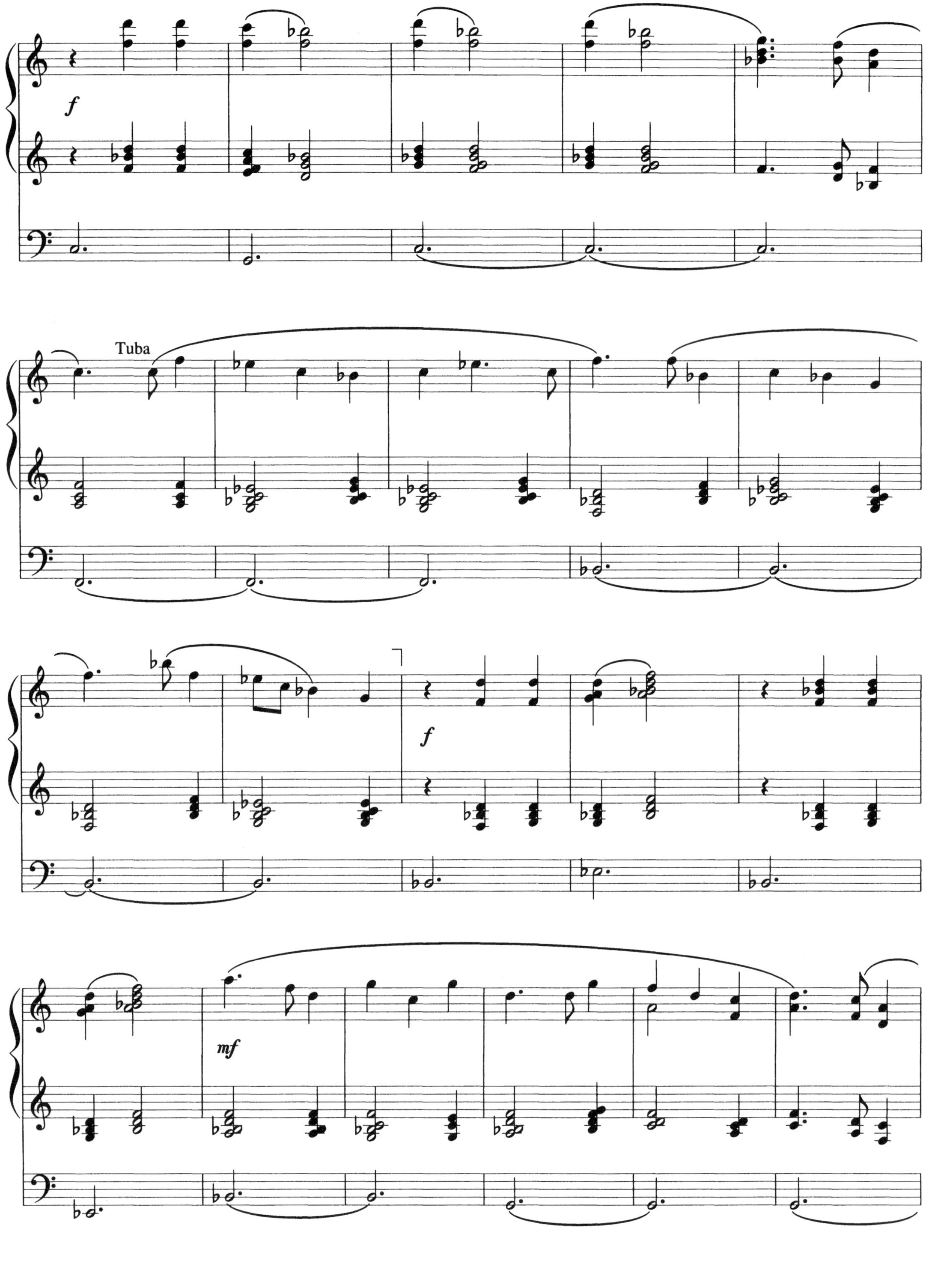
f
Tuba
f
mf

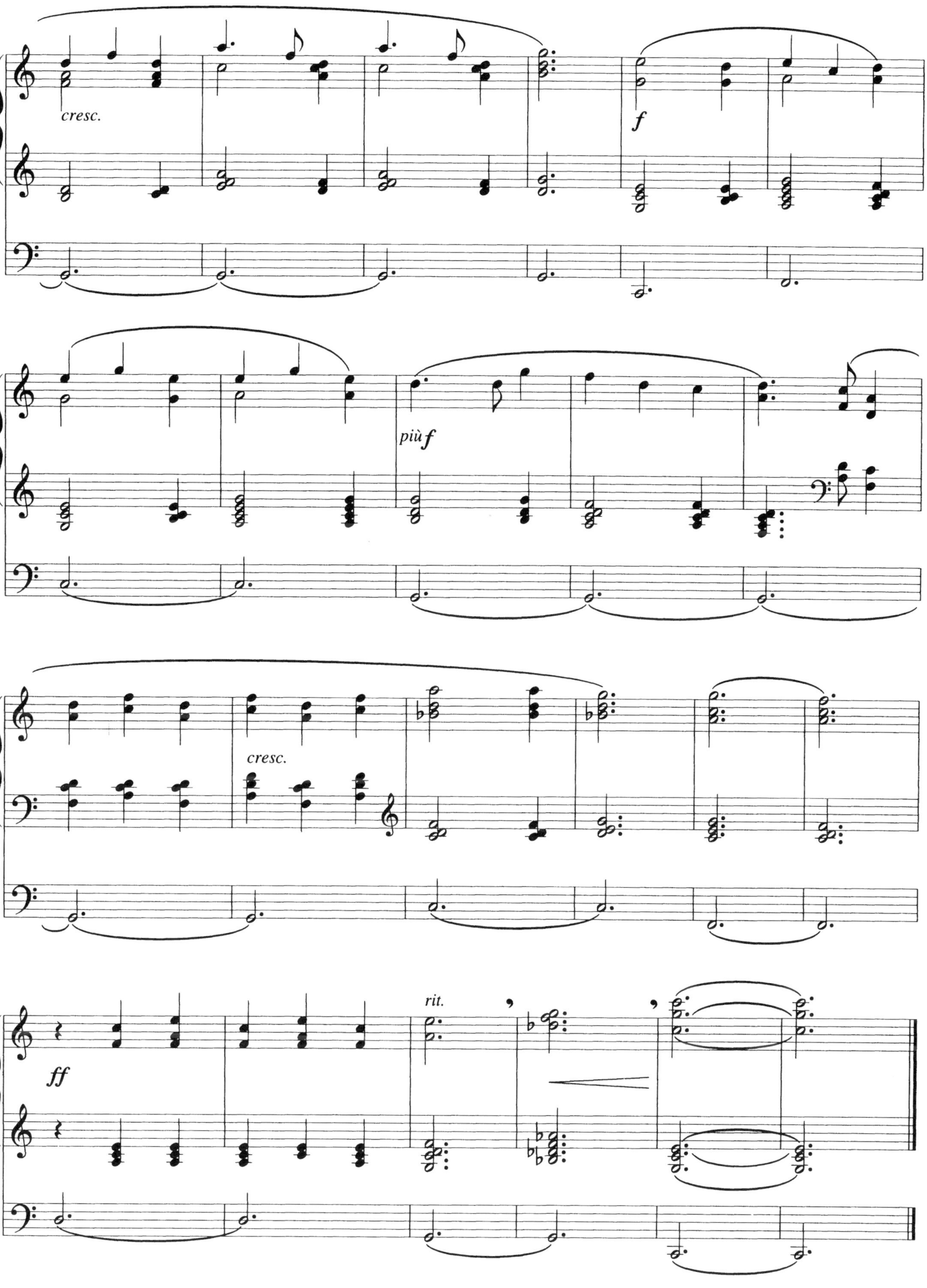

cresc.
f
più f
cresc.
ff
rit.

GRANDIOSO

Stanley Vann

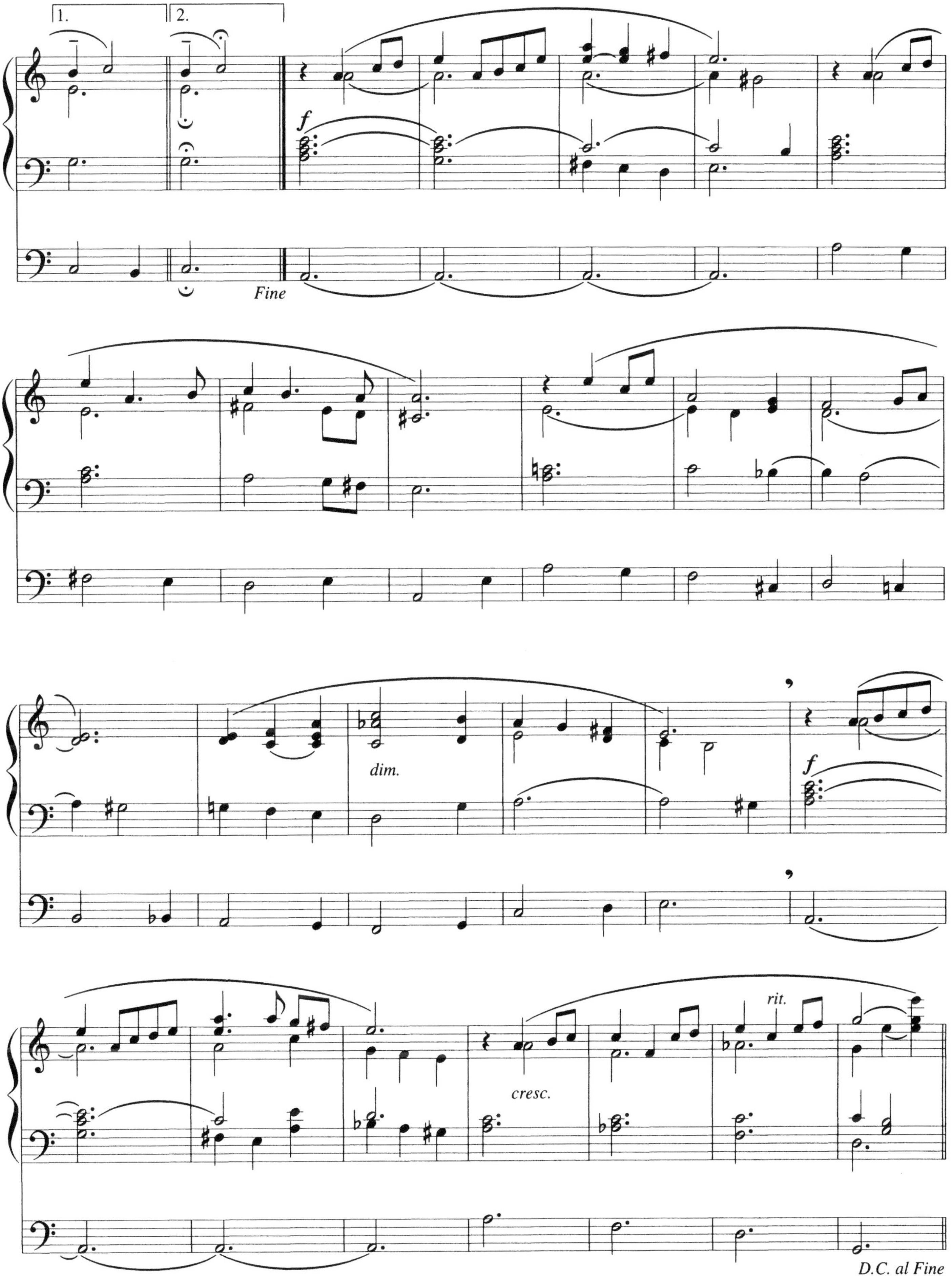
1.
2.
f
Fine
dim.
f
cresc.
rit.
D.C. al Fine

A QUICK MARCH

Robert Fielding

Allegro marziale (♩ = 84)

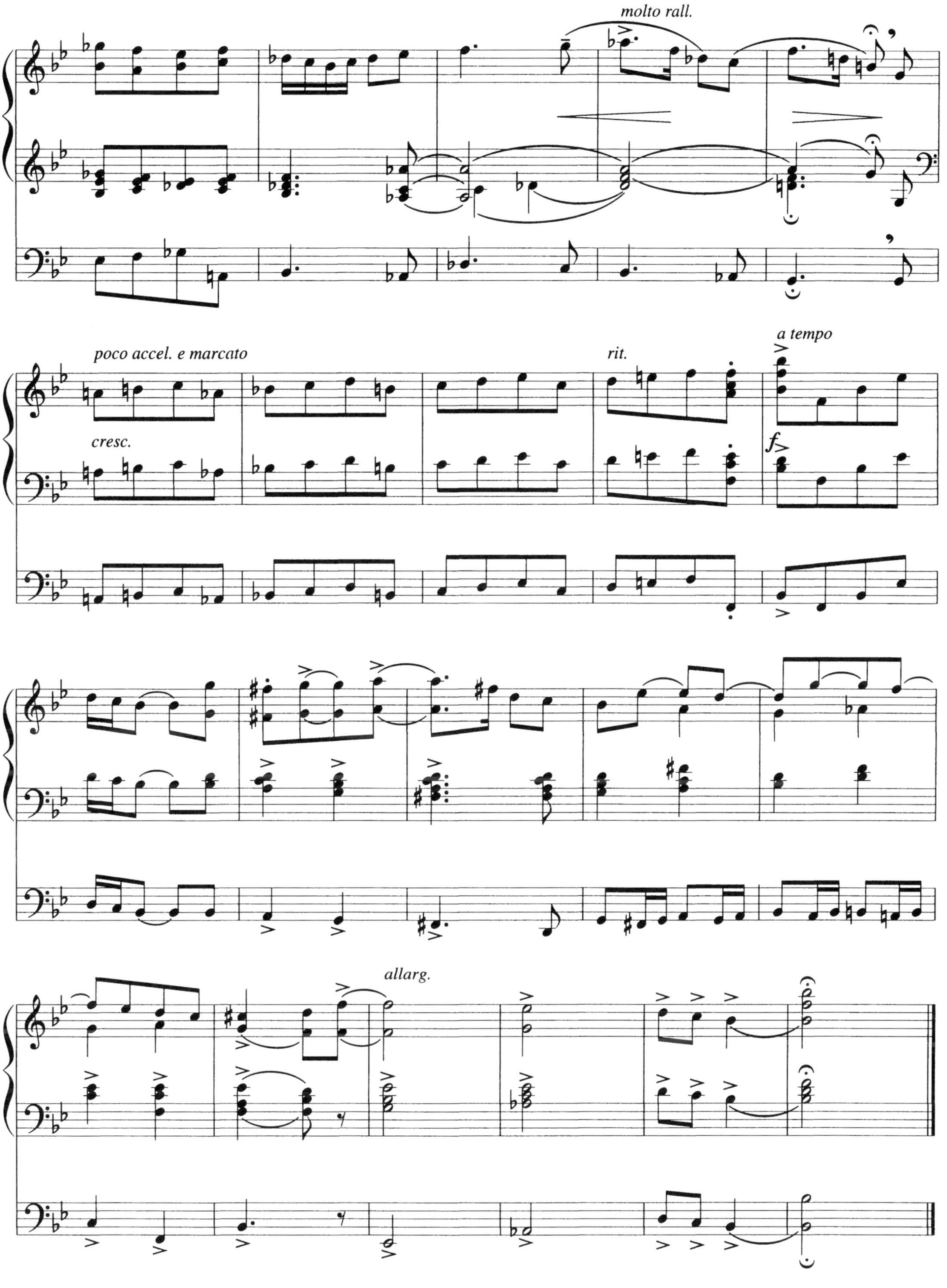
molto rall.
poco accel. e marcato
cresc.
rit.
a tempo
f
allarg.

PROMENADE

Rosalie Bonighton

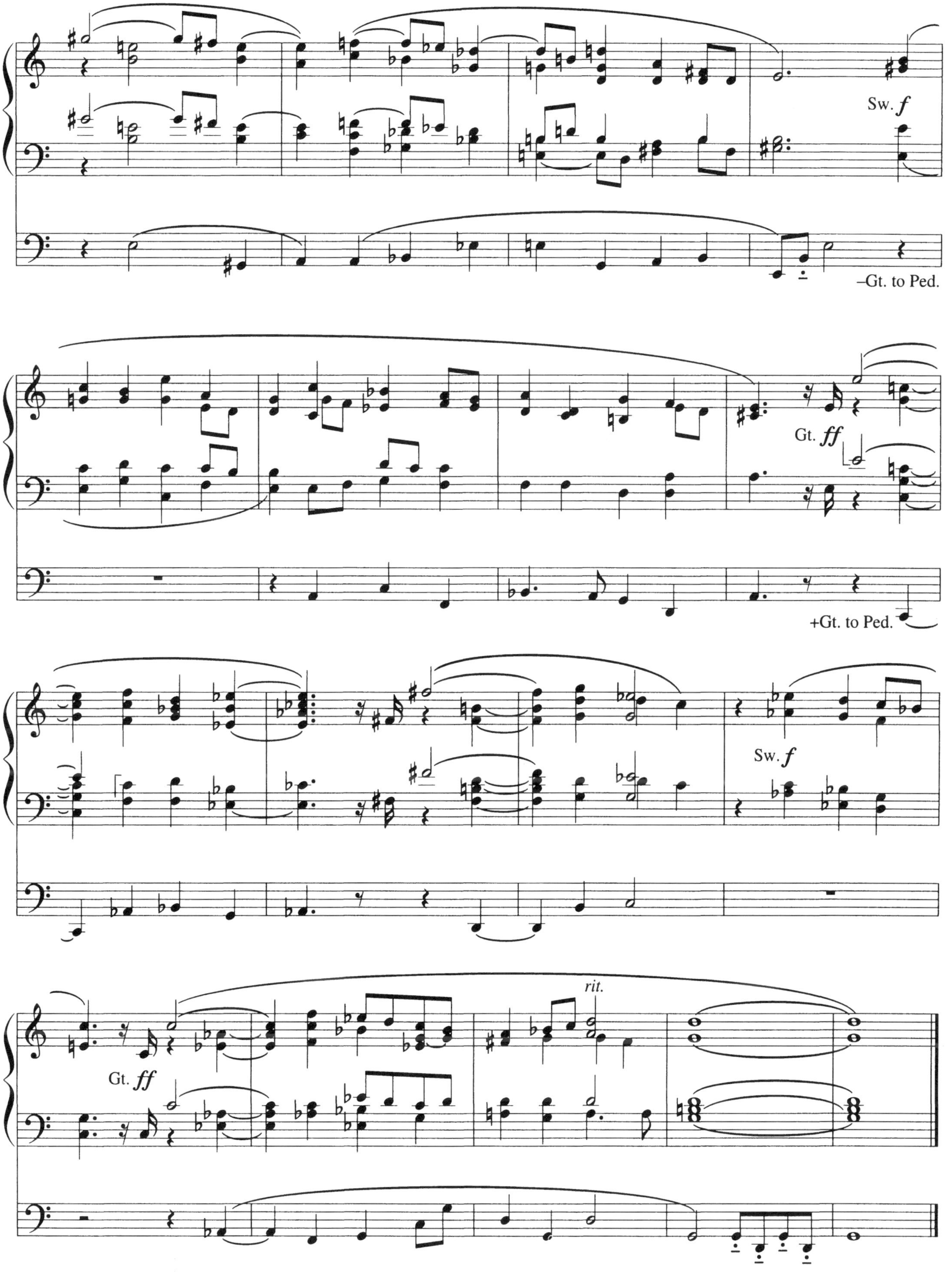
Sw. f
–Gt. to Ped.
Gt. ff
+Gt. to Ped.
Sw. f
Gt. ff
rit.

SORTIE IN SIX

Christopher Tambling

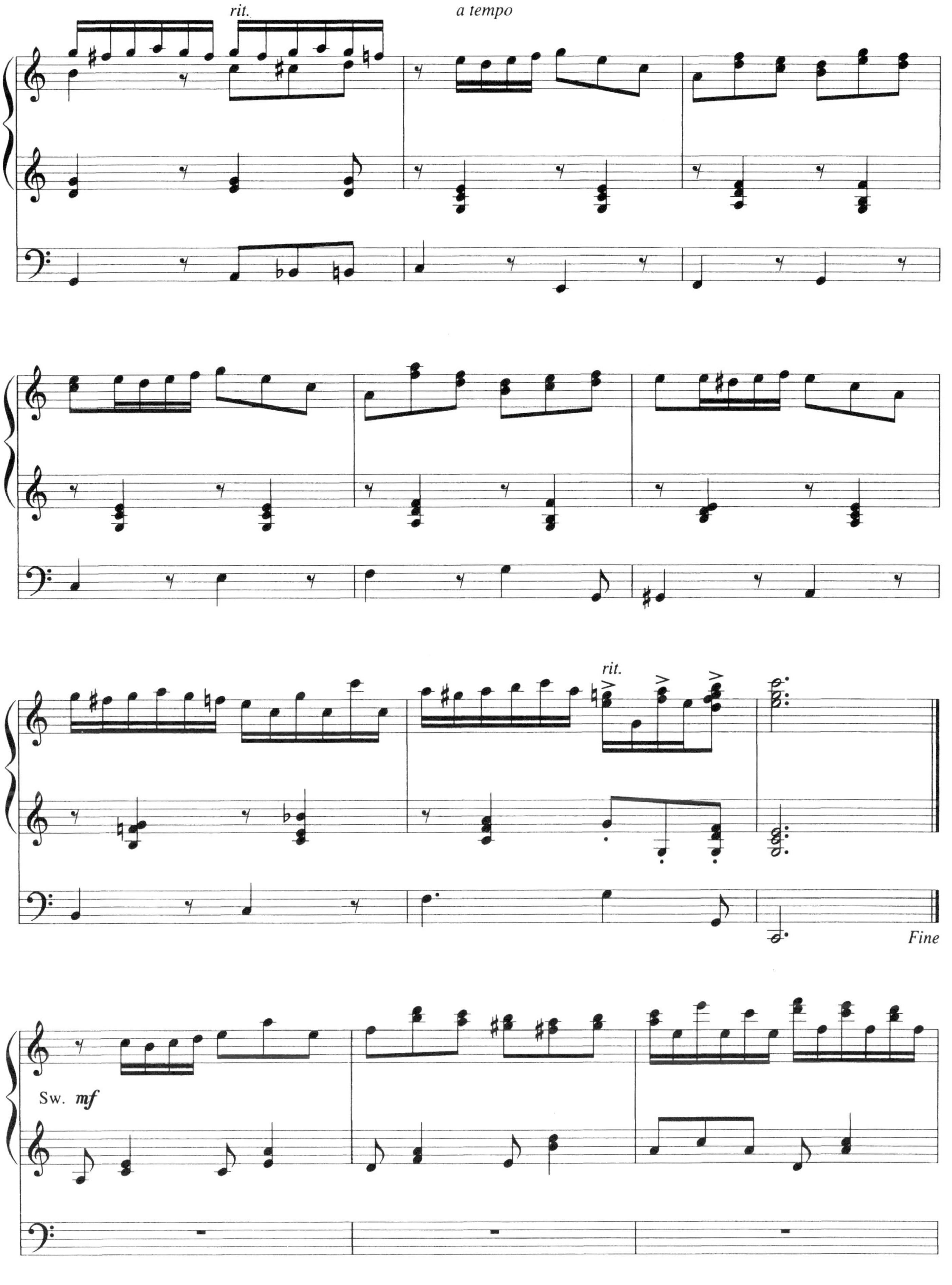
rit.
a tempo
rit.
Fine
Sw. mf

Ch.

+Full Sw. (Box closed)

cresc.

molto rit.

D.C. al Fine

To A D H

EASTER TUNE WITH SMOKE

Alan Ridout

Based on a traditional Breton melody – 'smoke' is Russian slang for tone clusters

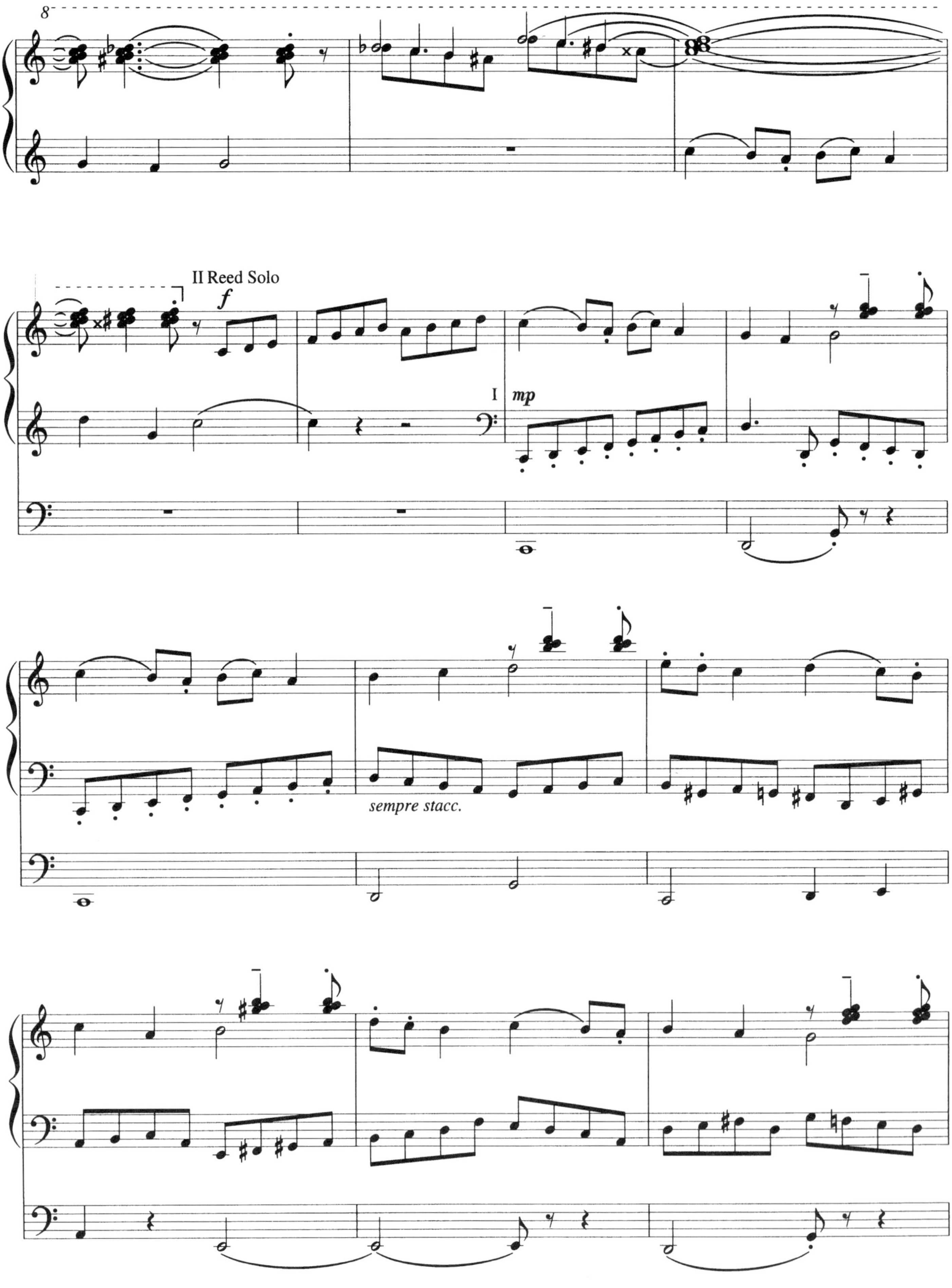
8
II Reed Solo
f
I
mp
sempre stacc.

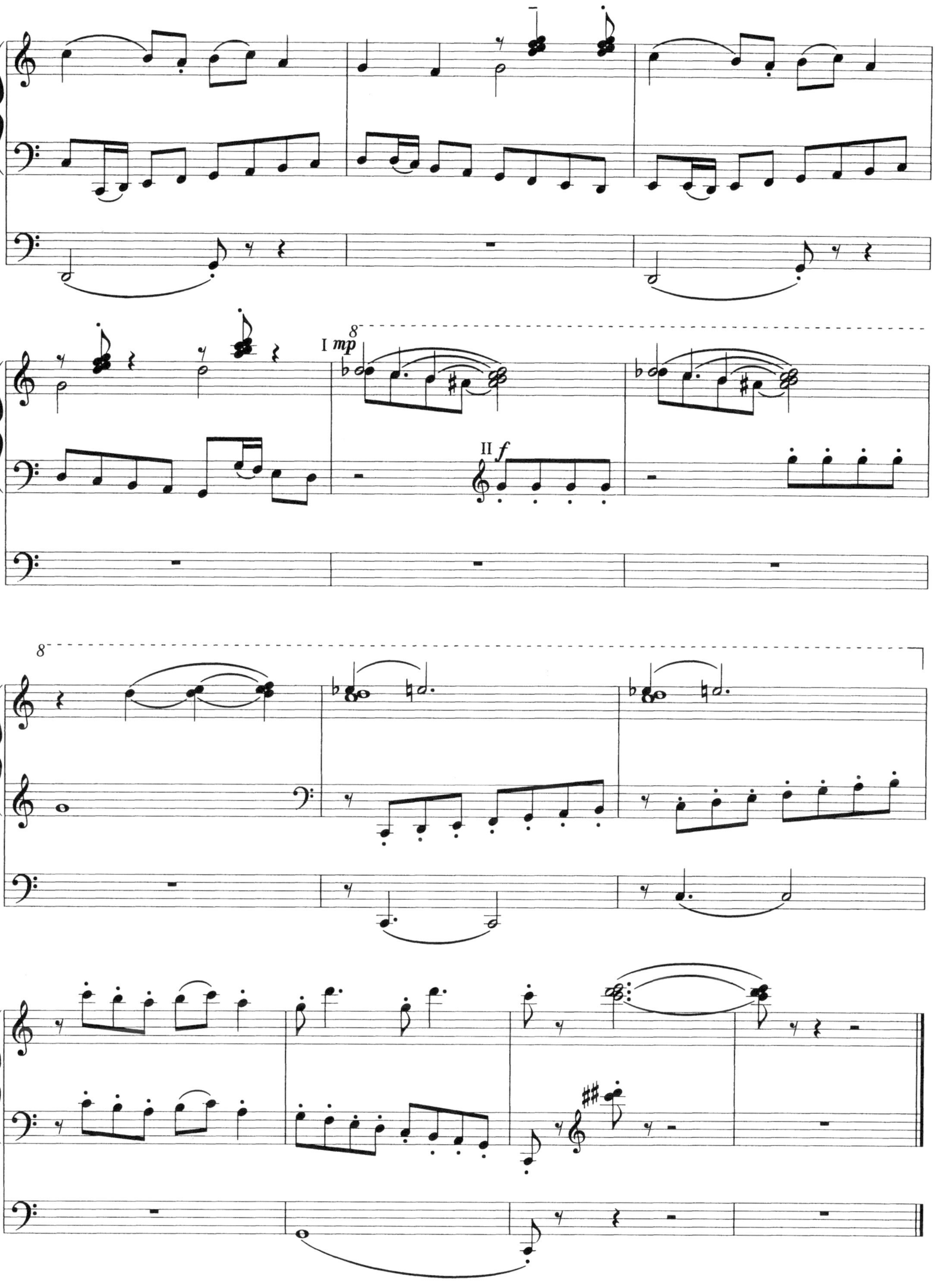
8
I mp
II f
8

for Ian Hunt
TRUMPET AIR
Paul Bryan

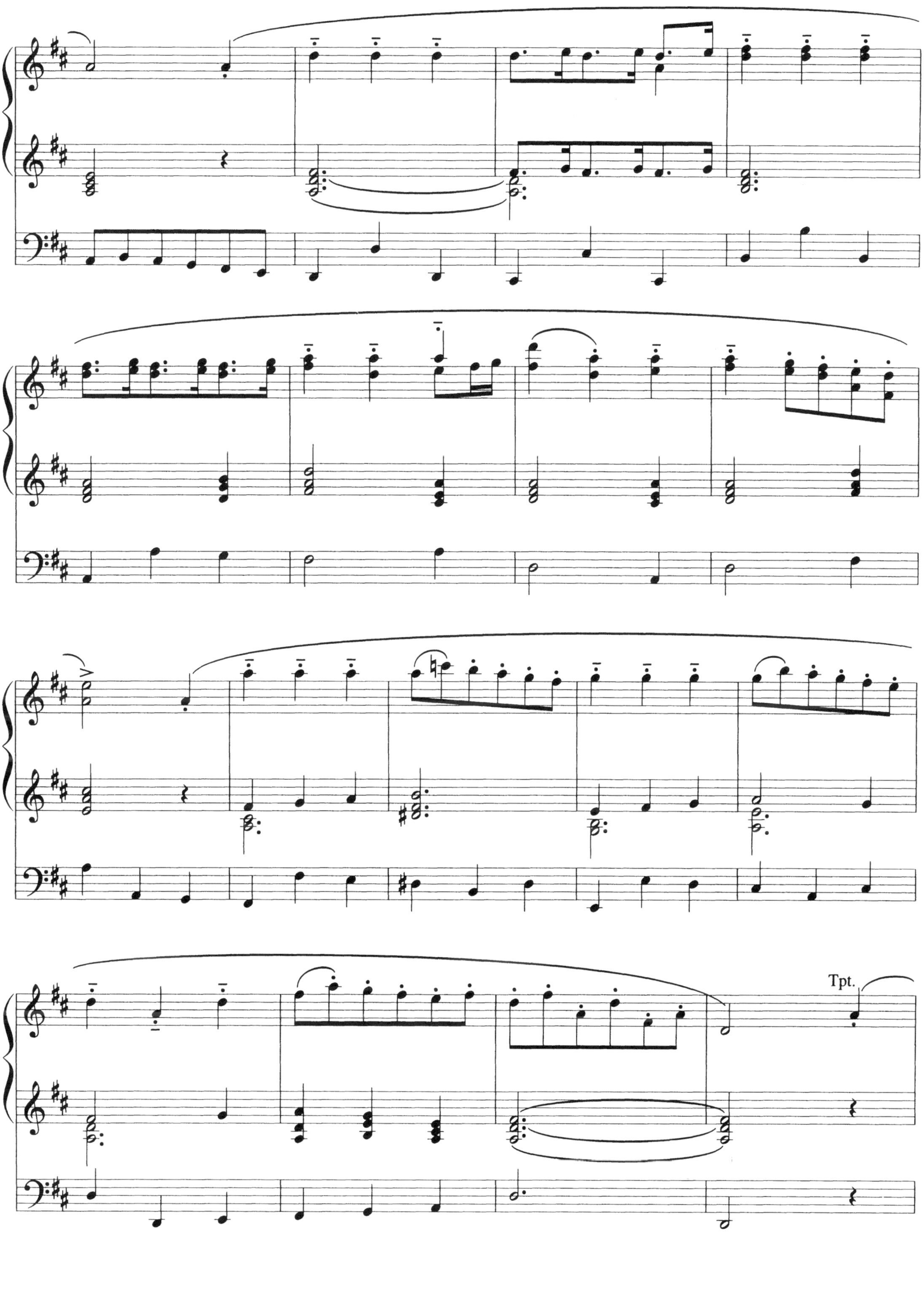
Tpt.

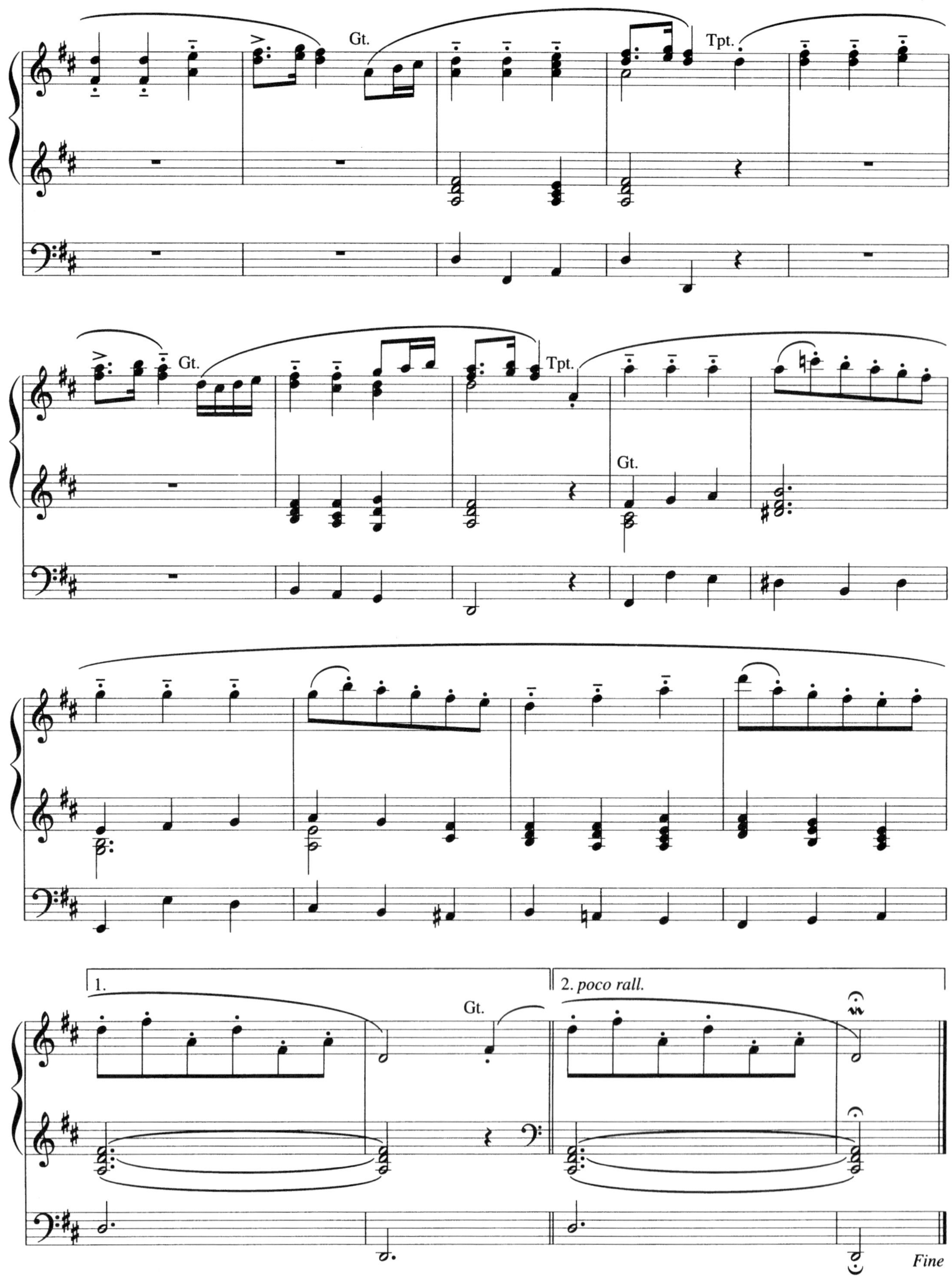
Gt.
Tpt.
Gt.
Tpt.
Gt.
1.
2. poco rall.
Gt.
Fine

poco rall.

D.C. al Fine

THE BISHOP'S PROCESSION

June Nixon

* optional Da Capo if required

SORTIE

Richard Shephard

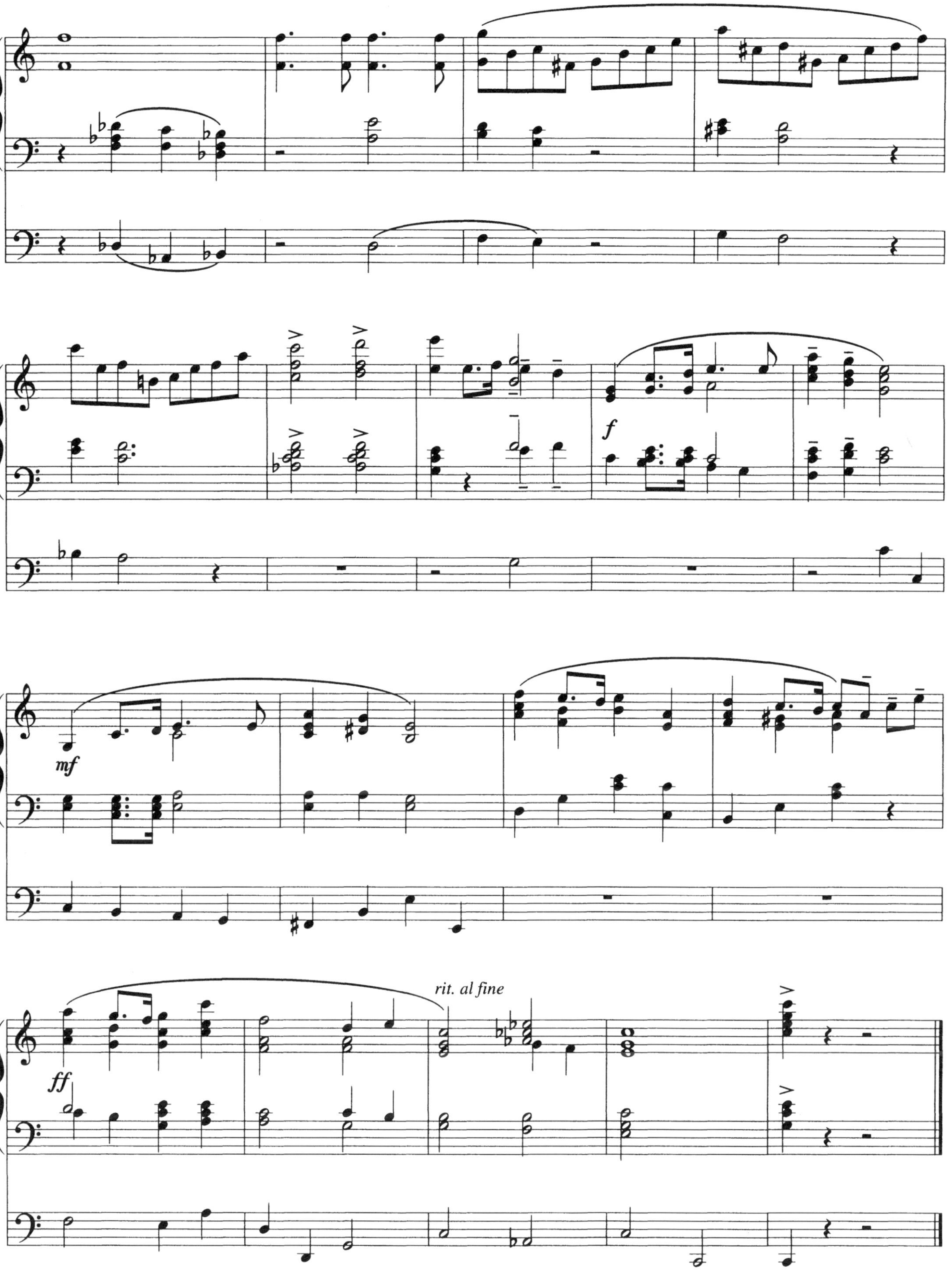

f
mf
ff
rit. al fine

GREAT AND GLORIOUS

Colin Hand

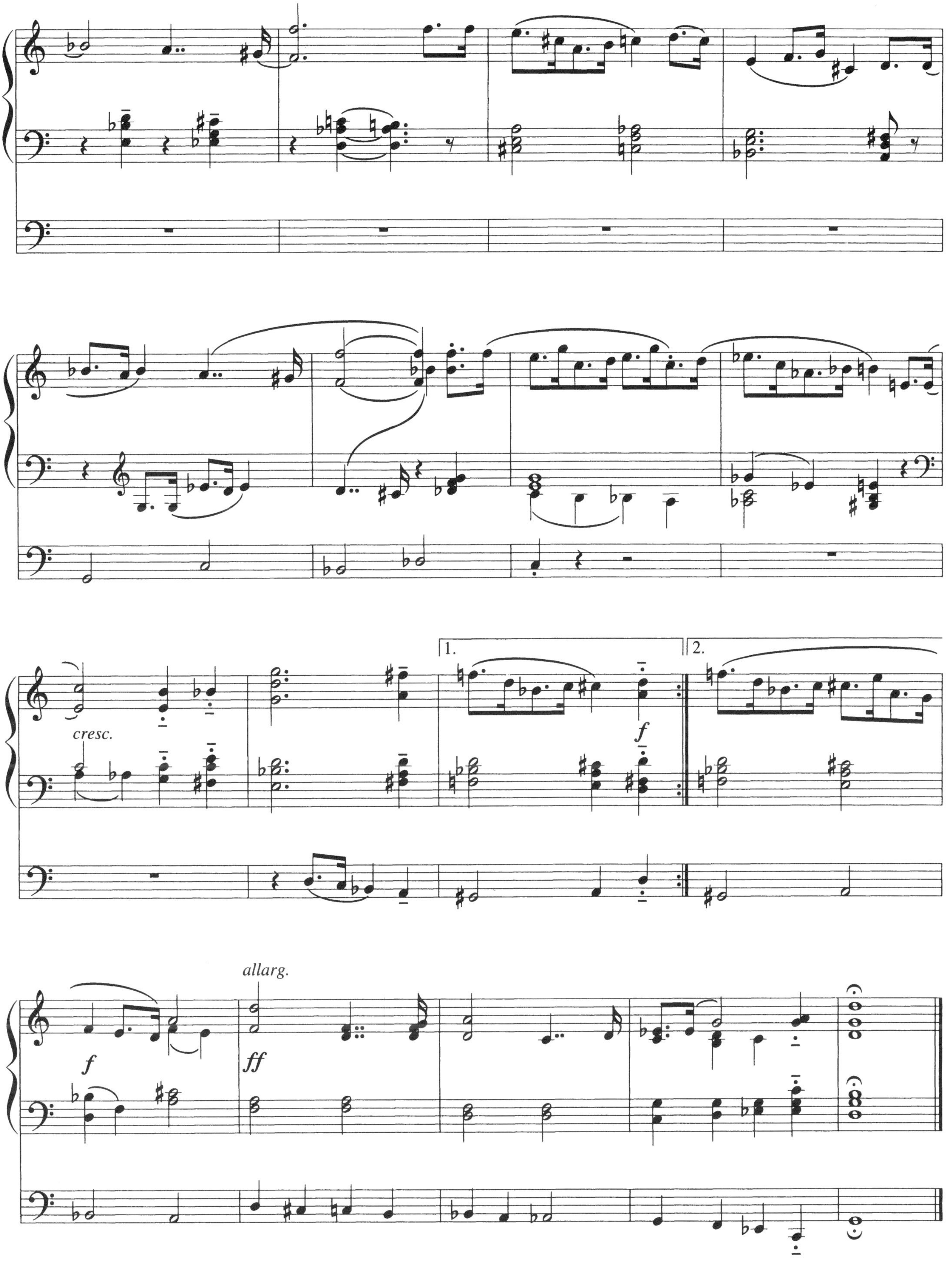
cresc.
1.
2.
f
allarg.
f
ff

FINALE

Alan Viner

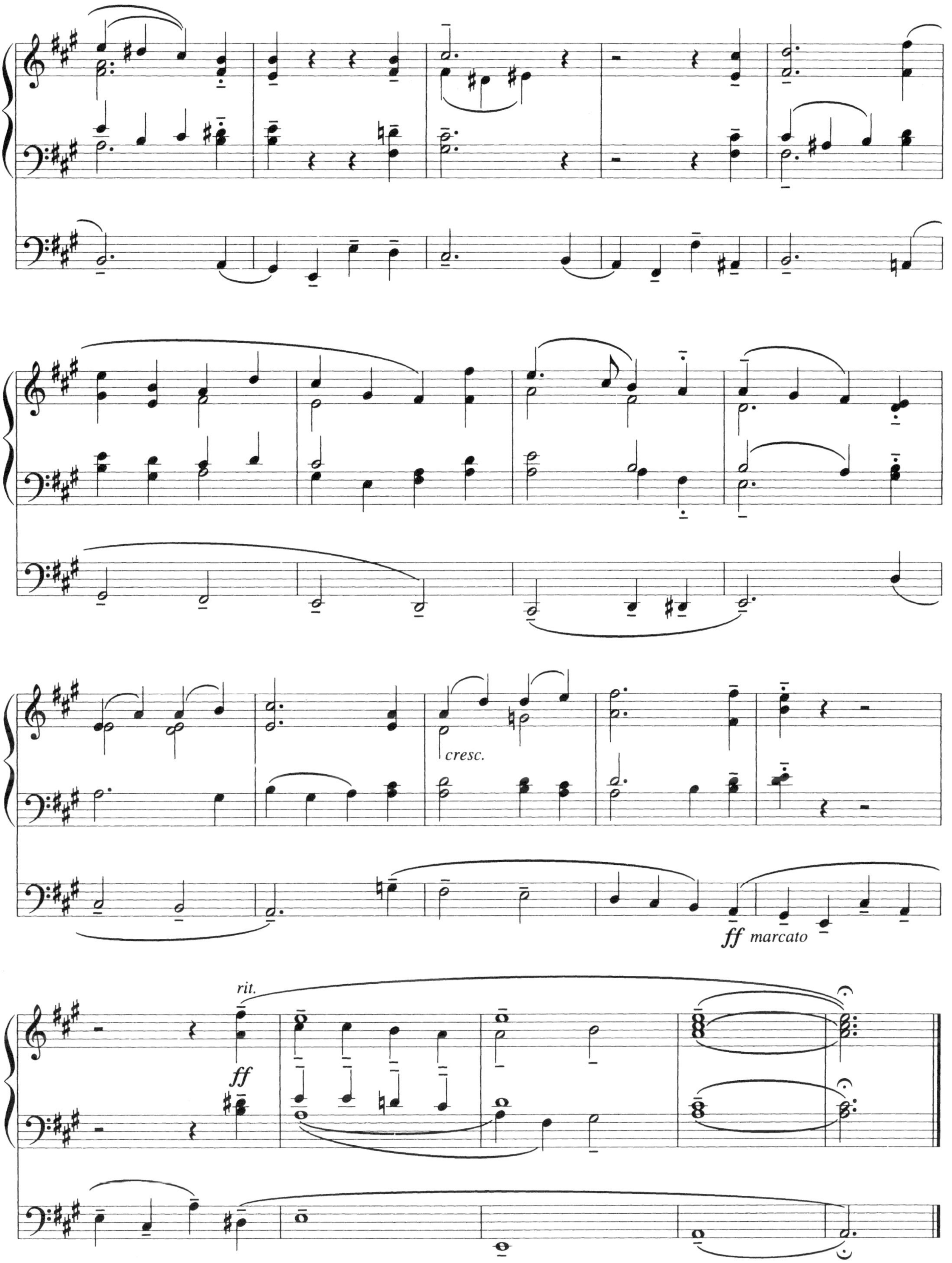
cresc.
ff marcato
rit.
ff

About the Composers

Malcolm Archer (*b.*1952), is Organist and Master of the Choristers at Wells Cathedral. He is conductor of the Wells Oratorio Society and the City of Bristol Choir. In addition to his work as a composer and recitalist.

Rosalie Bonighton (*b.*1946) is a composer, part-time teacher, and Organist and Music Director at St John the Evangelist Church, Ballarat, Australia. She writes for both professional and amateur performers, and has a special interest in music for liturgical needs.

Paul Bryan (*b.*1950) is Director of Music at St John's College School, Cambridge, where he also conducts the Walmisley Singers.

Owain Edwards (*b.*1940) is Professor of Music History at the Norwegian State Academy of Music, Oslo.

Robert Fielding (*b.*1956) is Director of Music at Clifton College Preparatory School, Bristol.

Andrew Fletcher (*b.*1950) is a Midlands-based church musician, choral director, teacher, composer, arranger and concert organist who regularly gives recitals, masterclasses and choral workshops both in England and the USA.

Andrew Gant (*b.*1963) is organist, choirmaster and composer at Her Majesty's Chapel Royal, St James's Palace.

Colin Hand (*b.*1929) is a composer of choral, orchestral and chamber music for both professional and amateur players.

Stephen Kemp (*b.*1947) studied harpsichord with Laurence Libin and composition with Robert Boury and Alan Ridout. He has both M.S. and Ph.D. degrees from the University of Chicago, and earns his living as a Pediatric Endocrinologist.

Richard Knight (*b.*1965), a former Organ Scholar at St John's College, Oxford, is now Director of Music at Dean Close School, Cheltenham.

Richard Lloyd (*b.*1933) was Assistant Organist of Salisbury Cathedral and successively Organist of Hereford and Durham Cathedrals. He now divides his time between examining and composing.

John Marsh (*b.*1939), formerly Organist and Director of Music at St Mary Redcliffe Church, Bristol, is now a member of the music staff at Clifton College, Bristol.

Colin Mawby (*b.*1936) has achieved an international reputation as a composer. His vocal writing is widely acknowledged to be 'masterly' and his music 'inspirational'. He was for many years Master of Music at Westminster Cathedral.

Andrew Moore (*b.*1954) is parish priest of St. Francis, Ascot.

Philip Moore (*b.*1943) is Organist and Master of the Music at York Minster.

June Nixon is one of Australia's best-known organists, choir trainers and composers. She is Organist and Director of Music at St Paul's Cathedral, Melbourne, and teaches at the Music Faculty of Melbourne University.

Richard Pantcheff (*b.*1959) lives in Oxford, where he specialises in writing choral and organ music. He composes frequently for cathedral and other choirs in the UK and Germany.

Alan Ridout (1934-1996) composed music in almost every form: symphonies, chamber music, choral and instrumental works.

Betty Roe (*b.*1930) studied music at the Royal Academy of Music and composition with Lennox Berkely. Best known for her music in the community, her works include many musicals for all ages, and four operas.

Richard Shephard (*b.*1949), is Headmaster of the Minster School, York, and Vicar Choral in York Minster. He has served on the Archbishops' Commission on Church Music and on Church Music Commissions on Cathedrals.

Christopher Tambling (*b.*1964) is Director of Music at Downside School and Master of the Schola Cantorum of Downside Abbey. He was previously Director of Music at Glenalmond College and Perth City Organist.

Quentin Thomas (*b.*1972) was organ scholar at Hertford College, Oxford, and studied composition and conducting at the Guildhall School of Music and Drama, London. He is active as a composer, conductor, organist and repetiteur.

Stanley Vann (*b.*1910) was Assistant Organist at Leicester Cathedral and Chorus Master of Leicester Philharmonic for Sir Henry Wood and Sir Malcolm Sargent; later successively Organist at Chelmsford and Peterborough Cathedrals. Composer of eight masses, fourteen Evening Service, many motets, anthems and organ peices.

Alan Viner (*b.*1951) was formerly Director of Music at the Priory Boys' Grammar School, Shrewsbury, and the Wakeman School, Shrewsbury. He now devotes his time to private teaching, composing and accompanying.

Norman Warren (*b.*1934) is a retired Archdeacon of Rochester. He is well known as a composer of hymns, and was a member of the music committee for *Hymns for Today's Chruch and Sing Glory*.